Discover more about one of the world's literary powerhouses; *Scandinavia*, home territory of some of the world's best-loved writers; Karen Blixen, Peter Høeg, August Strindberg, Jostein Gaarder, Kerstin Ekman and many others. Join them for tales of city and forest, for moral dilemmas and racy adventures, for trolls and transvestites — the *Babel Guide* will help you track down their best books for your greater reading pleasure.

Babel Guides are a new series on contemporary world fiction available in English. The *Reviews* introduce ninety of the best, most representative books, with a quotation as a taster. The *Database* gives useful details on fiction by Scandinavian and Baltic authors written in nine different languages and now available in English.

'a brilliant idea, well executed'

— *The Good Book Guide*

'accessible and entertaining'

— *Traveller's Literary Companion*

The Babel Guide to *Scandinavian and Baltic* Fiction

by Paul Binding

with

Ray Keenoy and Patrick Curry

Babel Guide to Scandinavian Fiction

First published 1999 by Boulevard Books
8 Aldbourne Road, London W12 OLN, UK
Tel/Fax 0181 743 5278
email: raybabel@dircon.co.uk
website: www.raybabel.dircon.co.uk

This publication received support from the Embassy of Sweden
and the Norwegian Ministry of Culture

Special thanks to;
Anders Clason, Per Sörbom, Gabriella Berggren, Joan Tate, Paul Binding and Michal Sapir

ISBN 1 899460 30 6

Boulevard Books are distributed in the UK & Europe by Kuperard/Bravo London
01714240554 fax 01714240556
and in the USA & Canada by Paul & Co. Publishers Consortium Inc. c/o
COSI 2 Christie Heights St.Leonia NJ 07605
tel 201 840 4748 fax 201 840 7148

Cover Art: Jackie Wrout
Typeset & Design: Studio Europa
Printed and bound by the Guernsey Press, Guernsey, C.I.

Index of authors reviewed

Anthologies

BALTICS

ANTHOLOGY

March, Michael (ed.)

Description of a Struggle. The Picador Book of Contemporary East European Prose

This high-powered anthology was produced in 1994 but still used the loose Cold War term of 'Eastern Europe' to mean 'the Communist lands of Europe plus Soviet Russia'. Hence we get, amidst many other very interesting things, two stories from Latvia, Lithuania and Estonia and, given the dearth of available translations from these nations' literature, we include a review.

The emphasis of *Description of a Struggle* is on more recent writing and Estonian Viivi Luik's *The Beauty of History* certainly hits a finely jaundiced post-modern tone with its allusions to communications that have to be endlessly hidden behind metaphor, ending her short piece with a splendid metaphor for the history of the Baltic nations since the middle ages; 'In the silence of the grave the night moves lands and peoples from West to East, so that not even a dog barks.' 327 Lithuanian Valdas Papievis attempts with *I'm Going Out, to Buy a Lightbulb* in a more difficult style, to transmit the feel of contemporary disillusion in his account of a disintegrating marriage, career and maybe mind...

Latvian Andrei Levkin in *History ofYellow* takes us on a train journey 'in search of one decent place on earth', passing through Volokolamsk, Irkutsk and Yaroslavl, not to mention Pavlosk, Industrialsk and 'totally incomprehensible Pustoshka'. It's a kind of mini Soviet *On the Road*, albeit this Russo-Latvian Kerouac is moving through vast mileage by train and not in a clapped-out roadster, with Dean Moriarty at the wheel...

More down to earth but equally atmospheric in its way Andra Neiburga's *Mousy Death* transmits a sense of life — queues, crowded trolly buses and an ever-present mild fear of the future — in Riga in the months before Latvia regained the political independence stolen by Stalin in 1940 and 1945.

Other stories by Baltic authors in this anthology are Jurga Ivanauskaitė's *Two Stories about Suicide* (Lithuania) and Estonian Rein Tootma's *We Gaze up into the Top of the Spruce Trees. (Ray Keenoy)*

'Remember that on the phone you should not use the words 'book', 'papers', 'document', 'briefcase', 'letter' or 'men'. A book can be forbidden, in its entirety, or can be printed abroad, papers are the same as documents but a document could always be a forgery. A briefcase gives away the fact that things are being moved from one place to another. But what things? And from what place? A letter could always be brought over the border by courier. Men could think *differently* for there are grounds for believing so. Men are always more suspicious than women. For safety's sake men's names should be changed to women's and Paris should be changed to Kiev, New York to Moscow. 'At auntie's' on the other hand, means in Kiev and 'at uncle's' means Moscow. The names Tallinn and Riga should also not cross one's lips unnecessarily. You can always speak about butter and eggs. It is even desirable to do so. You can speak about dogs but not about muzzles as muzzles attract unnecessary attention, and is that really a good thing? You can speak as much as you like about Aunt Olga, Mum, the polyclinic, cabbages and beets. Times mentioned should be during the day, as evenings are suspicious *per se*. It is better to say nothing at all about night, may God preserve you from the night.' 325-6 Viivi Luik *The Beauty of History*

'Then it will be quiet because our ears will have grown tired of listening to the railway, various stories, bottles rolling across the floor; swollen lips will no longer be able to carry on either about love or offence: everything finished long ago, only for some reason it continues travelling, if only in search of one decent place on earth, some sort of Irkutsk, Yaroslavl, Kostroma, which, should they appear en route, would turn out not to be them but Peremyshl, Voskresensk Sergiev Posad, Pavlovsk, Ustyug, Krasnodar, Taganrog, Oryol... Avtozavodsk, Industrialsk, Krasnofimsk, Ust-Labaz, Bishkek, Amu-Darinsk Volobuevsk and many other names, where we get so lost that there's nothing left for you to do but have a smoke with me at the end of the carriage as usual, leaning on your elbows, resting against me; although I now have no idea who you are...' 308 Andrei Levkin *History of Yellow*

'Were your parents repressed in 1941 or 1949, or were they perhaps among those who carried out the repression? Did your father serve in the Legion? Or was he perhaps a partisan? Don't tremble, my dear — did he shoot Jews? Or chase children destined for exile to Siberia across meadows of dandelions? And your grandmother — was she in the underground already at the time of the Czar (Jesus, how old is she?), did she survive 1937 by some miracle and in 1943 did she hide the very Jews that your father was, perhaps, shooting? Was she sent into exile again after the war? I don't know, I don't know, history presents so many possibilities, variations...' 315 Andra Neiburga *Mousy Death*

ANTHOLOGY

Moseley, Christopher (ed)

From Baltic Shores

This genial little anthology of Scandinavian and Baltic (three stories from each country) writers kicks off with Denmark's Suzanne Brøgger setting the scene of her writing in an old old place, a land full of menhirs, ancient grave-sites and the town of Løve 'a hundred kilometres away from Copenhagen by train — but thousands of kilometres away in time.' Svend Age Madsen's *The Man Who Created Woman* is set in 'an illustrious old library' and is something of a tribute to the Argentinean master Jorge Luis Borges. Dorrit Willumsen's *If it really was a film* efficiently explores the criminal career of an under-educated social reject — it's clearly not all sweetness and light in Social Democratic Denmark.

Estonian Einar Maasik's *Summer Rhapsody* is a kind of nature-poem celebrating the fish-soup, fir forests and fecundity of a homeland that he peoples with some fairly ferocious types... Mati Unt's *Saturday in the Sauna* also projects something of a crude rural world. Arvo Valton — who was deported by the Russians between 1949 and 1954 — dis-assembles another kind of crudity, the clanking bureaucratic collectivism of late Soviet Communism in his amusing *The Man with the Green Rucksack.*

Finnish Orvokki Autio's harsh *Thirty Pennies* bears the same fascination with squalid social realism as Dorrit Willumsen's *If it really was a film* as two drunken parents and a drunken lover argue over child-custody.

The celebrated Finland-Swedish (i.e. Swedish-speaking citizen of Finland) writer Bo Carpelan returns us to a calmer, more elegaic mood with his lyrical, nostalgic *The Storm* about a great 'yellow wind' that seems to blow around the margins of his childhood and then one day strikes the little provincial town where he grew up... Another noted writer from Finland is Rosa Liksom; in her rural paradise of *That Summer the Clouds Hung Low* the ill wind seems to be sexual desire and its consequences. In a brief piece she establishes a world of emotional and cultural claustrophobia, challenged by the fresh energy of a girl who turns into a woman, one unforgettable summer.

In Eeva Tikka's *The Aluminium Rings* Finland's fading rural certainties — symbolised by a faithful old couple living in their isolated cabin — lie uncomfortably side-by-side with the transient lifestyle of a typical young city-dweller.

Moving back across the Gulf of Finland to Latvia in Alberts Bels' *The Wrestler* we encounter the harsh conditions and stoicism of the peasant world in this story of a small farmer who goes to extraordinary lengths in his desperation to save his farm from the bank; it's a a wry and sympathetic story set in an impoverished landscape. Latvian Valentins Jakobsons, author of *The Fatherland is in Danger,* spent fifteen years in Soviet labour camps and his story, revealing the complacency and ignorance of Soviet jailers, stands as a little coda to the history of 'the Gulag Archipelago'.

Sometime Later by Aija Valoodze gives a cross section of middle-class lives in Soviet-era Latvia, in journalism and teaching, where the *leitmotiv* is frustration and hypocrisy. Meanwhile, in neighbouring Lithuania, a mysterious country famous as the last Pagan land of Europe, veteran writer Juozas Aputis portrays in his *Wild Boars on the Horizon* a rural world composed of natural forest beauty and extreme domestic violence. It's a story which has that unmistakeable aura of truth.

A truth that has happened all over Europe is the abandonment of rural homesteads in favour of cities or settlements nearer the main roads and the mod cons. In *The Dark Windows of Oblivion* Romualdas Lankauskas chronicles this sad process in a tiny hamlet of his native land, creating an elegy for a life lived in what would be today an unimaginable tranquility.

Rural peace is threatened by a kind of everyday erotic enchantment in the popular Swedish writer Göran Tunstrom's *Shadow of a Marriage*, even if everything ends happily (and boringly) ever after...

From Baltic Shores ends with its best story Marie Hermanson's *The Wandering Cook*, a 'simple little story' that actually brings together many grand themes of civilisation, philosophy and anthropology; it's as wise as it well-written. Bravo and thank-you Marie and the same to editor Christopher Moseley and the Norvik Press, a small but effective outfit that specialises in making Scandinavian fiction available in English. *Ray Keenoy*

'through contemplation I live in freedom and in peace and in connection with the world' Suzanne Brøgger *I Live As I Write And I Write As I Live* 34

'The men were sitting under the big birch-tree and drinking vodka in honour of Miners' Day. There weren't any miners amongst them, but a holiday is a holiday' Mati Unt *Saturday in the Sauna* 104

'to them she would always be just a 'teach' leading her insignificant grey life for a pittance of a wage — because what normal person goes to work in a school anyway? The normal ones head ministries and travel in luxury Zhigulis, appear on television, make films and get scientific degrees. And at least for the present Astrida did not have the power to demonstrate that in a couple of short years quite a few of these snobs, instead of the college auditorium and the laurels, would be having to put a gun across their shoulder and march 'left, left!', or weigh sausages behind a counter, but that is what Astrida wished for them with all her heart.' Aija Valoodze *Sometime Later* 181

'every time I came to this secluded village on the other side of an old pine forest, I liked to walk along the sandy path by the side of the forest that led to a pleasant little town with a small church solidly built out of field stones. It was pleasant to walk through the pine forest full of graceful juniper trees and breathe the air here. To the left of the pine forest stretched meadows and fields and further away flowed a stream winding its way past the banks overgrown with bushes and past another forest looking in the distance, probably larger and wider because it rose up to the sky as if it were a giant green fence that could not be scaled. Above the forest floated white clouds or when the days were sunny and fine a clear blue sky could be seen.' Romualdas Lankauskas *The Dark Windows of Oblivion* 219

ESTONIA

ANTHOLOGY

Estonian Short Stories (Pruul, Kajar & Reddaway, Darlene eds)

Estonian Short Stories (Puhvel, Heino ed.)

These two similarly-titled books come from each side of the perestroika and independence divide. The anthology edited by Heino Puhvel was published in Talinn, capital of Estonia while it was still under Soviet Rule in 1981 while the Kajar Pruul book is subtitled 'Writings from an unbound Europe' i.e. the big bad Russian Bear is not looking over anyone's shoulder anymore.

On the other hand the editors of the 'unbound' volume point out that Estonia's writers and artists had relatively greater freedom than other Soviet citizens as Soviet Estonia was a kind of shopwindow for the West to admire and in fact three Soviet-era writers make it into the post-Soviet book.

The older book, published in the Soviet Union, will today be found in libraries rather than bookshops but nevertheless contains interesting material, arranged chronologically as in the traditional type of literary anthology.

Eduard Vilde, part of the lively generation of Estonian journalists and writers that emerged at the turn of the century is represented with *His Daily Bread,* an entertaining and dramatic piece set in Italy.

A longer and more striking story by Vilde is *Casanova Makes his Farewells* which opens a tiny window on the Jewish presence in Estonia with the figure of Mirjam Gold. A romantic, slightly silly story but entertaining and accomplished with a very particular voice.

Jakob Mändmets, of the same generation as Vilde, wrote *The Old Shotgun*, set in the latter years of the Russian Empire. The rural peace of hard-working farmers is disturbed by an incredible bit of political skilduggery, all described in a plain, strong style.

Anton Hansen Tammsaare was a kind of grand old man of Estonian letters, churning out many novels including a noted five-volume work on village life in Estonia at the turn of the century. In *The Trip to Italy* he blends the sentimental and the realistic in a way that rings quite oddly today.

Friedebert Tuglas, writing a little later is clearly a talented and more modern writer than Vilde or Taamsaare and his story *The Shadow of a Man* is a grim and ghastly vision of the human damage wrought by the First World War when the soldiers of the Russian Empire were particularly poorly led and equipped. It's a story with the authentic chill of the devastation of this period.

Tuglas' style is described as 'Expressionist' and in the second of his pieces here *The Mirage* this style is applied to a happier theme.

Johannes Semper's story *A Mistake* is well written although in its account of political repression and brutality it is the 'Reds' who are the undisputed good guys. On the other hand the harsh pragmatism he describes seems to describe well Soviet political 'enforcement' too.

A difficulty with this anthology is that it doesn't indicate original publication dates for any of its stories and the motivation behind selecting stories is particularly well-hidden, although most of the pieces included are highly readable.

Peet Vallak, a skilled short story writer prominent in the independent Estonia of 1918-1940 contributes a wry and enjoyable little piece *Art and Crime*, lamenting the meagre earnings of the artist.

August Jakobson was a communist who ended up as a leading official in Soviet Estonia: the story here *The Great Shadow* is on the ponderous side.

Erni Krusten published inboth independent Estonia and its 'socialist' successor and a story from his Soviet period *Ashes* is about the isolation and nostalgia of exiles for the native land and its places; he writes quite delicately about the small inexorable tragedies of old age.

Rudolf Sirge's long short story *Stunted Bog Pines* is another Soviet story, a kind of political mystery tale — three men go fishing in a hamlet at the edge of a cold bog. It's an area that in the years after 1945 is still inhabited by anti-Soviet partrisans. The local people who live in isolated farmsteads are caught between Soviet authorities and armed fighters just as during World war Two they were caught between German occupiers and their local militia and Soviet partisans dropped in by air. This story expresses a degree of sympathy for their plight one might not expect in Soviet literature.

Lilli Promets, another writer of the Soviet period, writes a mean and succinct short story set in the immediate post (Second) war period. Her political slant atacking those who collaborated with or even fought for the Germans is pretty explicit.

Aadu Hint's *When the Ice Broke* addresses more or less the same theme but from an even more specifically Soviet point of view. The good storytelling though gives us a sense of the ultimately very difficult situation of Estonian contry people — here fishermen in particular — under Nazi rule during 1941 to 1944.

Ants Saar's Side by Side is the story of a young Estonian volunteer in the Red Army in 1941 who has been invalided out and is travelling to Siberia to join other Estonians. Somewhat sentimental, heroic stuff, it gives some of the war-time atmosphere too.

Paul Kuusberg's *The Rusty Watering-Can* is really a lot more interesting; there's a critique of everyday life, pollution, mismanagement, poor workmanship, lack of incentives and unavailablility of consumer goods — all those things the later Soviet Union was famous for. Juhan Smuul's *The Night the Pühadekari was Wrecked* is close to the natural world, the stormy seas of the Baltic and the lives of sailors. As the working-class is involved one has to expect some Soviet sentimentality and Smuul delivers; 'their young faces, their rough red workers' hands, with all the inner strength and frankness that emanateed from them'.

Mats Traat's *The Toy Water-Mill* has the atmosphere of late Sovietism; a husband-and-wife rather than a proletarian collective, involving themselves in simple (apolitical?) pleasures.

Arvo Valton's *The Torchbearers* which is carefully described as 'grotesque' in the book's introduction is a bleak and brief story of a 'dead man' waking in a mortuary to be told to shut up by the night watchman who won't help him get out of there back to the land of the living because it would foul up the paperwork. This 'grotesque' seems more of an arch allegory on the Soviet order of things, often cruel and hidebound.

Juri Tuulik ends the book with a story of heroic Russo-Estonian friendship which is also a story which tells us about the horrors of being a Soviet soldier captured by the Germans.

'But then, all of a sudden, spring was there. The sunshine was dazzling. The chalk cliffs of the outer islands dried and turned white in a few days. The exuberant grass grew perceptibly.

The gentle wind caressed the silvery branches of the willow tree as if they were the hair of a young girl. It came from the east, it came from the west, veering then to the southwest, dying down for days at a time. The firmament glowed like blue silk above a glittering sea.

When the shepherd Nikias, standing on the plain, raised his face upwards, he saw one heaven after another opening up. His young heart aching with sadness, he gazed at the expanses which grew out of one another like flowerbuds from flowerbuds.' 81 Friedebert Tuglas *The Mirage*

'The furnishings of the flat were the kind that no-one of us would crave for today. It was Frau Minna's flat.

That morning she drew up the dining-room blind and looked down into the yard. Nothing remarkable there, but the room was very dusty. There was never so much dust before, but who wants to listen to your complaints about whatever was different in the past. The war had left its mark on the ceiling of Frau Minna's dining-room, it had thumped a large piece of plaster loose. Deep cracks had also appeared, and that was where the dust came from.' *The German* 202 Lilli Promets

'And suddenly there came a break in the usual radio broadcast that could be heard over hundreds of blaring loudspeakers in all the halls, and hundred-metre-long corridors, in passages on the ground and underground, in dining-rooms and offices of the huge railway station. A military march, that was to inspire listeners, broke off in the middle of a bar; the Moscow radio announcer was stopped in the middle of his report about a heroic deed in the front: the manly, powerful voice of Leviathan was not able to complete the latest announcemet on military actions the day before. A hoarse voice from the station's own desk could be heard, announcing the departure and destination of an incoming train. People in the station got to their feet, hoisted all their bags and bundles, their suitcases sewn incloth and often tied together, onto their shoulders and made for the platform. They stepped over the sleeping people, stumbling upon their sprawling legs and arm, and obstructed all the passages to the platform.' 224 Ants Saar *Side by Side*

'All this lurching, he sure can't drive. Or he can drive, but doesn't care. State property, who cares! What if a spring or an axle breaks — shove in another. Roubles thrown to the winds, state's roubles, it isn't as if they came from your own pocket. The old bourgeois firm Motors would have sacked him there and then. No master to keep an eye on things, that's it. At the bus depot all they think of is fat bonuses, and to blazes with the passenger. Go on, step on the gas! And the roads look like if the pigs have been rooting them up. One paves it with asphalt, another breaks it all up again. The town fathers are busy welcoming visitors and making speeches. Visitors count, they are treated like tin gods. Leave your own townfolks to manage any way they can.' 242-3 Paul Kuusberg *The Rusty Watering-Can*

Estonian Short Stories (Puhvel, Heino ed.)

This 'post-Soviet' anthology of Estonian fiction begins with the 'grotesque' writer Arvo Valton with more allegories of Soviet life, as in the Communist-era anthology. Also in an elliptical, allegorical style Mati Unt's *The Fish's Revenge* displays Estonian avant-guardism, a kind of absurdism perhaps influenced by the Polish writer Slavomir Mrozek. Unt's second story here *The Black Motorcyclist* reads like a collage of references to what was (in 1974) chic modernism — with Africans on motorbikes, Erving Goffman's book *The Presentation of the Self in Everyday Life* and whatnot else. Not so much a story as a name-dropping exercise. Better is Unt's amusing *He Translated.*

The best-known Estonian writer internationally, Jaan Kross presents us with a very different kettle of fish in *Hallelujah*; a story from the Soviet Gulag of prison-camps where Kross himself served time and a picture too of muted, almost spiritual resistance to both Nazis and Soviets by those with the courage to entertain such a thing. *Hallelujah* is the story of a man driven mad by Nazi and Stalinist brutality and idiocy; a real twentieth century tale.

In *The Day his eyes are Opened* we get another slice of Kross' real writerly talent for finding and evoking essential humanity and we get a glimpse too into things that were clearly very hard to discuss in Soviet Estonia.

Toomas Vint's *The Swan-Stealing* written in 1974 is a parable about the 'end of ideology' while his *This So Embarassing and Unexpected a Death* written in 1983 explores the personal life and 'subjectivity' that was anathema to the busy politiking of Stalinist literature. As a family breaks up through mutual disinterest and adultery various drunks roll around stealing to finance bottles of beer and cheap wine. In fact we're shown a very unattractive and unheroic world that floats on alcohol...

Toomas Raudam's *Drooping Wings* is the reminiscence of a rural childhood while Mari Saat, one of the two women (out of nine) contributors to this book gives us the extremely finely-drawn miniature *Elsa Hermann*, an unsentimental picture of the intense relationship of two sisters who more or less bring each other up. Ülo Mattheus *Our Mother* gives a lovely sense of the rain-washed Baltic landscape of fir trees and dark earth while Maimu Berg, the other woman writer here, gives us a wry look at Russo-Estonian coexistence at the appartment-house level, drawn from a child's viewpoint. The story develops in a surprising way, bringing us an interesting taste of the strange cocktail of Estonia's contemporary history.

Her *The Mill Ghost* is also written in a quite light-hearted style and is a very enjoyable, ironic take on a writer's life.

Jüri Ehlvest, the youngest writer here (born in 1967) in *Disintegration of the Spiral* gives us a good and succinct ending to the book.

This is an impressive collection (once past the 'absurdist' work at the beginning) from what is an impressive literature especially if one thinks of Estonia's often difficult political history and its small population. *Ray Keenoy*

'I know many good translators. I communicate with them readily and gladly avail myself of their services. I don't know any language well enough that I could fully enjoy a work, especially a masterpiece, in the original.... And so I prefer a translator's version. They are, for the most part, educated and refined men, often entirely oriented toward their favorite country. This is betrayed by their use of wine, pipe, or women. A real translator is a clean type. Usually a tolerant man, often a good-hearted roly-poly. Seldom have I seen hysterical translators who chew their nails and tear their hair. A dark flame seldom burns in a translator's eyes. He is an altruist, a lover of someone else, he is not so much a sadist as a masochist. That is why it is pleasureable to drink good red wine with translators and to sniff their good tobacco. Translators seldom drink vodka. I repeat, they are not wild. But chance people do also happen among them. In fact, many a person who is more sensitive than average to the texture of the world, and who could express his sense perceptions in the form of an original creation, suddenly becomes a translator. Exactly so, I repeat at your astonished cry, a person suddenly becomes a translator, and it is not easy to tear him away from this work anymore. No-one has the courage to tell him outright that he smells differently, that he is strange. The errant glance that so readily betrays him bores into us with the frank question: well, what shall we translate today? And you are helpless before this naivete. You talk, suggest, mention what has not yet been translated, what is being translated. And that is how the days pass. And nothing changes. He is among us and sows a singular, perverse atmosphere. Many people have such an aura. But in particular those who have chanced to become translators.' Mati Unt 66-67 *He Translated*

'That was hard work, at times even dangerous work. If it was done in the slipshod, hasty manner characteristic of labor camp work and necessitated by the frequent -40 degree temperatures. Of course the men made great haste to return to the warming hut.... for there, within the shelter of the board walls, among a heap of men reeking of makhorka smoke, there was at least shelter from the wind and a spark of warmth near the iron stove.' 108 Jaan Kross *Hallelujah*

'A few years ago, when he had still been living in the center of the city, he very often went walking in this area — he had been captivated by the former gardens, their beds overgrown with weeds, and the fruit trees gone wild. No-one had come here to mow, and lush grass grew chest-high everywhere. The fact that vital nature had luxuriated almost in the center of the city had created in him the odd feeling that this was actually a country locale, and the daily cares that had only recently made his head ache had been replaced by the peace and carefree solace of being away. Now, however, there was a cultural park here, sterile roads strewn with gray gravel and a recently sown lawn that reminded Prants of the high-rise district he had become accustomed to in recent years, and he thought: at no period in history have such ugly boxes been built for habitation, they provide only alienation; even as they age, these buildings will not become more interesting — they're an absolutely impersonal, mass product like this newly created, senseless green space.' 155-156 Toomas Vint *This So Embarassing and Unexpected a Death*

'I rang the bell of the girl next door to invite her out into the yard. The neighbors had moved into our building after the war, and an extra word had also been thought up to specify them — *petsoora.* [Russian immigrants post-1945] They, too, were entirely deserving of that special label because they were different from the other people in our building. Among themselves they spoke Russian, but with me they spoke a peculiar Estonian nor exactly like that which we spoke at home. But I did indeed understand their conversation. The *petsooras* had two daughters — Anna and Yevgenia, however they were hardly ever referred to that way. Anna we called Nyura for some reason, and Yevgenia was referred to as Zenya. Their father, a perpetually somber man with a reddish face and sparse, light hair was a captain. He wore officer's dress, drank liquor and when he had drunk a great deal he fired a revolver in the yard. It was exciting except that his wife, Marusya, always prevented us from watching the captain shoot. After the first shot, Marusya's scream of desperation would sound from the buiding's direction, and she'd storm into the yard, seize us all into her arms as she herself would begin arguing with the captain in Russian. Then the captain would usually turn the revolver towards us, shout, and his face would turn bright red.' 140 Maimu Berg *The Rococo Lady*

KROSS
Jaan

The Conspiracy and Other Stories [Silmade avamise päev]

Jaan Kross (born 1920) is Estonia's best-known novelist, and a writer of world stature. His career reflects only too well the history of his country, small and powerless, yet with a strong identity and not without importance for greater states. Kross, born in the Estonian capital of Tallinn, studied law at the old university of Tartu (both cities are vividly described in *The Conspiracy and Other Stories*); he was briefly imprisoned by the Germans during their occupation of Estonia (1941-44) for suspected nationalist activity, and later, with Soviet domination, became a prisoner of the Russians. Eight years of his young life were passed in Soviet prison-camps. When he came back to Estonia he occupied himself with poetry and translation (translating Shakespeare among others) before turning to the novel, the genre in which he has excelled, particularly the historical novel.

The Conspiracy and Other Stories is a unified volume which should be read as such (almost as fragmented novel), its six stories dealing with the fortunes between 1939 and 1955 of one Peeter Mirk, who is obviously a stand-in for the author himself and who appears in other fictions by him — lawyer, academic, writer, anti-reactionary nationalist as well as internationalist. But at one point Mirk, who tells these stories in the first person, declines to say anything much about himself: 'I simply cannot.' Though a participant, who invites sympathy or censure from the reader, he is primarily an observer of his times and fellow-citizens, during the tragic instabilities and repressions of this century. But he is an observer with a lively fund of humour and empathic powers.

Three stories call for special attention; profoundly illuminative of the Estonian (and for that matter Baltic) predicament, they show Kross' all but miraculous literary skill, his enormous command over his material which nevertheless opens up to readers baffling territories beyond the narratives themselves. 'The Wound' which opens the volume takes us to the tense days of 1939 with Nazi Germany calling on German Balts (to which category Peeter Mirk's family in its origins belongs) to leave Estonia and accept repatriation in the Greater Reich. Peeter and his parents are not tempted by the offer, knowing full well that the homes found for them will have belonged to murdered or incarcerated Poles, but friends of his judge it best to leave Tallinn by such ships as *Der Deutsche*. We focus on one girl whose decision this is, a girl with whom Peeter has been involved and who has jilted him, Flora. Flora's plight, the central concern of the story, is at once representative and has its own ineluctable individuality and pathos.

The title story *The Conspiracy* must surely rank among the finest representations of prison life ever written; all the men cooped up in the one cell are there for political offences against the Russians, most of these trumped-up or based on flimsy evidence. Kross' delineation of the individuals (whose very individuality is under attack) is masterly, their interaction, their respective solitarinesses, their humiliation at the hands of guards. One prisoner, Lehtpuu, is an Estonian farmer whose vulgar manners and obscenity-littered garrulity grate on the others, including Peeter himself. Knowing of Lehtpuu's jealous attachment to his wife, Linda, after hearing rather too much about it, Peeter initiates a cruel joke against him — one he is intensely to regret. Peeter's cruelty — which he can barely comprehend himself — is but a reflection of the cruelty being evidenced in the larger world of which he is part.

The Days Eyes Were Opened (the title is a punning one) closes the collection; the time is September in the late 1950s, the scene a train travelling through Estonia. Peeter has been released from the camp, life can begin again. But are fresh beginnings really possible in a country which has suffered so acutely in the very recent past? Peeter listens to conversations in the railway carriage and appreciates the complexity, the delicacy of everyone's position. And — for the volume ends on a note of tentative optimism — he understands how what carries us through hardships are our affections for other people, our wish for their welfare.

'[Says Mrs. Kaasik] "The Professor said that August [her husband]'s case was a complicated one. The chances were fifty-fifty. We'll know how it went today. Today they'll be taking the dressings off his eyes."

"Oh.... So is that why you're travelling down to Tartu?" ...

"That's right," says Mrs. Kaasik, "I would have travelled anyway, of course. But the Professor phoned. We haven't got a phone ourselves in Varbola, but I gave him the number of the school. They don't mind. So he rang and asked me to travel down. Since he said he'd asked August, *what* he, August, would like to see first when they take off the bandages, assuming, that is, that he can see anything at all."

"And what did August say?" ...

"And August said...." says Mrs. Kaasik,... "August said that he would be grateful — if what he saw first was his wife!"

Mrs. Kaasik looks us straight in the eye, her silent smile implying: You all understand what I mean...

But then she feels there is a risk that her happy eyes could fill with tears right in front of us and that would be overdoing it, despite all this open-heartedness. So she snaps open her large handbag and hides her face behind the large flap (which has a mirror on the inside, no doubt) and begins to push strands of her grey hair under the edge of her headscarf and over the frame of her hearing device. Still wrestling with the constant smile of triumph on her lips. Just as, ten minutes before arrival in Tartu, the milk train crosses the ringing iron bridge over the river swollen by the September rains.' 236-237

KROSS
Jaan

The Czar's Madman [Keisri Hull]

Kross has given himself to the historical novel with a devotion rare in our times — and in doing so has transformed it in ways that are hard to describe. But transform the genre he undoubtedly has. Reading *The Czar's Madman* (which takes the form of a journal, admittedly a rather elaborate one with a systematic investigation of the ten-years-old past) one has a quite remarkable sense of being transported to a world in which ideological, political and social battles (whatever we know about them) are still being fought without any certainty of their outcome, of the characters being one's own kin, and a feeling that only through such a survey of action long accomplished (Kross' books are founded on vast and very detailed research) can our present be comprehended.

The Czar's Madman concerns the fate of Baron Timotheus (Timo) von Bock, enlightened German-Balt aristocrat who follows Rousseau in his belief in the possibilities for new democratic ways of living for mankind, and gets into trouble for putting them into practice. He marries a peasant-girl, Eeva, and, because he wishes to live on equal terms with her, has her educated to his level — together with her younger brother, Jakob, who tells the story (i.e.

keeps the journal we are given). Timo's utopian faith and trust in the essential goodness of humankind leads him to write to the Russian Czar a letter in which he outlines improvements that His Majesty should and could be making, in particular the liberation of the serfs. For this he is imprisoned in the famous Baltic fortress of Schlüsselberg for nine years. Eeva and her brother wait for him. When he comes out he is thought to have gone mad, and certainly many of his utterances and acts would suggest madness. But in other ways he appears observant, rational, indeed sane. Is therefore his madness feigned?

The novel has great narrative tension, a tension present as much in the pervading atmosphere as in specific happenings. Long imprisonment by the Russian authorities, a German-speaking upper-class, faith in humanity under test, the omnipresence of spies and informers and their presence in the least expected quarters — the parallels with Kross in 20th century Estonia are obvious. Yet one mustn't, I think, say that *The Czar's Madman* is a metaphor for the Estonia of our own times. Rather it is a demonstration, subtle and deeply satisfying as a novel, that all ages are agitated by comparable problems and struggles (some of them on-going despite temporary appearances to the contrary) and that belief in the rights of every individual is the only credo that can see us through.

'In the evenings Timo's friends would congregate either on University Street in his and Eeva's quarters, or elsewhere. Mostly these groups consisted of young aristocrats and literati, with a sprinkling of older gentlemen and university professors and their spouses. None of them showed any disdain for Eeva or acted as if they thought themselves superior to her. On the contrary: it seemed to them that they were trying to be especially amiable, which, on the other hand, sometimes seemed a little ridiculous — as when they would interrupt their conversations in French as soon as Eeva entered the room, and go on to address her in their often very stiff Estonian. And when she replied, with an almost imperceptible smile:

"*Mesdames et messieurs, continuez donc en français, pour moi c'est moins difficile que pour vous l'estonien*"

— some of them went slack-jawed with amazement ("So the pretty peasant girl that crazy Bock married really *did* get an education, just like people had been saying...."), others became instantly more talkative and inquisitive, even though they kept their curiosity about Eeva within the bounds appropriate to cultured society.' 29

DENMARK

ANTHOLOGY
Holm, Sven (ed.)

The Devil's Instrument and other Danish Stories

This excellent anthology focuses on Danish writing particularly of the 1960s. A later anthology *Double Danish: Contemporary Short Stories From Denmark* was published by Cormorant Books in Canada in 1991 and is no doubt worth tracking down to get an overview on more recent writing.

The title story *The Devil's Instrument* by Frank Jæger is a clever conceit that captures the sometimes light-hearted ease of sexual contact for the young 'as the snow falls lightly in the street' and the world is a simple, simply delightful place... Klaus Rifbjerg in contrast leaps right to the other end of the sexual spectrum with his portrait of the classic Dirty Old Man in *Old Man Jensen*. This seems though to be an honest and calm picture, graphic but not disgusting, picking up interestingly on the child's awe at the baffling sexuality of adults. Like *Old Man Jensen*, Hans Lyngby Jepsen's *The Blackbird* is a well-made little story but set in an older, simpler Denmark where the local community knows (and judges) everyone.

The next writer in this anythology, Villy Sørensen, has had three short story collections translated into English in the USA and his *In Strange Country* gives an inkling why; it is an intriguing, nightmarish but soberly described journey to the capital city of a dictatorship, a composite of Castro's Cuba, 1980s Czechoslovakia and Fascist Italy. It is also an ironic and very funny joke on gullible (Danish? American?) travellers who get out of their depth rather quickly.

Jørgen Gustava Brandt's *The Finnish Sailor* shows us life in a small fishing village through the story of 'the local tart' a woman now reduced by age to loneliness and universal general rejection as she tries for a last Saturday night fling of alcohol and sex. She finishes up in the arms of the (long-dead) Finnish sailor and this is hauntingly good writing.

The Man in the Cannon seems a very 1960s story; a bit absurdist, a bit sexually provocative while, in contrast, Ulla Ryum's *The Siamese Cat* is a fine evocation of quiet procvincial lives.

Albert Dam was a writer who first made his name as a novelist at the age of 82! His story here *The Mandrake* from the year of his breakthrough as a writer is an excellent, mystery-laden re-telling of the Robin Hood legend with extra sexual and occult elements that spice it up considerably into an effective allegory on power, corruption and social idealism. Keeping up the dark atmosphere Poul Ørum's *The Rat* is a nasty and powerful encounter with poverty and......a large black rat.

Absence by Christian Kampmann is an accurate glimpse of a marriage, its long drawn-out subterranean battles as well as its felicities, rhythms and acheivements. Anders Bodelsen's *Success* is set in executive suites and on freeways; the Denmark of identikit middle-managers and their beloved motors looms up in appalling, crushing clarity. Leif Panduro's *'Röslein auf der Heide'* cuts away from that vision of traffic lights, lane-hopping and synthetic-mix suits back into the fabulistic upper-middle class seventeenth century beloved of many Scandinavian authors. This curious story is composed largely of undertones of uneasy feelings that somehow together form a narrative...

Editor Sven Holm's *Miss Urst visits the Deer Park* is sensuoius and bizarre. The tale includes the re-birth of Miss Urst and the death of her poodles who one feels sorry for, unlike Miss Urst. Benny Andersen ends the book, he is another Danish writer who has had several books translated in the US, by Curbstone Press of Conneticut. As well as a writer he is a Jazz panist and his story *The Passage* is suitabley wacky and as much not about anything in particular as a good jazz riff. Just go with the swing. *(Ray Keenoy)*

"' Mosetta," he said, since she couldn't understand him anyway," you are maladjusted, but it is to be reckoned to your credit that when in Rome you do not shout as the Romans do and that you prefer to keep quiet altogether. The language of your country is corrupt, especially the nost important words: words like father, mother, love — because the Dictator is called the Country's Father and the country is called the Mother and they both demand to be loved.'" 65
Villy Sørensen *In Strange Country*

ANDERSEN
Hans Christian

Fairy Tales [Eventyr]

Hans Andersen called his autobiography of 1855 *Min livs eventyr* (*The Fairy Tale of My Life*); like a fairy-tale hero he had emerged from the poverty, obscurity and suffering of his early life in Denmark's second city, Odense to receive the personal and financial support of important Copenhagen families. He would embark on a literary career that brought him worldwide fame and increased Denmark's cultural prestige. Though the author of novels, plays, poetry, travel-books, Andersen owed this fame to his fairy tales. Though his resentment of this has been exaggerated, he repeatedly insisted (rightly) that these fairy tales were not merely for children but were a contribution to adult literature as well, that their most important quality was not the naivete, the child's vision, universally acknowledged, but his humour. As much as Dickens, who greatly admired him, humour is the inimitable indispensable element, funny-sad, bittersweet, at once innocent and sophisticated. To which attribute we must add stylistically flexible and frequently colloquial language which brought something new and vernacular into Danish writing, his extraordinary ability within a single tale to synthesize genres and unify them by means of narrative manner and controlling vision (a story like *The Travelling Companion* partakes — often, amazingly, at one and the same time — of the traditional folk-tale, the vignette of country life, the Gothic horror-tale, the humorous anecdote, the religious or moral parable, and the poetic excursion into supra-realistic realms) and finally what can only be termed the mystical. *The Little Mermaid* and *The Snow Queen*, to take the best-known instances, are two of the great transfiguring imaginative literary journeys of the 19th century.

Andersen's father was a shoemaker who died when his son was eleven; a radical intellectual prevented by poverty from the full realisation of his gifts, he built for Andersen the toy theatre that was to be so important to his development. An interesting thesis could be written on the effect of toy theatres on writers who became representative national figures drawing on a rich folklore: Ibsen, Dickens, Robert Louis Stevenson, García Lorca. Andersen's ability to condense material and to produce work on a miniature scale that seems inexhaustible in its content must derive from this childhood passion. Andersen's mother was much older than her husband, a woman of indomitable character whose will-power Hans — appearances often to the contrary for he had a histrionic side — inherited. Her daughter, Hans' half-sister, worked as a prostitute for a time; she was to cause her brother a deep unease. The contrast between the deprivations of his early years and family and the success and wealth he became familiar with acted as a galvanising creative force, as in the case of Dickens himself; throughout the stories menace can be felt, security is threatened, identity is challenged and undermined. Andersen repeatedly appears himself in his work — usually as a listener, a travelling collector of stories (he was a considerable and restless traveller, particularly devoted, like so many Scandinavian artists, to Italy) — but of course the stories at their best are almost more often than not dramatisations of internal conflicts, of the three-sided battle between cruel memory, ambition and the desire to know happiness in life.

Andersen had a difficult temperament, he was emotionally unfulfilled, bedazzled by the idea of greatness and by those who had known it, sexually ambiguous, both lonely and sociable. It is impossible surely not to read perhaps the finest story of all, *The Little Mermaid,* as a heartfelt cry of longing for an ordinary human life and love that he was from the earliest denied, for an appreciation in warm and physical terms for those excellences of character which had to have principally literary recognition.

On the other hand Andersen's nearness to both the peasantry and the urban proletariat is responsible for the two remarkable features of his *oeuvre* which have given him his firm position in world literature: his ability to crystallise a common human predicament in a story that is a memorable, psyche-addressing metaphor; his ceaseless sympathy for the unfortunate, the downtrodden, those obscure as he once felt himself to be, like the Little Match-Maker and the poor families who live in the attics of tenement buildings whom we meet in *The Snow Queen*. It is worth pointing out that a majority of the most famous and impressive tales feature female characters and seem, at one level, even when overt fantasies, pleas for women to be released from oppression. *Thumbelina* and *The Little Mermaid* lend themselves to this reading, while of the marvellous *Snow Queen* children's literature critic Naomi Lewis writes: 'How many of us notice that it is the one great fairy tale where all the main characters (eight or more of them) are girls or women, while the victim who must be saved is a boy? Did Andersen realise this himself?'

As one can say about Dickens (whom he visited, outstaying his welcome by being a guest for five weeks!) Andersen has become part of the climate of the West. *The Emperor's New Clothes*, *The Ugly Duckling* — these are familiar to many millions and have become instruments of our self-definition. He has been influential not only on children's literature (it is possible to find him in the stories of Astrid Lindgren and C.S. Lewis) and not only in Denmark (though his influence can be found in Isak Dinesen and Peter Høeg) and not only in Scandinavia (where P.O. Enquist has written a play, *Rainsnakes*, about him) but continuingly throughout the world's generations: Lord David Cecil, W.H. Auden, Q.D. Leavis, Angus Wilson, Cees Nooteboom are just five eminent twentieth-century writers who have gratefully paid tribute to his genius. There are many, many editions, but the World's Classics selection (Oxford University Press) can be particularly recommended — for L.W. Kingsland's fluent-reading translation, for Naomi Lewis' percipient introduction and for the beautiful original illustrations by Vilhelm Pedersen and Lorenz Frølich.

'When it grew dark many-coloured lamps were lit, and the sailors danced merry dances on deck. The little mermaid could not help thinking of the first time she had dived up to the surface of the sea and had seen the same splendour and rejoicing, and she whirled in the dance with the rest, swerving as a swallow swerves when it is pursued, and they all applauded her in admiration, for never before had she danced so brilliantly. Sharp knives seemed to cut into her delicate feet, but she did not feel it, for the pain in her heart cut yet more sharply. She knew this was the last evening she would ever see him for whom she had forsaken her kindred and her home, given up her lovely voice, and daily suffered unending torment — and he had no idea of it. This was the last night she would breathe the same air as he, or look upon the deep sea and the starry blue sky; an everlasting night without thoughts or dreams awaited her, for she had no soul and could not gain one. And all was rejoicing and merrymaking on board until well gone midnight. She laughed and danced with the thought of death in her heart...

The ship grew still and quiet: only the helmsman stood by the wheel. The little mermaid laid her white arms upon the rail and looked towards the east for the first red of morning — the first ray of the sun, she knew, would kill her. Then she saw her sister rise up to the surface of the sea.' *The Little Mermaid* 103-4

BLIXEN
Karen (DINESEN Isak)

Out of Africa

Out of Africa was published in 1937, only six years after Karen Blixen's return to Europe from Kenya where since 1941 she had lived on and run a coffee-farm — for the last ten years, after her divorce, in sole command of it. The book therefore has an elegiac quality; profound feeling for a place, a way of life, a network of relationships that can never come back, that already partakes of the *paradis perdu*, permeates every page. Even the marvellously simple opening sentence suggests this: 'I had a farm in Africa, at the foot of the Ngong Hills.' And it is with a salutation to the Ngong Hills that the book ends: 'The outline of the mountain was slowly smoothed and levelled out by the hand of distance.'

Though a memoir, not a novel, *Out of Africa* is as good as one — succeeding by those very means that novels at their best work on us: characterisation, the loving attentive portraits of the Africans she comes to know so intimately and yet who always remain mysterious to her, the delineation of a relationship in her love for Denys Finch-Hatton, her marriage to her cousin who gave her syphilis and which was unsatisfactory almost from the first and finally an intense sense of place. The book has variety — its mining of African (Kikuyu) lore, its rapturous descriptions of plant and animal life — and shape; its form is almost symphonic.

It was on the coffee-farm, in the evenings, that the Baroness Blixen began writing what she refers to here as 'fairy-tales'. In fact, under the pseudonym of Isak Dinesen, her *Seven Gothic Tales* came out three years before *Out of Africa* (for a long time her most famous work). Is Isak Dinesen the same as Karen Blixen? Certainly we can ascribe to both a great poetic sensibility and literary power. Certainly there is in both an almost uncanny sense of significant and appropriate structure for her material. Isak Dinesen's stories are often praised for their 'aristocratic' attributes (their feeling for *bon ton*, their exquisitely civilised standards that coexist with an exemplary toughness). But it is *Out of Africa* that for me is the more aristocratic in viewpoint, and not, one has to confess, always in the complimentary sense of that term. There is a certain loftiness, a concentration on aethetic sensations that is not always sympathetic, and for me this is revelaed in her relish for shooting — for taking the lives of wild animals (whom no-one could appreciate more finely) as though she had the right to obey whatever impulses were hers. Perhaps her later experience of occupied Denmark chastened and even humbled her proud nature for the better.

This is a full and rewarding book, readers of which should put the Robert Redford/Meryl Streep movie out of their minds as thoroughly as possible:

'When Denys Finch-Hatton came back after one of his long expeditions, he was starved for talk, and found me on the farm starved for talk, so that we sat over the dinner-table into the small hours of the morning, talking of all the things we could think of, and mastering them all, and laughing at them. White people, who for a long time live alone with Natives, get into the habit of saying what they mean, because they have no reason or opportunity for dissimulation, and when they meet again their conversation keeps the Native tone. We then kept up the theory that the wild Masai tribe, in their Menyatta under the hills, would see the house all afire, like a star in the night, as the peasants of Umbria saw the house wherein Saint Francis and Saint Clare were entertaining one another upon theology.' 141

BLIXEN
Karen [DINESEN Isak]

Seven Gothic Tales

Winter's Tales

Last Tales

Anecdotes of Destiny

Isak Dinesen would seem one of those writers who are truly sui generis. Affinities can be found for her — eminently with Hans Christian Andersen himself; her place in twentieth-century Danish literature is comparable to his in the nineteenth century — but so original are her tales that she seems to have arrived in the literary world, her creative mind sharpened and intensified no doubt by her African life, like Athene springing fully armed from the brow of Zeus. The comparison is apt since what her stories generate above all is a sense of the writer's wisdom, evidenced in their mesmeric narrative thrust, their purposeful, resonant, imaginative language and their wide canvas, born of a fully lived and complicated life. Her tales span over many countries and times, but their breadth does not lie in this so much as in their emotional range and their coverage of many different social milieus and predicaments. (Incidentally Dinesen, if anybody, could lead one to speak of a `Scandinavian' sensibility; though, for obvious reasons, Denmark features the most frequently in her work, she is clearly equally at home in Sweden and Norway; indeed her evocation of the Norwegian landscape in such stories as *The Pearls* in *Winter's Tales* and *Tempests* in *Anecdotes of Destiny* is surely unequalled even by writers from Norway itself.)

'Romance' or 'romantic', 'fairy tale', 'Gothic' — these are terms employed (not least by Dinesen herself) in relation to her fiction and understandably, but they mustn't be allowed to obscure her grasp of complex human psychology including her subtle understanding of mixed motives and her almost eerie ability to render sexual longing, her understanding of the prevalent standards of many societies and her intellectual comprehension of metaphysical aspirations. Her aristocratic cast of mind is frequently commented on — but in many of the tales it is far less apparent than in *Out of Africa*; in some of the finest a very 'Scandinavian' democratic vista is in command, for instance in *The Dreaming Child* (in *Winter's Tales*). She is also one of the rare writers to be able to pass from female to male, even in their specifically sexual aspects, with equal empathy.

Her four volumes differ from one another, though they are all very palpably the work of the same hugely individual writer. *Seven Gothic Tales* (1934), as its title proclaims, is the book in which her feeling for the exotic, for the triumphantly and romantically exceptional, as a kind of laboratory in which to examine the workings of the human heart has its richest expression. In *The Old Chevalier* about a Danish nobleman's relationship with a French prostitute we read:

> 'I thought of the goddess Nemesis, and I believed that had I not had the moment of doubt and fear in the night, I might have felt, in the morning, the strength in me, and the right, to move her destiny and mine. It is said about the highwaymen who in the old days haunted the forests of Denmark that they used to have a wire stretched across the road with a bell attached. The coaches in passing would touch the wire and the bell would ring within their den and call out the robbers. I had touched the wire and a bell had rung somewhere. the girl had not been afraid, but I had been afraid, I had asked: "What am I to pay for this?" and the goddess herself had answered: "Twenty francs," and with her you cannot bargain. You think of many things, when you are young.'

Winter's Tales (1942) was Isak Dinesen's favourite among her collections, partly because the stories were written during the Nazi occupation of Denmark and mine the wealth of Danish folklore. The stories here are perhaps of all hers the closest to the fairy-tale, even the folktale: *The Pearls* is an inventive variant on the Brothers Grimm's *The Boy Who Set Out to Learn How to Shudder*, actually referred to in the text, the wonderful *Sailor-Boy's Tale* makes use of the common folk theme of instinctual kindness to a bird (or animal) in distress being unexpectedly rewarded in a completely different context. The volume contains one of her most sophisticated productions, *The Dreaming Child*, yet this too has folk origins — in stories of foundlings who are princes in disguise, of changelings who possess and exercise extraordinary talents. But the story is also a sensitive and mature study of a marriage, of the parental impulse, of the necessary power of fantasy. Of the effect of the child Jens on the household which has adopted him, Isak Dinesen writes:

'One effect of this particular spell was this: that people were made to see themselves with the eyes of the dreamer, and were impelled to live up to an ideal, and that for this their higher existence, they became dependent upon him. During the time that Jens lived in the house, it was much changed, and dissimilar from the other houses of the town, it became a Mount Olympus, the abode of divinites.'

Last Tales (1957) partake of all categories of Isak Dinesen's art: from the Gothic in *The Caryatids* to the evocation of past social mores in *Copenhagen Season*. Reviewing it in the 'New York Times' Eudora Welty wrote:

'Her tales are glimpses out of, rather than into, an extraordinary mind. Sometimes one feels that Isak Dinesen's stories come toward one like the flashes and signal-beams from a lighthouse on a strange and infrequently sighted coast — a coast beautiful and precarious, for it may be the last out-reach of magic, but resting on bedrock.'

But, in my view, her last volume, *Anecdotes of Destiny* (1958) is, as a book, the finest, the five stories, three of them of 'novella' length, being united by the theme (not always explicitly stated) of Ariel, of reach and over-reach, of the undismissable dictates of the spirit in a world apprently intent on frustrating them and distinguished by a limpidity of style and by rapt, intent economy in narration. Of the three substantial tales *Babette's Feast*, set in Norway, has been made famous by Bille August's film; its subject and surprise ending, of the servant turned genius, belong to both fairy-tale and *commedia dell'arte*, to say which isn't at all to diminish the portrayal of a social world and of individual motives.

An Immortal Story describes — movingly and memorably — a doomed attempt to convert into reality the old seamen's story of the young sailor who, ashore, is offered five guineas by an elderly man to make love to his young wife. *Tempests*, again taking place in Norway, is perhaps, were one asked to make such a choice, Isak Dinesen's supreme story, the one that represents her mind and art at the height of their powers. A touring theatrical company is shipwrecked in bad weather in a remote Norwegian town, and the girl, Malli, who has played Ariel, wins the hearts of the community through her beauty and her bravery during the storm, especially that of the son of its leading family. But she cannot accept the new part found for her; her spirit says otherwise:

'I will sit quite still and wait an hour before I close my letter.... Now the hour is at an end. Within it I have thought of two things.

...That when soon I sail from here, I may again run into such a storm as the one in Kvasefjord. But that this time I shall clearly understand that it is not a play in the theatre, but it is death. And it seems to me that then, in the last moment before we go down, I can in all truth be yours....

But the other of the two is this: If now I heard your steps on the stairs from the office, and you came into the room to me! It seems to me now that those moments in which I did so hear your steps on the stairs were the happiest in my whole life....Farewell.' 94-5 *Tempests*

BRØGGER
Suzanne

A Fighting Pig's Too Tough to Eat [En gris som har vaeret at slås kan man ikke stege]

Since the early 1970s Suzanne Brøgger, journalist, iconoclastic novelist and poet, born into a partly Jewish family affected by World War Two and the German Occupation, has been living in the quiet rural district of Løve in West Sjaelland. As she herself says in her essay *I Live as I Write and I Write as I Live*: 'I live in a rather invisible place where progress has passed right by, and I am happy about that.... In terms of train tracks, I live only 100km from Copenhagen — but in terms of time, I live thousands of kilometres away. I live by the marshes where the marshwoman brews her mist and I write my books — it comes to the same thing. From my window I can see where the world ends.'

A Fighting Pig is a fictionalised diary of Suzanne Brøgger's life in Løve, its strange title deriving from a folk belief firmly held by her neighbours which made a strong impression on her. From the literary point of view the work has two sources: the famous Gobelin tapestries depicting the six senses, 'The Lady and the Unicorn' and Rainer Maria Rilke's *Notebooks of Malte Laurids Brigge* which pays homage to these same tapestries and is allegedly written by an aristocratic poet of Scandinavian provenance. Brøgger adopts Rilke's form of notebook observations, jotting down both impressions of the external country world and internal reflections and divides these up — *pace* the tapestries — according to the six senses (though the division isn't especially rigid).

Suzanne Brøgger comes over as an urbane, highly intelligent, eccentric, bohemian individual — with an exhibitionist streak and a warm heart. She is often in love. At times I feel the journalistic breeziness is too obtrusive, and there are certain areas — in particular her attitude to animals — when, despite her Green credentials (study of Lovelock and Gaia, interest in Tibetan Buddhism etc.) she appears quite superficial in her responses, refusing to do justice to the harsher truths in their exploitation by human beings. But at other times she displays a Colette-like engagement with the natural world — her accounts of the cat Shabanou are quite delightful — sensuous, feminine if not positively feminist, and attentive to detail. Above all she enjoys an easy and sensitive relation with her neighbours, thoroughly conservative, indeed tenaciously so, (reading about them is to be given a key to the widespread Danish Euroscepticism) — and very unlike herself. She is able nevertheless to enter into a real dialogue with them and bring them to life on her pages. Though her landscape is a Danish one, and intimately known, Trelleborg, 'the best preserved Viking monument in Europe' is close to hand, her notebook novella is true to the urban-rural dichotomies experienced by most Western communities today, and, taken in context with her frequently incisive essays, provides a memorable and very enjoyable addition to their serious discussion.

'It's Helmut who's ploughed the black field.

Helmut can plough, but he can't walk. For once upon a time he fell in the barn and broke his pelvis, and because he didn't want to go to the doctor, the bones didn't set properly. So now Helmut can only get around by pulling himself up in jumps and jerks using a broomstick. But every morning at five they move him out in the field or up on a tractor. His hair is grey, his complexion like apples and his eyes as shiny as those of a virgin. But it isn't a man you're talking to, he's too sublime for that. You automatically make a slight curtsy when passing him at the edge of the field.

Next to the black field is a strip of green, a ditch with a black bird. That means infinite happiness.' 95

HØEG
Peter

Borderliners [De Måske Egnede]

This, Peter Høeg's third novel, is arguably the finest of the prodigiously successful Danish writer's productions, more elusive than its fellows and making harder demands on its readers. Set in a special school and centring on three disturbed adolescents one of whom bears Peter Høeg's own name, it is obsessed with the conflict between linear and circular time, and presents key events elliptically, often interspersing scenes — both dramatic ones and vignettes of school life — with philosophical speculations.

The school is a government-blessed experiment, a private establishment catering for intelligent privileged children but also taking in difficult pupils from special institutions in order to 'normalise' them. Peter, the 'I' of the novel, the suicidal and murderous August, and the girl Katerina with her terrible omnipresent familial past are candidates for this process. A humane venture? Possibly — though Peter in particular comes to loathe Biehl's Academy, above all for its preoccupation with conformity. The re-education of mavericks is carried through without open or honest dealings with the adolescents themselves; the school head (Biehl) and his deputy are revealed as essentially self-deceiving bullies, and their lack of feeling justifies Peter's hostility. There is a sense in which the whole rehabilitation enterprise is a paradigm for Denmark — and indeed any prosperous developed Western society. There is continual exasperated reference throughout the novel to Bishop Grundtvig, nineteenth century architect of modern Denmark; indeed Biehl is the author of a book about him. The fact that Denmark is, quite literally, one of the world's most civilised societies, doesn't diminish Høeg's accusations of smugness, of ultimate intolerance. Even the smoothest-running society will produce a misfit like the novel's Peter — who will one day become the creative writer, Peter Høeg. Also, even the smoothest-running society has to acknowledge a kind of time that is beyond clock measurement,and which challenges all its assumptions:

'There we sat... I kept going...

"There is a selection that takes place. People are selected according to the laws of nature. The school is an instrument dedicated to eleveation. It works like this. If you achieve in the way you're supposed to, time raises you up. That's why the classrooms are arranged as they are. From Primary I to III you're on the ground floor, then you move up to the first floor, then the second, then to the Secondary on the third, until at last — at the very top, in the assembly hall — you receive your certificate from Biehl. And then you can fly out into the world."

There, I had said it. We were nearing the conclusion.

"I've been wondering why it is so hard for them, why there are so many rules. And it occurred to me that it is because they have to keep the outside world out. Because out there it's not everywhere that it raises up. There are lots of places out there where time drags you downwards towards destruction. That is what they must keep out. You must be left in no doubt that the world raises you up, otherwise it would be impossible to cope with the expectations. Coping is something you do best when you believe in time. If you believe the whole world is an instrument through which you become elevated, just so long as you do your best — that is the metaphor the school presents. It's brilliant.'" 69

HØEG
Peter

History of Danish Dreams [Forestilling om det Tyvende Arhundrede]

In 1987, in a north Copenhagen suburb, a young man of thirty arrived at the private house premises of a small but distinguished publishing company, Rosinante. He had, he said, written a novel — rather a long one, it turned out — which he would like the firm's founder, Merete Ries, to read. He was working as a dancer, and had not met with much response in his dealings with the publishing world. Editors have good reason to be wary of people presenting themselves on their doorsteps asking to be read, but Merete Ries found something serious and appealing about her caller — Peter Høeg. And his novel proved to be both ambitious and accomplished, a picture of Danish life through the development of four families — with contrasting stylistic mirroring of their attitudes to life. Rosinante published the novel (the literal meaning of its Danish title is 'Introduction to the Twentieth Century') in 1988, and it was at once seen as the début of a quite remarkable talent.

Only on the last page of the book do we learn the identity of the 'I' who has periodically made authorial intrusions into the long, many-stranded narrative. It is Mads, the descendant of every person we have engaged with, and we at last realise that what we have been receiving as objective pictures of people and times past are a part of his subjective being, and therefore, by extension, of our own. Like his grandfather, Carl Laurids, Mads Mahogni was born on New Year's Eve, and this date has an unashamedly symbolic resonance. This is reinforced by Mad's own resemblance to Peter Høeg himself: they have the same adventurous predisposition, loving fencing, mountaineering, skiing. Mads is thus the very opposite of the sensitive, enervated youth who ends the history of Thomas Mann's *Buddenbrooks*, with which this novel has certain affinities. Mads stands rather as the inheritor of energies which were destructive in his forebears but which can eventually lead to freedom of expression. Høeg sees that, since the second World War, Western society has swept away not only old hierarchies, but also the beliefs that sustained them. And we are the better for their destruction.

Mads' ancestry is various and vigorous enough. His paternal grandfather was an amoral, hugely successful entrepreneur, his paternal grandmother a high-class whore. His maternal grandfather, Adonis — still alive at the end of the book — comes from a long line of master criminals, but is himself, though a proficient pickpocket, a musician-cum-stunt-artist of great integrity. His maternal grandmother, Anna, was believed as a child to be the future mother of the Saviour of Mankind, and was therefore kept in a cage to protect her from the attentions of ordinary male progenitors. She escaped to run off with Adonis. The histories of his grandparents' fortunes as presented partake of Magic Realism; the later sections of the novel dealing with the meeting and marriage of Mads' father and mother are closer to actual experience, constitute a brilliant metaphor for prosperous bourgeois society and are very moving. The layers of meaning behind the tensions and inconsistencies in Carlsten and Maria's life are many and rewarding.

'Riding [on bicycles] side by side along the byways, under the sun and the sky and the larks, and eating liver pâté with cucumber on wholemeal bread in the fresh air, they [Carlsten and Maria] resemble the Fifties' dream, our dream, of young love; and the only thing that might seem surprising is that their past did not really exist; that they rode through Denmark without any sign of recognition and without visiting one single person and without really seeing anything at all except each other's eyes and each other's sun-kissed freckles. And perhaps this says something about the price of that impending freedom which was already making its presence felt... And a moment later their infatuation was no longer doubled, but trebled, when — on the top of that hill which we Danes call Himmelbjerget, Mountain to the Heavens — Maria suddenly found herself with something in her hand: something light-coloured — her diaphragm — and she drew her hand back and sent the soft rubber discs spinning far off into space. And because, that summer, everything fell into place with such perfect and intimate timing, she became pregnant that very evening.' 30

HØEG
Peter

Miss Smilla's Feeling for Snow [Frøken Smillas Fornemmelse for Sne]

A case could be made for naming this the European novel which made the greatest impact on the widest readership during the 1990s. Despite the acclaim given *A History of Danish Dreams* and a volume of short stories, nothing quite prepared publishers and author for the enormous success, critical and commercial, of this ingenious and imaginative thriller; it changed Peter Høeg's whole life — and income. It often seems impossible to meet someone who has not read and been captivated by the book — and for a time it made the Arctic terrains almost fashionable. Director Bille August turned it into a film.

The strange memorable title of the novel sums up its central character's predicament. Smilla lives uneasily in Denmark, her affluent doctor father's country, remembering with sad intensity her childhood in Greenland with her strong-willed Innuit hunter mother. A physicist of some accomplishment, she has proved quite unable to follow projects through, to hold jobs down. ("Is there any institution you haven't been thrown out of, Miss Jaspersen?" she's asked.) She chooses to make her home not in some suburb for professional people, but in one of the bleak apartment blocks down by the Copenhagen docks where so many Greenlanders live. Because as she puts it:

> 'I feel a connection to the Eskimos... because of their ability to know, without a shadow of a doubt, that life is meaningful. Because of the way, in their consciousness, they can live with the tension between irreconilable contradictions, without sinking into despair and without looking for a simplified solution. Because of their short, short path to ecstasy. because they can meet a fellow human being, and see him for what he is, without judging, their clarity not weakened by prejudice.'

Her intransigence and aggression don't make her many friends. Nor, as it turns out, do her gifts: she can distinguish and classify the numerous types of snow and ice that ordinary Europeans fail to notice. This gift has an uncomfortable application when she realises from looking at his footprints in the snow that a little Greenlandic boy, Isaiah, who fell off the roof of her apartment block was being chased. It's an extremely hard business convincing others that this was the case, but her dogged nature means that Smilla is up to this and more, indeed a great deal more.

For she has stumbled on a lengthy chain of deception,

exploitation and suppression which she feels morally compelled to follow to its furthest conclusion — to be attained at the end of a hazardous voyage to north-east Greenland and the lonely islands off its ice-bound coast.

It is extremely hard to put this long novel down, and the excitement it engenders spills over into your reluctant time away from it. But this is only one of its attributes; it is also a novel of a riven society, of the relations between Europe and an under-considered part of the world, of science versus the atavistic, of humankind against the terrifying vastness and power of Nature.

'How bright the roof is in front of me.As if it was the snow, in a layer maybe ten centimetres thick, which has all along created the light on this winter day, and which still shines with a sporadic glitter like brilliant little grey beads.

At ground level the snow melts slightly, even in hard frost, because of the heat of the city. But up here it lies loosely, the way it fell. Only Isaiah has walked on it.

Even when there's no heat, no new snow, no wind, even then the snow changes.As if it were breathing, as if it condenses and rises and sinks and disintegrates.

He wore sneakers, even in winter, and those are his footprints, the worn-down sole of his basketball boots with the barely visible outline of concentric circles in front of the arch on which the player is supposed to pirouette.

He stepped out into the snow from where we're standing.The footprints head diagonally towards the edge and continue along the roof for maybe ten metres.There they stop.And then continue towards the corner and end of the building.Then they follow the edge at a distance of about half a metre, up to the corner facing the other warehouse. from there he has turned approximately three metres in towards the centre to get a running start.Then the tracks go straight for the edge where he jumped off.' 7

HØEG
Peter

The Woman and the Ape [Kvinden og Aben]

In the near future a new extension is added to London Zoo, to promote the exciting discoveries about humankind's kinship to the animal world. Headed by the intensely ambitious Adam Burden, whose thirst for success exceeds both his moral sense and his power of empathy with other creatures, the Zoo is to feature at the opening of this extension a remarkable specimen, an anthropoid ape whose labyrinthine brain may well challenge all convenient assumptions about the gulf between humans and non-humans. The word 'challenge' has a double sense for the brain of the ape Erasmus (in point of fact superior to a human's) is very active and resourceful, and more than up to working out how best to outwit his exploiters. For that, as Madelene, Burden's beautiful acoholic Danish wife, perceives is what the director and his colleagues are — willing, indeed anxious to carry out hideous experiments to prove their theories, blind to the complex world of emotion that the ape, like all sensate beings, carries within him, and not above using criminal assistance. Something about Erasmus galvanises Madelene out of her bored, rich, upholstered life, something it would be too easy to dismiss as attraction, or even 'animal magnetism', though it partakes of these. Certainly the beautifully described moment when the ape, captive and resident in the grounds of her own home, reaches out with his great arm and plucks a peach for her, is decisive. But perhaps it is principally that the ape's situation, which he so patently comprehends, brings home to Madelene just how restricted and disadvantaged her own is.

So she abandons the consolations of alcohol and sets about not only freeing Erasmus but uncovering what misuses are in store for him. But as she becomes more deeply involved with his plight, sex asserts itself — and love too. The scenes of love-making between ape and woman brought the novel a certain *succès de scandale*.

A tightly-plotted and fast-moving thriller this novel — in its theme and perhaps also in its central female character — resembles *Miss Smilla* more than any of Hoeg's other books. It is more overtly ideological too. There is great beauty in its evocations of animal life, both in contact with and away from human beings, a beauty that gains rather than otherwise from its unflinching look at the cruelty and suffering that run through the creature world.

'She unlocked the cage and remained in the doorway for a moment looking at the animal. She was never going to see it again and so she tried to imprint its image on her memory, to take a mental farewell photograph.

The ape was in the process of feeding. It ate absorbedly, egoistically, as Madelene herself always dreamed of eating, with every sense other than those of taste and smell suspended, stripped of all mannerliness and with that same fearlessness which had from the beginning, seemed like a question aimed at her. A question which, she now realised, had been asking: How do you really want to be? And to this question her heart had answered: I want — in some way — to be like you.

"I've come to let you out," she said.

The ape rose. It placed its fists on the ground and pushed itself into a position which, while erect, still left it on all fours. From there it kept on going, relinquished its hold on the ground, straightened its back, lifted its head and clasped its hand across its chest.

Madelene had been aware that the ape had — to some degree and in a way she did not understand — been learning from the people and goings-on around it. Even so, she was staggered. For a moment they stood there, quite still, she and the ape face to face. Then she turned towards the grille and opened first it and then the conservatory door. They stepped out into the park.' 73-4

STANGERUP
Henrik

The Road to Lagoa Santa [Vejen til Lagoa Santa]

This novel is the distinguished Danish novelist's recreation (aided by his own personal investigations) of the mysterious and never satisfactorily explained story of the once reknowned Danish naturalist, Wilhelm Lund, who, in 1933 ventured into the Brazilian interior. Here for ten years he was to pursue his researches against the appalling odds presented by hostile indigenous people and an appalling climate. Known as the White Bone collector, Lund had come across the fossils of animals never before known. His attempts to place them scientifically belong to that phase when the prehistoric period was being re-written, when eras of unbelievable duration and complex make-up were having to be pasted over the conventional wisdom about God's creation of the Earth.

At the end of the ten years the obsessive Lund, attended by his close friend the artist P.A. Brandt, stopped working and enetered a distressing mental state. He never returned to Europe. The power of the hostile, magnificent landscape around him and of the significance of his own tremendous discoveries overwhelmed him.

This is a powerful and intellectually challenging novel, and in its fascination with Nature and its apprehension of places beyond the reaches of Western civilisation, it is informed by a very Scandinavian love of adventure and desire to understand the widest of all possible worlds.

'Brazil, Java, Spitzbergen, the North Pole. Where does Earth begin? Wilhelm makes the globe spin round and round. Suddenly he stops it with his finger. The Earth begins there! And the Earth turns round the Sun and the Moon turns round the Earth. But right now the Earth is standing still because he has stopped it just where Europe merges into Asia. What if he had been born there? Would he have had slanting eyes and high cheekbones? Would he still have been named Wilhelm — just in a different way? He once lived out on a star, said his father after he had climbed the stairs from the draper's shop, changed to his slippers in the corridor, and come all the way through the apartment into the room where Wilhelm has been lying in bed for almost ten days. Now he is feeling a little better. The worst fever attacks are over. His father's globe has been placed on a small low table by the head of his bed so that he can learn all about the countries of the world. It is brown where there are mountains and has yellow markings where there are steppes and white ones indicating desert and striped and dots across the oceans where Columbus and Vasco da Gama sailed with their men.' 31

FAROES

ANTHOLOGY

Brønner, Hedin (ed.)

Faroese Short Stories

The Faroes, an island group North of Scotland but politically part of Denmark, have only the population of a small town but have managed all the same to produce a quite disproportionate literature, well and genialy presented in this collection. It starts off with an amusing, sympathetic story by pioneer Faroes author Mads Andrias Winther *The Battle of Klandurskot* — a sort of Clochemerle tale set in an isolated island parish. The dynamic new young parson tries to introduce a school and even, God forbid, update the old-established hymn tunes. The conservatism humorously explored here stems no doubt from a patriarchal and conformist life-style that evolved in cold treeless lands where everyone had to pull together to guarantee survival. Winther's second piece here *To Catch a Thief* is a splendid story, a real popular tale passed from mouth to mouth, like a fresh and socially critical folktale.

Sverri Patursson, like Winther a turn of the century writer, gives us a story of the sea in *Eliezer and the Basking Shark* rather than of the village — it too is a fine bit of storytelling; full of human conflict and the struggle with nature.

The anthology also contains six stories from the acknowledged star of Faroese litereature William Heinesen. The first, *Gamaliel's Bewitchment,* is a rollicking tale set in the fish processing works of the Faroese capital Tórshavn, a tale peopled by commanding sea-captains, beautiful women and dull merchants all behaving very oddly one mad summer's day... More bewitchment in *In the Madman's Garden,* the enchanted scary world of children's discoveries, the discovery of a secret garden, of secret sadness and secret pleasures. *The Night of the Storm* is more dramatic; an expressionist romp which begins with a devastating North Atlantic storm hitting Tórshavn and which ends with a kick in the belly to self-righteous moralists. The last of the Heinesen stories here is the lyrical *Celestial Journey* which demonstrates how Heinesen loved his flights of fancy as much as his famous psychological realism.

Heðin Brú born in 1901 was of the same generation as Heinesen. His *Lice* is a very funny (and disgusting) example of what one might call the 'folksy' (as opposed to folk) tale. It's the sad story of a very old man and his littly itchy pets. There's another old chap in the equally folksy *Emanuel* but *The Long Darkness* is the poignant account of a blind man in an all-hunting, all-fishing all-farming society which had no place for a young shepherd who had lost his sight. Brú's *Men of Letters* in contrast is a hilarious story of young sailors.

Author Martin Joensen was from a rural part of these predominantly rural islands and his *To Be A Dentist* has fascinating social detail of life at the turn of the century in isolated places while Valdemar Poulsen's *The Huntsman* will please those not enamoured by Nordic enthusiasm for hunting. Karsten Hoydal who contributes *Summer Eve at the 'Rockall'* had a day job as a fisheries inspector while the youngest writer here, Jens Pauli Heinesen, a distant relation of William Heinesen was born in 1932 and his *Little Frants Vilhelm* is a fine story of a child and his odd pet while *Gestur* is also an animal story, about a dog, a good honest old dog, a fine thing on the Faroes or anywhere else. *Ray Keenoy*

'Long before they anchored, they sent a boat ashore for mail, and before the crew had secured the sails, it was back. But they all agreed to wait with the reading till they had finished their work and cleaned themselves up.

There were other Faroese vessels in the harbor. Boats passing between them were hailed so that bits of news could be shared. Poor people from shore came out to pay visits on board. Here came a gnarled old man and held up a battered tin can, asking them to give him a fish liver. The men hung over the rail joking with him, asking if there were plenty of nice girls on shore — and liquor as well. *Jú,* he could vouch for that! And when they threw some food down into his boat, his eyes lit up within his tangled beard, and he thanked them eagerly and cast off.

Another fellow came alongside and climbed on board and went around begging for everything he laid eyes on. They took him forward to the bow and showed him the starboard anchor hanging on the rail. "See this anchor hanging here? The skipper is going to throw it away. Why don't you go down and ask him for it."

The man went below right away, but it appeared he wasn't too well received. Out he came again like a whirlwind, jumped in his boat, shoved off and rowed ashore as if for his life.' *Men of Letters* Heðin Brú 207

'Sakaris Mortansson was the only shopkeeper in the district. His place was not particularly large, but the area didn't need a large store. The fishing and farming were good. The sea, the soil, and the bird cliffs filled the larders with food, and the sheep provided wool enough to clothe each body. So what Sakaris sold was mostly a sprinkling of flour, cereal, and tobacco — and then some coffee and syrup. A drop of coffee was a veritable gift from heaven for old, shivery people to have standing in some sooty pot all through the day. They would come to Sakaris with a handful of wool in the fold of an apron, or with a few ounces of feathers in a white bag. Sakaris was a bit annoyed whenever he had to weigh these trifles; he wasn't very well supplied with weights, either. (Some said, though perhaps only in malice, that he used small pebbles to put on the scales instead of the missing weights.) They rarely bought more than a quarter or a half pound. And they didn't buy much more of the other wares either. They were thrifty and would feel uncomfortable about bringing home armfuls of expensive boughten goods.' Martin Joensen *To Be A Dentist* 225

'Tórshavn, the ludicrous old capital of the Faroes, has not, curiously enough, picked itself a sensible location on any of the numerous calm and quiet fjords of these islands, but has grown on a precipitous open shoreline that the ocean has chewed up into countless promontories and skerries, and in winter the surf often reaches in among the houses and fills the narrow and steep alleyways with its salty spray. The so'westers sometimes take the form of hurricanes and cause damage to life and property.' William Heinesen *Night of the Storm* 117

HEINESEN
William

The Black Cauldron [Den Sorte Gryde]

A novel from the Faroes, an island group North of Scotland, politically part of Denmark but with a distinct culture and language. What, if anything, does a reader expect from such a source? Probably not this racy, conversational satire, set in the period of British occupation during World War II. War time means Kingsport or 'The Cauldron' is filled with 'déracinés and refugees' and has become 'a cosy nest for profiteers of every kind'. It is also very much a place filled with great characters, amongst them the voluptuous but bewhiskered young woman Thomea and her admirer a bedraggled Iclelander, Engilbert, a scholar of a mystical kind who makes a living lugging tubs of whale blubber around.

As in Nietzche's phrase, 'Alcohol and Christianity' are rife amongst the islanders, who habitually imbibe the cocktail of stern religion and hard drink common on Europe's North-Western fringes.

The Faroes evidently had a strange war, in that while many of their seamen were killed in German attacks on allied commercial shipping, at the same time unprecedented amounts of money poured in for their products and labour. This is Heinesen's main theme, the moral corruption of the powerful in the pursuit of wealth and the destruction of the powerless through death at sea and that disease of the poor life, TB.

Less prosaically one also gets a sense of this land encircled by nature (the seas) and hence more magical than those places where man has broken the link, the narrow bridge, between himself and the natural world and its dreams and visions, its waves of feeling and delight. These are things suggested by the Dedalus edition's jacket cover image; a night-set painting of boats, seals and mythical animals out in the fjord, from a painting by the multi-talented Heinesen himself.

It's not just love of nature that Heinesen celebrates; there is plenty too of what flows between man and woman, particularly in war-time when men don't know how much of life's fruits they'll ever live to taste; the islands are awash with foreign soldiers and sailors pursuing the island women, both single and married...

Meanwhile German raiders machine gun fishermen and torpedo boats carrying cargo to Britain — towards the end of the book Heinesen's satirical tone darkens and we discover why it's called *The Black Cauldron*, as more and more young men are killed bringing in and trans-shipping from Iceland fish catches that bring their owners record prices, and wealth is made amongst great misery. This is not a 'war book' but a work by a brilliant witness to this cataclysmic period, seen from an unusually far-off viewpoint but with perhaps all the more perspective for that, particularly relevant today as we discover just how much money was made (and in such evil ways) on both sides of the war that Heinesen's Faroes played a minor part in. *(Ray Keenoy)*

'Ivar and Frederik were not allowed to go before they had had a cup of coffee. Ivar poured a snaps for his father. The old man sipped it slowly; he held the glass gingerly and took great care not to spill a single drop, and with every sip he breathed a wish for thousandfold good fortune and then called down Christ's blessing and grace on them.

Ivar watched him impatiently. His father had always been like this, tender, delicate, almost womanish, full of pious apologies, excessively grateful for little things. Ivar could not help thinking of his mother, whom he clearly remembered, although he had only been five years old when she died: she was the opposite of her husband, big-boned and tough, mannish in temperament, kind and patient with her children, but taciturn and bitter when confronting strangers. Aye, his parents had been very different in nature and background; his father had come from poor stock, his mother from an affluent farming family. Yet despite this their married life had been happy, and they had left behind them the achievement of a lifetime: they had cleared the virgin land under the outcrop known as the Angelica Wall, where there was now a potato patch, meadows and a small herd of cattle. A peaceful locality, well hidden from the world, aye, merciful heavens, a happy place, a paradise to look back on when you were out there on the sea.' 101

FINLAND

ANTHOLOGY

Bo Carpelan, Veijo Meri & Matti Suurpää (eds)

A Way to Measure Time: Contemporary Finnish Literature

Perhaps the best piece to read first in this rich, splendid anthology is the last, written specially for the book by Matti Klinge: *A history of Finland in fourteen paragraphs*. This gives an excellent overview of the very particular historical and cultural circumstances in which Finnish writers have had to work. Finland entered this century as 'an autonomous state under Russian rule', an inheritance of 1809 when Finland was separated from Sweden, a significant Swedish minority however remaining a constituent of the new Duchy of Finland. Despite its subjection to Russia, Finland developed both a strong nationalist movement and a western-style (Swedish-influenced) democratic polity, both of which were to stand it in good cultural stead later on. Helsinki was a self-conscious, forward-looking capital city (waiting for the country's independence); egalitarian institutions and infra-structure evolved.

Finland broke from Russia during the 1917 revolution, and achieved recognised independence in 1918. The story of between-the-wars Finland is palpable in many a piece in this book: the growing prosperity and corresponding confidence, combined with an increased trust in Germany in the event of any conflict with the Soviet Union. This trust was to be cruelly betrayed by the Molotov-Ribbentrop pact which assigned Finland to the Soviet sphere of influence. In the 'winter war' (1939-40) Finland held off Soviet attack for 100 days before defeat and the surrender of Karelia. When Germany attacked Russia in 1941, Finland was an ally of Nazi Germany. From 1941 to 1944 Finnish soldiers were once again engaged against the Red Army. One does not have to read very far in this anthology to realise the tremendous effect on the Finnish national psyche of these, in effect, two separate wars: the savagery and inequality of the fighting, the dubiousness of the ally, the desperate recognition of the unlikelihood of success. A major Finnish prose-writer, Veijo Meri (born 1928), one of the editors of this volume, has made war experience a major theme. An extract from his fine story, *Boxes of Nails* is given below. See also the work of Väinö Linna (1920-92) whose novel *The Unknown Soldier (Tuntematon sotilas [1954])* has achieved classic status and is excerpted here: a horrifying account of physical deprivation, a young commander blinded by shell-fire in *Before Battle*.

Finland did not recover her pre-war territories but had to accommodate their fleeing inhabitants; further, she had to pay reparations to the Soviet Union. However in other respects she emerged secure from the aftermath of the Second World War, and was able to pursue social and economic policies making her one of the most affluent and egalitarian countries in Europe. Industrialisation and urbanisation proceeded; the Finnish imagination, nourished on an empty atavistic landscape of forest and lake and coast, had to come to terms with this while not foregoing an inherited sense of kinship with nature. Matti Klinge writes of the post-war period:

'The 1950s were very European, the 1960s American-influenced, the 1970s oriented toward the political Left. In the 1980s cultural life, along with economics and foreign policy, experienced a strong emphasis on international relations and inter-dependence, in which the provincialism engendered by Finland's size and internal interests was consciously rejected.' In 1994 Finland, together with Sweden and Austria, joined the European Union, in itself a significant marker of the 'new world order'.

Of the stories of contemporary life included here, read in particular *Melancholy Tale* by Antti Tuuri (born 1944) and *The Guest of Honour* by Martti Joenpolvi (born 1936), a poignant tale of an old labour dignitary at an official function. *Fury* by Alpo Ruuth (born 1943) is a nerve-rasping little study of gratuitous urban sadism and violence. Rural life continues to be a great inspiration to the Finnish literary mind, however, and — because of the inevitable slenderness of Finnish-language fiction recommended in this *Babel Guide* (because so few books have been translated) a second quotation from

A Way to Measure Time follows that from Veijo Meri.

Novelist and short-story-writer, Veikko Huovinen (born 1927) is famous for his renderings of backwoodsmen's lives; the story *Hirri* is a poignant and beautiful example of his gifts.

'To the right was the Gulf of Finland, grey, vast, as smooth as death. Even at midday its horizon was like a dark corner. The waves appeared motionless no matter how long and hard you looked at them. The sandy shoreline went on and on. In front of us spread a small valley three kilometres wide, in which a scraggly forest of leafy trees was growing. On the ridge beyond the valley was a pine forest, just like the one we were standing in. It was raining, but had gone on raining for so long it hardly mattered any more. It was as if the trees were shooting out long streams of spit from time to time.

The front line ran along the ridge beyond the valley. The pioneers were setting up barbed-wire barricades and clearing visats by chopping down trees. We went over to our own ridge to dig the third line of trenches. They were planning to move the front line here, further back, to a more advantageous position without the enemy realizing it.

The trench site had been marked out for us with chalk lines.... It was best to do the digging in pairs. I had a strong buddy, stronger than myself.

We finished our stint in a couple of hours and left. We ate at our gun positions and then calmly sat around chatting. In the distance you could hear a rumbling noise like a pot of potatoes boiling; the Germans were shooting, bombarding Leningrad.

"No-one's got it very good over there right now," my buddy said.

"Have we got it good here, then?" I asked.' Veijo Meri *Boxes of Nails* 175-6

'But the dead Hirri hears nothing now: he is frozen to the sphagnum moss, to be found there the next day and carted off to the village. The gravedigger will make a hole in the sandy soil, the parson will say a few warm words, and the cantor will sing, pulling his coat collar to his throat to protect it from the wind scurrying in from the lake. But where will a graveside-speaker be found who might recall the old man's life-work, as happens at the funeral of a person who has served the community usefully? No-one will tell the scanty cortège about the frail man's struggles in the harsh forest. There'll be no mention of Hirri's efforts with the log-piles, or his struggles in the icy mist on the logging river at night. His work is in fact so ordinary, so taken-for-granted, it would be unable to move the survivors.

Was it mere accident that Hirri nevertheless received, even before the funeral, a handsome memorial service — a kind influential men never receive? ... After midnight the humped clouds began to release a shower of snowflakes. The storm took hold of them and sped them along, spreading a white deck over the pine swamp, trailing a ribbon through the thickly clustered young spruce. By morning the wind was dropping, and the snow was beginning to come down peacefully, decorating every stone, stump, juniper-branch or elder-sprout with a white cloak of ermine. When a coppery flame began to rise in the eastern sky, the last storm-cloud disappeared behind the opposite horizon.

Light came filtering into the great forests.' Veikko Huovinen *Hirri* 134-5

IDSTRÖM
Annika

My Brother Sebastian [Veljeni Sebastian]

Despite her Swedish name, Annika Idström writes in Finnish and about Finnish-speaking people, as the names of the characters in this lively and affecting novel from 1985 proclaim. English-language readers, however, have *My Brother Sebastian* in a translation —a very supple and vigorous one, by the excellent Joan Tate — from the Swedish version.

Antti, eleven years old and small for his age, tells his own story. He is at once precocious, being very articulate and unafraid of philosophic speculations and pronouncements, even though these earn him mockery, and ineluctably childish, a prisoner of fantasies, unbridled prejudices, hatreds and superstitions. His home life is hardly satisfactory, and its chaos spills into his 'public' life — at school and with other children, who mostly detest him. His mother, Kaarina, who writes fiction, staves off her loneliness and feelings of emotional claustrophobia with promiscuous associations with men which often mean her having to keep the bedroom door firmly shut against the inquisitive, resentful yet comprehending Antti.

At school there is his lisping teacher Kerttu Sivonen, who thinks Antti would benefit from a psychiatrist, the clinging yet treacherous classmate, Taru, whose mouth is often wet and black as a result of her penchant for sucking liquorice, and some horrible bullying. Antti's fellows force him to put a safety pin through his ear and to sit for an hour on a drawing-pin and they shut him up in the girls' changing-room. It is in the last ignominious position that he has his first meeting with the man he comes to loathe more than any other, Mika, his mother's lover and once the lover of Taru's mother; he moves into Antti's home, with disastrous results. No wonder Antti comes to rely on an imaginary companion, Sebastian, independent enough to defy anyone.

In addition to its presentation of a disturbed child's mind and its depiction of his failure to communicate his deeper selves to the outside world, *My Brother Sebastian* tellingly evokes the contemporary world — not just in Finland or Scandinavia — of dissolved families, children's enforced access to adult sexuality, urban and domestic violence, ethical confusion and unsatisfactory dependence on institutions as a way of evading emotional or intellectual solutions.

'The alarm went off and it was time to go to school. My cold had got worse in the night and although I had slept badly, I hadn't heard Kaarina coming in. I dressed and went into the kitchen. She was stirring the gruel, the cream cake lying untouched on the table. I sneezed. She put her hand on my forehead. 'Well, at least you haven't got a temperature,' she said indifferently, then started humming quietly. She was in a good mood. I stared at the two liver-pâté sandwiches and the mug of cocoa. A red candle was burning in the middle of the table. I sneezed again, really loudly this time. Kaarina turned the volume up on the radio! I felt faint, yet managed to admire her beauty, her fair hair loose over her shoulders, her mild blue eyes, her long white nightgown: she looked like an angel. I pushed aside the plate of gruel, feeling sick. Kaarina dipped her finger into the gruel, popped it into her mouth and sucked on it for a long time with her eyes closed. The gruel was like thin white slime. 'But this is good,' she said finally. 'Why aren't you eating ?' I went to the bathroom because I thought I was going to be sick. I cleaned my teeth, combed my hair, took my backpack from inside the door and put on my jacket. Kaarina was leafing through the newspaper. She looked up and smiled as if she had remembered something amusing. The candlelight created a cosy atmosphere in the room and I had to make myself go, otherwise I would have stood in the doorway for the rest of the day.' 22

PAASILINNA
Arto

The Year of the Hare [Jäniksen vuosi]

'Two dissatisfied cynical men, getting on for middle age' are driving along a country road in southern Finland one fine early June evening. The one at the wheel is a photographer, the other a journalist, and they are on a mutual assignment for a well-known weekly. Suddenly, in the middle of the quiet road, they encounter a young hare, 'tipsy with summer', trying out its jumps.

The driver reacts too slowly, and the hare hits the windscreen, is bounced back off it and can be seen hastening off into the forest. Vatanen, the journalist, goes after the animal and finds it has done no more than break a hind leg, for which he improvises a splint with a twig and a strip of his handkerchief. The photographer grows impatient and angry, and drives off, leaving his colleague and the hare to themselves in this remote spot. In a sense it is he who has performed the crucial existential act of the novel, from which everything else derives. Alone with the hare who is grateful to and trusting of him, the journalist realises that they have bonded, and that the bond is indissoluble. He realises too that he doesn't want to return to his job, which bores him, or to his Helsinki home, which costs too much, or to his wife, with whom he's no more in love than she with him. The hare, the recipient of his own spontaneous benevolence, appears itself benevolent, so why not throw his lot in with the animal, and chuck everything else in?

This Vatanen does. Finnish law makes it illegal to keep a wild animal captive, so Vatanen seeks out a game warden to explain how the hare's injury came about, and how he saved it. He thus gets an official declaration that the hare 'belongs' to him; this proves invaluable in the many adventures and narrow escapes in this picaresque (but artistically designed) novel.

The hare lives in Vatanen's knapsack and when not inside it, is following him at close range as he makes his way through the vast Finnish forest country. Almost always the little animal delights and inspires kindness in the people who meet this unusual pair. Vatanen has sold his one valuable asset, his boat, and with the proceeds, and money from casual labouring jobs, manages to support himself on a journey far into the north and north-east of Finland. He returns to Helsinki only when the hare is ill, so that it can be properly treated by a vet.

You can follow the route Vatanen and his hare take on any map of reasonably large scale, and I strongly recommend readers to do so. It reinforces the authenticity of this remarkable book, and makes it easier to grasp the significance of certain episodes — for instance, the tragi-comic crossing into Russia. As the two travel on, summer becomes autumn and autumn winter, and the young hare grows a white coat for camouflage against the snow.

In many cultures, perhaps a majority, the hare has become endowed with magic properties and Paasilinna (born in 1942), a journalist like his protagonist, is aware of this, but essentially he resists such associations. In the course of the book Vatanen meets a young man, Kaartinen, who has taken to the ancient religion of the atavistic forest — and tries to sacrifice the hare. There is a message here. Vatanen, appalled, wants none of any 'strange world'; he wants only *this* one, so varied and so fine, and to be able to respect and act compassionately towards it. Hare is hare, forest is forest. Why ask for more?

At the end of the novel the elaborations of organised human society, so often tedious and life-denying, are mocked. The Russian authorities return Vatanen and the hare to the Finnish authorities who have compiled a long and ludicrous list of transgressions. The novel ends, however, with the triumphant vindication of Vatanen who escapes with his hare from gaol. Tenderness, devotion, love, between two different species of the creature world, have won through in the end. This is a wonderful book, which has enjoyed cult status, not only in Scandinavia but in France. Risto Jarva's film of 1977, which Paasilinna helped to script has also been widely admired. English-language readers are very fortunate, for the translator is Herbert Lomas, himself a poet of real distinction, who brings his gift of language, sharp but lyrical, to bear on his rendering of Paasilinna's unique work.

'It was a hot, sunny morning, and Saturday as well. He took a stroll round the village streets and, in his search for a good spot for the hare to browse, he came across the cemetery.

The herbaceous arrangements on the little hillocks were very much to the hare's taste. It particularly relished the rye-grass on the recent spring graves.

The church door was unlocked. Vatanen called the hare away from the grave-plots and took it inside. What a wonderful coolness and peace! Though Vatanen had long since given up church, it didn't stop him relishing the silence of the huge space.

The hare hopped along the central aisle to the chancel, dropped a few innocent pills in front of the altar, and then began studying the church more systematically.

Vatanen sat down in a pew, observing the altar painting and the architecture of the nave. There were places for about six hundred people there, he estimated. The nave was partially two-level: both side-walls were lined full-length with galleries that joined under the organ-loft at the back. Wooden staircases led to the galleries from either sides of the altar. A looming light from the high, narrow windows evoked a dreamy, peaceful ambience.

He gathered up the hare-droppings from the altar and slipped them in his pocket. He picked his way down a side-aisle to a pew tucked away at the back, removed his shiny new boots, stretched out on the bench, settled the knapsack under his head and prepared for a doze. This was a much more agreeable place for sleeping than the boarding-house. The eye could travel into the lofty Christian spaces of the ceiling, and the still, pitch-pine columns adorned with verses were a fine contrast to the grubby designs on the peeling boarding-house wallpaper. The hare was silently pottering about by the sacristy door behind the altar. Let it, Vatanen thought, and dozed off.

While he was sleeping, an elderly man came into the church: the pastor, here to do a few ecclesiastical chores. He was wearing his ministerial garb, a black cassock with the white tabs of his clerical bands at the neck. He walked briskly past the altar to the sacristy without noticing the hare near the door. It stared in astonishment at this apparition of a black-cassocked man....

When (the pastor) came back, he was holding several sheets of paper, probably sermons.

Only now did he perceive the hare, which had lolloped its way up to the altar. It had profanely left a few droppings by the sacred place, and now it was sniffing the flower arrangements on the altar steps.

The pastor was shocked into letting the sheets of paper slip from his hands and float down to the floor.

Lord, help us!'

The hare hopped down the altar steps and vanished into a side-aisle.' 58-60

WALTARI
Mika

The Egyptian [Sinuhe egyptiläinen]

In exile at the end of his life, Sinuhe, royal physician in fourteenth-century BCE Egypt, is writing his memoirs. Wily and tough, he is no innocent, but Sinuhe (as he realises in hindsight) is rarely if ever in charge of his own fate. His personal life is dominated by the ruthless courtesan Nefernefernefer and a fiery Cretan bull-dancer, Minea. Viable love (in the form of Merit, a Theban tavern-owner) finally arrives, only to fall victim to the parallel and increasingly tumultuous political and social changes at the heart of which Sinuhe, thanks to his position, constantly finds himself.

These have been set in motion by the pharaoh Akhnaton, who is attempting to replace Egypt's ancient pantheon with Aton, a single solar god. Akhnaton — possessed by the vision of a single, loving god — takes on the established worship of Ammon and other lesser deities. This sets him at odds with both the powerful hierarchical priesthood and the popular sentiments of the people, and his pyrrhic victory bears out the truth of Machiavelli's observation (which Sinuhe would have reluctantly endorsed) that 'a man who wants to act virtuously in every way necessarily comes to grief among so many who are not virtuous.' Chief among those are the Princess Baketamon; Kaptah, the head priest of Aton; and Horemheb, the general of the royal army. This last — with the collusion of Kaptah, and despite the hatred of the Princess — accedes as pharaoh, and eventually banishes Sinuhe.

Like the best of its genre, reading Waltari's *The Egyptian* one quickly forgets that it is an 'historical novel' and becomes immersed in its particular period and story. Among the incidental pleasures here are the relationship between Sinuhe and his irrepressible servant Kaptah and their travels in contemporary Babylonia and Syria as well as Egypt. Crete in particular (including an unforgettably macabre Minotaur) is as vivid as an eyewitness report. And intertwined into the dramatic events centre-stage is Sinuhe's personal discovery — inadvertent and gradual, but equally compelling — of his own true origins. *Patrick Curry*

'The people must be controlled by fear. If the gods govern them, the throne needs no weapons to support it. Were Ammon content to be Pharaoh's servant, he would fully deserve his place, for no nations can be ruled without fear. That is why Aton, with his gentleness and his cross of love, is an exceedingly dangerous god.' 269

FINLAND-SWEDISH

CARPELAN
Bo

Axel [Axel]

Bo Carpelan (born in Helsinki in 1926) is one of the leading Swedish-language poets of his generation; two selections, *Room Without Walls* and *Homecoming*, are available in English, both containing poems from *The Courtyard*, the watershed volume in which Carpelan adapted his Wallace Stevens-like modernism to the rendering of the familiar and homely, discovering their strangeness and quiddity. He is also the author of three novels. *Axel* is a recreation of the life of his own great-uncle, the Baron Axel Carpelan (1858-1919), partly in third person narrative, but for by far the greater part of the novel in the form of an imaginary (but perfectly possible) diary. What makes Axel Carpelan a fascinating figure for later generations is his creative friendship with the most famous of Finns, the composer Jean Sibelius (1865-1967). Bo Carpelan relates that he knew very little about his curious relation until he read, in the late 1930s, a book about Sibelius, his name having never been mentioned in his family; then in the second volume of the massive life of Sibelius by Erik Tawastjerna (1967) he read of his uncle as 'a fully fledged figure' in the composer's story and his curiosity and creative energy were aroused.

As a child, Axel was sickly, stunted, lonely, sensitive. These characteristics remained with him in youth and young manhood. He was frequently severely ill, and he lost his parents and elder brother in quick succession. The one way in which he hoped to transcend the miseries of his condition was through music of which, from his earliest years, he was a passionate lover — and a learned one as well. He knew classical works intimately, was a perceptive analyst, and had ideas for quartets, oratorios etc. But he hadn't been endowed with the necessary vital spark or perhaps it was outward-turned energy that was lacking. However an outlet for his deep musical feelings, and belief in the art-form, was at hand. Carpelan heard the early music of Sibelius and realised the true genius behind it. He also, he felt, knew which direction it should take, directions its owner might not have thought of.

Sibelius was a composer with deep meaning for his contemporaries, especially his Nordic ones. He voiced the Finnish people's desire for liberation, before 1917, from the repressive rule of the Russian Tsar; he expressed a rapport with Nature, with the wild fierce nature of the Finnish forests and lakes, that seemed like a plea on behalf of a freer mankind; he explored the ancient Finnish myths, and saw their profound significance for modern man, while in his music he broke away from artifice and emotional indulgence to make symphonies of organic growth combined with concentration of form — 'cold water' after the heady brews of Vienna and Paris.

Carpelan gave Sibelius (who was to dedicate the second Symphony to him) needed money. He wanted Sibelius to create symphonies that drew on the sounds and feeling of the forest; he realised that the one-time violin virtuoso should compose a major concerto for his instrument, he divined that Sibelius and his wife would be the better for a visit to the South, to Italy, from there to look back over the whole Northern heritage. Here is an extraordinary case of one of the greatest of artists owing guidance onto the genuine creative paths to an obscure other, an admirer, a sick man, possibly a neurasthenic, a refugee from the hurly-burly of life. Sibelius himself was to exclaim in his own diary: 'Now Axel is being lowered into the earth's cold arms. It feels deeply, deeply tragic. For whom will I compose now?'

'The new villa, smelling of fresh wood, comfortable and stately but not too big, not an ostentatious structure. Aino (Sibelius' wife) and Janne (Sibelius) showed me the greatest solicitude and joy at my presence... I told Janne that when I am seized by thoughts that are too gloomy I consciously divert them along channels that bring consolation: with the reflection that life is full of chance, man is a speck of dust (in Janne's case a rather large one, it must be admitted) and yet as eternal as the atom. Perhaps death is not so dreadful, after all? Will not my dead body be just as near the sun as my living one? Janne did not want to talk about this, moved the subject to music...[I] brought up the subject of Janne's leaning towards the classical, which he confirmed. The Third Symphony ought to lead out across clear waters with lofty space above it. Lay in the guest bedroom, listening to the soughing of the wind in the trees, and there was a great sense of calm there... The whole of Ainola [the Sibelius' villa] smelt of forest, Janne must be taking it with him into the Third Symphony.' 242-243

FAGERHOLM
Monika

Wonderful Women by the Water [Underbara kvinnor vid vatten]

Along with such films of Ingmar Bergman's as *Summer Interlude* and *Summer with Monika*, this book (a first novel which has had a tremendous success in the Nordic countries) must constitute one of the greatest artistic tributes ever made to that unforgettable magical phenomenon, the Scandinavian summer. Monika Fagerholm's unique achievement is to make us realise the significance of these months of unending, unbounded sun and light in the totality of Scandinavian life, cultural and psycho-social — and the ambiguity of that significance.

The novel opens in the early 1960s, a time of great prosperity throughout Europe, but nowhere more so than in democratic Finland. A young couple, Kajus and Bella, acquire first a grey cottage, which they paint red, and then a white villa, by the wooded shores of an inlet of the sea. All around them in similar accommodations are similar couples and their families, all possessed by similar desires: to surrender themselves to sun and water. By the sea it is surely more real than back in the city! Each summer suggests that it might go on for eternity; and every year of course it does end, and the seaside house has to be shut up, and the city returned to. But life by the water will be taken up once the next summer begins, and the dullness of the between-time can be rejected. And so on!

Although, compared with the routines of office and apartment, these months are indeed blissfully free, they are not lived as unmaterialistically as those enjoying them like to think, a point that emerges fully if subtly from Monika Fagerholm's novel. Houses, speedboats, water-skis, snorkelling gear, barbecue equipment, cameras, furniture for studio or verandah all cost money. But to these Swedish-speaking Finns, such is the affluence of their society, that all the accoutrements of pleasure seem as natural to living as the play of sun on sea, or the picking of cloudberries.

For the most part we see this water-centric life through the eyes of Thomas, Kajus and Bella's son, who is seven when the White Villa becomes theirs. Childhood too feels as if it will continue for ever. It can't, and doesn't — obviously! Anyway Kajus and Bella themselves are changing, without wholly realising it. Inside the bodies tanned by sun and braced by sea-breezes, unexpected, unasked-for emotions are developing.

Kajus becomes more and more content, in a very male way, with just pottering about and reading detective stories. Bella's sensibility grows, on the other hand; she finds far more satisfaction in the company of her summer-neighbour, Rosa, than she does in that of her husband and son — who, to tell the truth, bore her. A relationship blossoms between Bella and Rosa that defies easy analysis, but becomes the most important feature in both their lives. Eventually, defying the eventless fluidity of summertime, they run away together....

Monika Fagerholm's style and presentation of her characters and their changing situations brilliantly echo her subject. She avoids scenes of dilemma or confrontation, preferring instead to make a collage of summer activities that do seem to exist free of our nervous conventional measurement of time passing, and yet — when viewed from an appropriate angle — seamlesly contribute to it. *Wonderful Women by the Water* is a profoundly original novel, lively, thoughtful, sensuous and springing from a real concern with how difficult ordinary people find acceptance of maturing and aging. One side of us, whether male or female, wants to be forever at play by the eternal sea.

'Why are water skiing shore women beautiful? Irresistible? Inescapable? In their yellow and white bathing costumes, although one of them even has an orange life jacket?

Philosophical questions. Thomas is nine, nearly ten. He has no tendencies towards philosophising. Nor later either, for that matter. He is just like his mother, a person who will never have a philosophical disposition. It is concrete. To him everything is concrete.

He is in his summer paradise, trying to do all kinds of things. Spying and sabotaging and being in the forest, getting interested in new things and meeting new people. But it is pointless. He always ends up there again. On the shore, that is. Where the shore women are in the bay. Water skiing behind the Lindberghs' glossy mahogany speedboat. The one, then the other, taking turns..... Off they go. Wheee, and they have gone. The joy of speed. And everyone claps.... everyone is down on the shore all right. Has finally ended up there.' II2

KIHLMAN
Christer

All My Sons [Alla mina söner]

Though written as a first-person novel, and having the emotional intensity and the sense of other people's lives associated with fiction rather than non-fiction, *All My Sons* follows experiences of Christer Kihlman's own in the mid-to-late 1970s. For its autobiographical nature alone the book attracted a great deal of attention (by no means all favourable) in Scandinavia when it first appeared in 1980. On a visit to Buenos Aires for literary purposes, Kihlman meets, through a contact Q., in the smart Union Bar a handsome young man of twenty, Juan, a 'taxi-boy' as Kihlman soon, fascinatedly, comes to realise — ie. he supports himself by sex. Though Juan has already had experience of girls and women beyond counting (including French pop star, Sylvie Vartan), and though he is engaged to Lilita, someone he genuinely loves, the majority of his trade is with men, older men. ('Five paying clients a night. Five completed sexual acts, that is, with five different men, all utter strangers? Exactly.') In a sense the (married) Kihlman joins the rank of these men (though he doesn't make clear the sexual interactions between himself and the youth for some time in his narrative). He speaks but little Spanish, Juan's only language; nevertheless these five weeks of the taxi-boy's almost daily company give him an intensity of happiness such as he's never known before. He even becomes fond of Lilita too, and of Juan's working-class, part-Indian, part-Italian family. Juan must come to Sweden and Finland, where perhaps Juan can become again the tango-singer he was in his mid-teens; Kihlman must write a book about him.

Both ambitions are realised (though Juan's attempts at breaking into the Finnish music scene don't amount to anything), and one can say that the ultimate failure of the first is what really makes for the success of the second.

This is a painfully affecting yet artistically satisfying work, both subtle and bold in its depictions of the erratic movements of the human heart, and, self-willed and self-obsessed though he shows himself as being, Kihlman portrays Juan and Lilita (by now his wife) with a paradoxically selfless understanding of their dilemmas, personal, cultural, sexual, even geographical. Juan's time in Scandinavia (Stockholm, which he comes to loathe, and Helsinki, which he prefers) is largely unhappy, and Lilita's only slightly less so. Why? Because, Juan in particular, they are bored, they have little curiosity or knowledge of any society outside the Argentinian, and of all societies perhaps, Swedo-Finnish is baffling to them in its particular combination of civic consciousness and individual liberty. Finnish women feel themselves free to make their own sexual decisions; Finns of either sex do not feel it necessary to be surrounded by miscellaneous other people all day long but cherish solitude. On the other hand the men (and Kihlman conspicuously) seek solace in drink, and drunkennness disgusts Juan. Moreover there is dishonesty in the very nature of the relationship that the older writer and the young man enjoy, compounded by efforts to rationalise it socially to others. Yet their story is not one of unrelieved disaster; affection and even a sort of respect remains, and if Kihlman's later return to Argentina and to Juan and Lilita was to strip him of certain illusions, there was also a partial resolution.

A major theme of this book is exploitation, and it was this that shocked its first readers. Kihlman was evidently (and, it would seem, comparatively unashamedly) prepared to buy a young man's affections and attention, to sever for his own satisfaction Juan's intimate connections with his background, to take control over his life while lowering his own moral standards and significant obligations to others in order to do this. And yet some good did come out of the entanglement, not least among them the kind of self-knowledge which enriches this book.

'To me, Juan was unique. In reality, he was not unique. in Juan's mind, I was... I don't actually know what I was, but it was equally divorced from reality. And when reality collided head-on with illusion, with the romantic dream, with the misunderstandings of ignorance, then the difficulties arose. They crept up on us slowly. I don't really know when they began. Or when they ceased, if they have ceased now. Or ever will cease. For they have not ceased. I still carry him with me just as much, in my heart. Just as he carries me, in his.

When Juan came to Europe, we had known each other for no more than a month. In relation to me, he had been a taxi-boy for most of that month. The point was that I had never directly sought him out in that capacity. He had from the first been a human being to me. In the end I became the same for him, despite all the differences between us, which were a constant obstacle...

At the time, I was still convinced Juan was unique. It wasn't until my second visit to Buenos Aires in the autumn of 1978 that I realized he was not that at all. My feelings for him did not change in any way as a result, but deepened. That was what was strange. I couldn't have enough of him. We couldn't have enough of each other. There were days of silence and despair, days when we almost hated each other. But hatred, what is hatred? The black lining of the cloak of love. And whoever rips off the cloak of love makes himself bleed.' 95-96

KIHLMAN
Christer

The Blue Mother [Den blå modern]

An immensely powerful and ambitious novel, *The Blue Mother* amply shows one of Kihlman's major influences and affinities (perhaps indeed *the* major influence and affinity): William Faulkner. Like the great American Southerner, Kihlman, in writing of his characters' emotional lives releases in often frenzied-seeming passages whole pent-up worlds of desires, yearnings, fantasies, terrors; he draws back from nothing, and — consonant with his own time and culture — is far more overtly concerned with ambivalent and devouring sexuality than is the older writer. Yet — again as with Faulkner — Kihlman's concerns with the external world match in obsessive feeling and observation those with the inner. His novels too inter-relate, so one can say that Kihlman, studying the often ingrown society of Finnish Swedes, has made for Finland a kind of Yoknapatawpha County, Faulkner's literary homeland.

If the Faulknerian parallel holds good, one could say that *The Blue Mother* — with its in-depth, at times passionately done portraits of three brothers, one dead before the main action of the novel — is his *The Sound and the Fury*. (There is even a correspondence between the name of Faulkner's 'idiot', Benjy, and that of Kihlman's withdrawn and psychosis-plagued character, Benno, though the comparision should not be pursued too far; Kihlman is a highly original and personal writer.)

The family of *The Blue Mother* belong to the prosperous, self-satisfied Swedish-speaking haute bourgeoisie against which the two brothers who alternately tell the story, Benno and Raf, have in their contrasting way rebelled. Both feel they have been insufficiently loved. The sensitive Benno — after an initiatory sexual experience with a pastor — is drawn to his own sex, later embodied by The Boy, and his successors; sometimes his sexual aspirations take the form of lurid fantasies, the graphic nature of which — one centres on Auschwitz — shocked earlier critics and readers. Raf, the writer, representing, one surmises, another very important side of Kihlman, has tormented heterosexual relations, and takes refuge from his pains in frenetic drinking bouts. (Alcohol has dogged Kihlman's own life.) There is much that is disturbing and even horrifying in this story of the brothers and their emotional associates, yet there is redemptive beauty as well — prefigured early in the accounts of their relationship with older brother, Robby, killed in the War, whose feeling for Nature was so acute and empathic:

'Robby tells me about the life of a butterfly. They don't eat, but are content to suck honey from the flowers. The eating has already been done by the caterpillar, which naturally needs nourishment because it is growing. The butterfly doesn't grow any more. It is complete, and its only remaining task in life is to....well. He stops there, and looks very important and knowing and avuncular, and explains that perhaps it is not suitable to tell me about that now, but he will when I'm older....Yes, I learned a lot about the wonderful wealth of nature during these conversations or lessons with Robby.... How little you think about the endurance of butterflies, their will to struggle and their courage, when, for instance, you see a Swallowtail on its leisurely flight from flower to flower, apparently so light-hearted one light-hearted summer day. You don't think then about the twilight sovereigns of the air, the moths, their narrow wings reinforced with powerful crossbars, and their streamlined bodies, those unsurpassable flyers which can achieve speeds up to fifteen metres a second, the same as some birds, including the sparrow.' 24

KIHLMAN
Christer

The Downfall of Gerdt Bladh [Gerdt Bladhs Untergang]

Perhaps Christer Kihlman's most haunting and tightly constructed novel, this novel is concerned with the plight of a Helsinki business man, Gerdt Bladh, head of a major department store, and member of a family which crops up throughout Kihlman's fiction. Back from a visit to Switzerland to prepare a Swiss Week for the store, Bladh returns to Finland to make two terrible discoveries: that his wife is having an affair with a friend, and that there are plans to oust him from the board of the directors of his own family's firm. To make matters worse the instigator of the latter, Ari Sarkama — a Finnish Finn in distinction to a Swedish Finn like himself — is someone he has personally assisted. Ari Sarkama has uncovered rumours greatly to Gerdh's discredit, that, when abroad, he frequents boy-bars, availing himself of those who proffer themselves, and that he has been involved in a homosexual murder.

It is at a comparatively late point in the novel that we appreciate that these rumours are indeed with foundation, so completely have we entered Gerdt Bladh's schizoid mentality — which can for stretches of time believe the cultivated professional man's persona as his only reality. Certainly he has taken many boy lovers, and if he is no murderer, he has behaved in a cowardly fashion when his young boyfriend, Jürgen, was set on in a New York street and killed. A tragedy in the past is uncovered, and we understand one of Gerdt's deepest and most hidden convictions: that he has been possessed by the soul of a cousin who committed suicide, enabling him to be the successful male he has become rather than the timid half-feminine boy he once was.

Gerdt's end, like his whole predicament, is tragic; Kihlman's is a dark imagination, yet the novel does not leave us entirely with hopelessness so keen is the intelligence and sensibility controlling it, confronting life at its saddest and starkest.

'Sometimes when he had been to a meeting or met some business contact in a smaller place like Dortmund or Heidelberg, when his official work had been completed, he had hired a car, in the evening or afternoon (sometimes declining the obligatory dinner on the pretext of a migraine or an old ulcer), turned into his hotel and quickly changed into leisure clothes and set off at a furious speed to the nearest city, from Dortmund to Cologne and from Heidelberg to Frankfurt, driving like a maniac along the autobahn to be there in time, in large Mercedes cars that easily did 220, through the night on almost empty motorways, to be there in time for what? Driven by the unattainable, pounding and imperative, to be in time at the bar and the velvety dimness and the music and the world of night and the security of the world of night with its snug cosiness and inviting smiles and the last business deal of the day and the morning hours in a humble, shabby little hotel in a shabby little room with no shower, only a small washbasin and tap and towel (sometimes already used) and a bed. And never alone in bed. Hunting through the cities of the world, in a desire that knew no satisfaction. Hunting for beauty and the ultimately secure, hunting what was straightforward and ultimately liberating, hunting liberation, without even the slightest inkling of what he was doing.' 201-202

SCHOULTZ
Solveig von

Heartwork. Selected short stories.

Solveig von Schoultz (born 1907) is, says the biographical note to this volume, 'the undisputed grande dame of Finland-Swedish literature', and reading through these seven magnificent short stories (she is also a very distinguished poet), it is not hard to see why. Bo Carpelan, who like her is equally at home in prose and verse, defines in his introduction her genius in words hard to improve on:

'In addition to a rich and perceptive portrayal of humanity, her stories present a comprehensive view of existence itself with all its undercurrents, hidden springs, blood circulation; a mystic conception of reality which marks much of what is most expressive and alive in Finland-Swedish modernism, whether poetry or prose.'

In the story *Room for the Night* we enter — physically as well as emotionally — the being of an eighteen-year-old girl who, lying to her mother about her whereabouts, takes the ferry over to Stockholm to meet the father she hasn't seen for eleven years. On the boat a (Finnish) boy is attracted to her; they dance, he scribbles her his Stockholm address. Meeting father turns out a disaster, a Finland-Swede who has now put on Stockholm airs with prosperity, his cold wife and business-partner so jealous of his past. She doesn't want to stay with them, but where can she go in the Swedish capital but the flat of the boy from the boat? — and a real dump it turns out to be. She surprises both him and herself with her pasionate weeping at what has happened.

Summary cannot do justice to the story's multi-layered subtlety. Greatly depending on imaginatively selected dialogue, it opens up severeal independent yet temporarily connecting lives for us — sees them too, for all the sharp observation of the contemporary world, *sub specie aeternitatis*. *Morning Coffee* is the portrait of a long-married couple, now dependent on their daughter, who have come greatly to bore and irritate one another. *The Victor* shows us an unmarried mother's frantic subservience to a wilful baby whom her current boy-friend is, mysteriously, able to control. *Grasshoppers* must surely be one of the finest studies in the contrast between age and youth ever written; a writer and his perhaps too perceptive wife are offset, in their early old age, by their son and his girl-friend of the moment (with whom a serious relationship is beginning). I know little in post-war fiction more moving than the old couple's coming together at the story's close, a physical and emotional rapprochement made with the acknowledgement that the writer isn't as good as he once was, that he has 'survived himself'.

'"One more thing. In the long run, what does it matter whether you were at your best in the middle, at the beginning or at the end? It's only now that you can feel."

"But you don't know how it feels."

It was almost inaudible; perhaps he hadn't meant to speak. Just so softly, out into the darkness too, she whispered:

"Do you really think I don't know? You're a part of me."

He didn't hear her, but it didn't matter. He held her so tightly that she could feel his body along the whole length of hers, his long, stirring body. His pyjama jacket was undone; the hair on his chest rubbed against her chin, and there was the broken button she'd forgotten to mend. Inside, his heart was beating steadily; she knew that soon it would be beating more quickly and more loudly.

"Have you been lonely?" he murmured. She didn't reply, but she could feel his body waiting. He held her more tightly; his body jerked, and they were both waiting; he would rise more slowly than before, but from a deeper level.

And as they listened, while there was still time, as their grey hair mingled on the pillow, she heard the curtain flutter inwards, and on the scent of the hay the thin, intoxicating notes of the grasshoppers' song floated in.' 128

ICELAND

BERGSSON
Gudbergur

The Swan [Svanurinn]

To an unnamed farm in the interior of Iceland, an unnamed little girl of nine is sent to spend the summer, with a man and his wife also nameless. This is the first time the girl has left the coast; on the coach-journey away 'from the sea's waves to green, arched hills,' she has the sensation she's 'withering and dying'. Though hers is essentially a story of an individual's growth, she's never wholly to lose this feeling.

The girl has been caught stealing from shops — sweets, sandwiches and marmalade (which she's devoured actually on the premises!). The juvenile court passes what in Iceland is a not uncommon sentence: she's to be exiled to the country. In the words of her own mother: 'You ought to live in harmony with nature in the countryside... and uproot from within you, with God, all that is evil in your own bad nature.'

Just as there is an ironic contrast between the little girl's peccadillos and the thrill they give her (of almost metaphysical excitement), so there is between authority's kindly, rational decision and the actual experiences that come the child's way in consequence of it. Certainly nature can and does provide healing images of harmony and of the continuance of life (and its beauty is celebrated throughout the novel in sharp poetic prose, a thing of beauty in itself). But it is at best an ambivalent mentor. Farming in the Icelandic interior is no unmitigated idyll. The little girl, new to country experiences, witnesses the difficult birth of a calf; not long afterwards she has also to witness its death (it's slaughtered), and see how its mother loses her wits with distress at its loss. In one of the most powerful passages of the novel the girl and the farmer on whom she is billeted rescue an errant mare. On the way back home they have to force the animal to swim a river in full spate. The mare is terrified, and the girl suffers acutely on her behalf. Yet only a matter of minutes after she's emerged from the water, the mare becomes an ordinary, glossy, serviceable animal again. There's a resilience in nature that partakes of amorality.

Gudbergur Bergsson (born 1932) is the author of nearly twenty novels (as well as of short-stories and poetry) and is looked up to as a modernist master. He divides his life between Iceland and Spain, on the literature of which he is an expert, translating and lecturing on it. *The Swan* is a novel of exceptional distinction, and perhaps its fineness can in part be attributed to a marriage of its author's involvement with Spanish culture (characterised by the spirit known as 'duende', an 'openness to death') and his spiritual penetration of his own country's landscape. The girl at the centre is at once a convincingly rendered individual and a folktale-like representative of human nature, while the other characters — the unhappy, trustworthy farmhand and the farouche farmer's daughter so unfortunate in love — give density to her story while never ceasing to be autonomous persons. The adventure with which the book closes, a transcendent experience, relates to the eponymous swan and its role in folklore. It admits of no easy explanation, however; here mystery is all.

'And so she went on. It was calm and still around her as before, absolutely calm weather, but then she began to feel a slight breeze. She walked into it, farther, farther, and the breeze got up and turned into a rough wind. Now she could see over the mountain. The countryside was bathed in sunshine, a much clearer light than on the mountain's far side. She was still expecting a shadow to descend upon her, so that the swan would plunge down and sweep her off the mountain with its wings. But it was her feet that carried her on. They were tired, but she could make her way on them. Now she could see down to the flat plain, as if looking down into vast watery depths. She saw the grey circle of fog a little below her and headed into it. The wind greeted her, welling up against her like a powerful river. It was trying to throw her over backwards, over the edge of the mountain and straight into the lake, but the slope was downwards, her feet found it and overcame her fatigue. She knew she would reach her destination, however exhausted she might be. For that reason she stretched out an arm. The wind whisked her skirt up. The cold latched itself into her bare body, but she took to the air, she felt herself flying onwards, plunged down into the circle of fog, and easily slipped through it. Then she saw everything in an instant: the vast panorama, the house at the foot of the mountain, and the fact that all the horses had gone, except the farmer's daughter's horse. And she saw, too, something she could not understand: she saw the snow-white swan flying ahead of her, apparently showing her the way.' 143

GUDMUNDSSON
Einar Már

Angels of the Universe [Englar alheimsins]

For this novel, narrated by Paul, the protagonist, Einar Már Gudmundsson (born 1954) drew on the tragic and all-too-short life of his older brother, Pálmi Örn (1949-1992) to whom it is dedicated. Paul is much preoccupied with his date of birth, March 30th, 1949, the day that Iceland joined NATO despite violent protests by Communists and other dissidents. Though the symbolism is never laboured, Paul's instability, which leads to many years' incarceration in the psychiatric hospital, Klepp, mirrors the instability of thinking behind this political decision of commitment.

It is commitment that Paul has always found difficult. The novel is divided into two parts. In the first we watch Paul trying to cope with the problems of maintaining his identity in the ordinary world. In many ways no more lawless or defiant than his friends (for example, the two pairs of brothers in his neighbourhood) he finds such difficulty in adapting his personality to others that he takes refuge in frenetic drinking bouts and explosions of ferocious temper.

Paul is born into a section of society which, even in egalitarian Iceland, is identifiably working-class. His father is a taxi-driver, one of his uncles was in his youth a passionate Communist (as was Gudmundsson's own), a fighter for the proletariat in the International Brigade in the Spanish Civil War. Older people tend to treat Paul kindly, less so his contemporaries who dub him 'Muzzy Softie' despite his acts of aggression and leave his companionship behind for the easy thrills of cars and money-making.

The second part of the novel covers Paul's time in Klepp, and leads up to his eventual realisation that he must 'bid farewell to the monolith of solitude and this earthly world'. For this is a posthumously narrated novel: Paul has killed himself, and is looking back over the confusions and sadness of his life from the vast tranquility of death.

Yet the final effect of the novel, for all the miseries it records, and the desolation of the last chapter, is celebratory. In the world's eyes Paul is a casualty, a failure who cannot even be permitted freedom, but in the author's — and at times his own — he is a vessel of powerful feelings, responsive, passionate, able at times to see into the depths of existence. Nor is humour missing: the other inmates of Klapp are shown as possessing a vitality in their craziness: Oli who imagines he has written the Beatles' lyrics, Viktor, who lives vicariously as Shakespeare. The humour is attendant on the compassion that is so striking a feature of Gudmundsson's art. In Iceland he is credited with having liberated serious writing from an overawed preoccupation with its own cultural past, by turning for inspiration to the creative minds of rock and punk. Here his Paul is more moved by the Beatles, Frank Zappa and David Bowie than he is by the sagas' Njal and Egil. And his rememberings have an irresistible directness.

'...I have been painting a picture of the girl I love. Her name is Dagny, and she is incredibly beautiful, with breasts like beech trees and eyes like heather, but when I stroke her curvaceous hips and touch her breasts she vanishes, leaving nothing but the window where she stood, my frame on to the world, my life and my death....

But while Dagny was still a girl in reality, where people live healthy and happy lives, I loved her so passionately that she moved across my heart like an eraser, rubbing out all other girls.

Immediately I felt the way she rhymed with my turbulent blood and the drumbeat of my soul, even though now, much later, I see her only in my mind's eye.

She is sitting beside the ocean, waiting to see my window reflected in the waves. When I open it, she crawls in and stands on the floor in front of me.

I sense the aroma of birch from her breasts and the scent of flowers and summer that buds like heather in her eyes.

For an instant, her blood races through my veins while the fires from old wines blaze beneath my heels.

Then I stand naked and alone.' 77-78

GUNNARSSON
Ólafur

Trolls' Cathedral [Tröllakirkja]

At the centre of this immensely powerful novel, shamefully neglected so far by English-language readers, stands a successful Reykjavik architect, Sigurbjörn Helgason. Two events in his earlier life still haunt his maturity: the death of his brother, Johannes, a devout Christian, who rejected the priesthood to lead a Christ-like life among ordinary folk, and his own confrontation, as a student visiting Europe, with Gaudi's unfinished masterpiece, the great cathedral of the Sagrada Familia in Barcelona. His ambition has long been to design for Iceland a comparable cathedral, on a lofty headland, that will honour God through its ability to withstand the elements. But by the time we get to know Sigurbjörn (June 1953) he has to be satisfied merely with being responsible for Reykjavík's first-ever franchised department store, in conjunction with his partner. Are we to see Sigurbjörn as a modern-day Prometheus punished for the audacity of his dreams? Certainly the fate that is his could suggest such a reading.

Outwardly Sigurbjörn's life is at once ordinary and that of an eminent and prosperous man: an attractive and sensitive wife, and four children, one of whom, Helgi, is an Icelandic football star, picked for leading London team Arsenal, the other (the closest in temperament to himself) an imaginative boy of eleven, Tóti. A grand celebration is held for the opening of the great store, and at it Sigurbjörn gets rather drunk, and entrusts a key to the whole new edifice to Tóti. Out by himself, Tóti gets into conversation with a vagrant he and Sigurbjörn have already seen hanging about the city. Won over by the man's facetious talk, Tóti uses the key to let himself and this man into the deserted mall. Tóti is then assaulted, sexually one assumes, and for a while is very seriously ill in hospital.

The event alters the lives of the entire family. Icelandic justice sends the offending vagrant to prison for what seems to the suffering Sigurbjörn an insultingly short time. The necessary emotional sequel to this violation of the innocent has not occurred. The architect's obsession with the tragedies of his past now recurs and intensifies. He longs to put a stop to his torment by destructive action, a longing that undermines both the continuing work on the department store and his dreams of the cathedral of the future. It is realised in a ghastly — and to the reader wholly unexpected — murder.

Olafur Gunnarson (born 1948) is a Roman Catholic, and his themes of overreaching and redemption, acted out in a secular society, are treated in a manner not dissimilar to the great Japanese Catholic novelist, Shusaku Endo. Like Endo, Gunnarson is not only a novelist of spiritual crisis, he works his story of sin and expiation into a vivid and realistically evoked milieu. Sigurbjörn's family life — especially perhaps his relationship with his football-star son — is most convincingly done. But for all the Catholicism, the novel (hence its title) is also concerned with the Icelandic troll as an embodiment of gratuitous malice, of evil. In conversation Ólafur Gunnarson has said that Icelanders are the only contemporary people he knows of who have retained their mythological beings in their proper proportions; the British have shrunk their elves and goblins to diminutive beings, but the troll is human-size or larger, denizen of rock and crevice, enemy of the civic and civilised, of church and department store alike. Certainly the novel evokes unforgettably, with great narrative drive, the powerlessness of people, no matter how great their intellect and their position in society, against what often seems a force of sheer motiveless malevolence abroad in our world. All the same the inherent desire to create, to achieve, to defy this force must be seen to prevail, however hopeless-seeming the tasks involved.

"'Look at the sandbanks...' Sigurbjörn raised both hands in the air."They're like snowdrifts honed by the wind. Anyone building a church in a place like this should take those shapes as his guide. Look! Don't you think such a building would look good over there where the terns are?" Sigurbjörn pointed up at the grassy mounds of the breeding area and spread out his arms, paced the sand and moulded a church in the air with his hands."And the roof would look like a sea-lashed rock."' 60

LAXNESS
Halldór

Independent People [Sjálfstaett fólk]

Nonni, the poet-to-be in *Independent People* is described as destined to become 'greater than all other Icelanders', and it is generally thought that, when writing this, Laxness (who, born in 1902, won the Nobel Prize for literature in 1955) had himself in mind. His position as man and writer in his own country was unassailable, and hard to parallel: far and away the most famous Icelander of his times. Born of a farming family, he published his first novel when he was seventeen, travelled extensively and made himself precociously familiar with international artistic movements. He became both Roman Catholic and Communist, and created virtually singlehandedly the modern Icelandic novel, for which he drew both from the considerable long-lineaged Icelandic eddic tradition and from modernist thinking about fiction, from traditional repositories of lore and legend and from his own experiences and observations.

Independent People, for which the greatest critical claims have been made, takes place in a remote valley in Iceland cursed according to folklore by the early Irish sorcerer Kolumkilli (Columbkill) and his later partner, the witch Gunnvor. Their malign presences are to be felt throughout the novel which is set in the early twentieth century. But our preoccupation is with a sheep-farmer, Bjartur (whose hard life is rendered with a multiplicity of careful and informed observations) and his family. Bjartur's character seems to have been twisted by his unsatisfactory relationships with both his wives. His first wife died giving birth to a child not his own, Asta. Asta is both daughter and not-daughter (younger woman) to him; she brings out both the sympathetic and the harsh side of his nature. While portraying a dominating relationship of great psycho-cultural significance, Laxness also offers us a paradigm of Iceland, and even of its relation to the world beyond, though, in the remoteness of his existence, Bjartur chooses scarcely to acknowledge much beyond his own bleak valley and husbanded sheep.

'...Bjartur had been brought up on the old measures of the eighteenth-century ballads and had always despised the writing of hymns and new-fangled lyrics as much as he despised any other form of empty-headed fantasy. "My father," said he, "was a great man for poetry and was gifted with the tongue; and I owe it to him that I learned the rules of metre when I was still a youngster and have kept them since in spite of all the newfangled theories of the great poets... I inherited my copies of the rhymes from my father, seven of them belonging to the days when there were men of genius in Iceland, men who only needed four lines to the verse and yet you could read it in in forty-eight ways and always it made sense .... But mind you, if they heard tell of a famous woman they didn't stop to count the cost even if she lived in another hemisphere; no, they were off after her with the light of battle in their eyes, to conquer kings and kingdoms and heap the slain higher than the hills." 63

NORWAY

ANTHOLOGY

Hanson, Katherine

An Everyday Story. Norwegian Women's Fiction

An Everyday Story is an interesting showcase for Norwegian women writing over a period of 130 years from Seal Press, an independent West Coast publishing house active in Scandinavian literature and international womens' writing.

The anthology kicks off with Camilla Collett, one of the founders of modern Norwegian writing, represented here with

Storyteller Sara. This is a curious piece, mixing a fine and loving description of landscape, a forest awakening after the storm — 'rooks...cawing...rose up from the wet branches as though anticpating the rich broth of insects and worms seduced forth by the rain' — with images of rural poverty and desperation.

Certainly very startling too, at the time it was first published (1885), was Amalie Skram's *Constance Ring,* excerpted here, and being the 'scandalous' portrayal of a woman's marital *un*bliss. In the section here we see Constance trapped by convention inside a marriage where her sole purpose for existing is to make the awful boor she's married happy.

There's a similar theme in Dikken Zwilgmeyer's title piece *An Everyday Story,* but rather than a middle-class woman's boredom and disgust here we have a lower middle class woman's life of killing drudgery in trying to keep her sons looking respectable on the pittance her husband spares her. Social-feminist agit-prop this may be but it's convincing agit-prop...

Régine Normann was a writer a little younger than Zwilgmeyer but born in the distant Vesterålen islands and her *Love-Root* shows elements of rural folk tradition in its story of youthful passions.

Ragnhild Jølsen was a lively Bohemian character and her fine story *The Twelfth in the Cabin* suggests a Scandinavian light-heartedness and frankness about the facts of life in contrast to the harsh Protestant morality other writers describe. Gro Holm also grew up at the turn of the century and experienced rural life and gives us a picture, in an excerpt from her trilogy *Løstølsfolket* (the story of life on the *Løstøl* farm), of a young wife's tough and claustrophobic existence, living in the same small wooden house as her mother-in-law.

Nini Roll Anker's *A Crime* is very suggestive — a perfect, tight little Free Church ('free' in the opposite sense as to how it is used today) family — and the youngest daughter has just killed herself! Why? Can too much parental control kill? Anker's understated anger here gives the story its bite.

Sigrid Undset was one of Norway's most internationally-known writers and here in *The Charity Ball* she flexes literary muscle with modesty and force, there's steel under the kid gloves.

Cora Sandel was also internationally successful with her *Alberta* trilogy; here in *The Child Who Loved Roads* we meet one of her archetypes; the rebellious, sensitive girl who has to find the world on her own, away from all the supervision and control of the conventional. In her other piece here, *A Mystery,* we encounter more specifically the kind of cruel narrow-mindedness and the harsh thriftiness with money and feeling implied in the first story. Sandel was clearly a great writer, human and defiant.

Ingeborg Refling Hagen's *Borrowing Fire* is a tremendous story of an isolated farmhouse in a forest full of foxes, terrifiying hungry wolves and... ghosts. And then the fire goes out!

Magnhild Haalke's *Stormaja and Lilmarja* is equally beautiful and has a folktale's mysterious resonances and repetitions in its story of two sisters divided and united by love of a fey young man.

Åsta Holth's *Salt* is impossibly elegant agit-prop — and interesting for what it tells us about minorities and the poor in pre-war Norway, in this case the Finnish-speaking minority of Finnskog province.

Torborg Nedreaas' *Achtung Gnädiges Fräulein* also alludes to a darker aspect of Norwegian history — the German occupation during World War Two — in its story of a naive young girl exploited by a Nazi officer.

In *The Paradise Fish* by Solveig Christov we travel to a small community that lives on the edge of town in a kind of semi-rural state. In a few dazzling pages we run through love, desertion and death. It's clear from this and many other pieces in this collection that the short story has reached an advanced level in Norwegian literature.

Various brands of Protestant soul-searching and devil-fearing were abroad in Scandinavia in the early twentieth century and Ebba Haslund's *Santa Simplicitas* reflects this in its story of a life utterly moulded by (exagerrated) Christian piety. It's a story written on the fine line between anger and irony — Haslund is cited as one of Norway's 'leading feminist writers' and she mixes a pretty stiff cocktail of sexual and religious strands to make her point.

Continuing the feminist vein Margaret Johansen's *The Office Party* is a funny and well-written bit of feminist agit-prop about entrenched attitudes.

A Vietnamese Doll by Vigdis Stikkelien also seems at first rather agit-prop with its sensitive subject matter of 'trans-national adoption' as a Vietnamese orphan is adopted by wealthy Norwegians but in fact the theme is sympathetically and interestingly treated.

Bjørg Vik though reads much more vividly, this is 'real' writing rather than pushing buttons according to a political agenda. In her *The Entryways* we encounter a writer who has extensively explored working-class life in Norway, especially the lives of women and girls. Her second piece here *The Breakup* is a very sensitive and realistic view of 'the new freedom' in the contemporary ease of family dissolution which impacts here on a couple who have been together for sixteen years. The woman has found a new love leaving her old partner calmly and wistfully to point out everything they've built together will have to be dismantled. The woman finds herself losing 'something different from what she had expected'. Food for thought here no doubt; perhaps couples shouldn't behave as if they're going to spend their whole lives together if actually they most probably won't?

This collection contains authors born between 1813 and 1952 and with Karin Sveen it moves into the younger generation (of 1984 when the book was published). Sveen is from a working-class family and her story here *A Good Heart* is a glimpse of very poor hardworking people whose allegiances were equally divided between communism and evangelism. This is an exemplary short story; 'a whole world in a drop of water...' Sveen's excellent piece compensates for the fairly unreadable early work posted here from Kari Bøge, Tove Nilsen, Cecilie Løveid and Katrin Moe.

Apart from this well-meaning attempt to put a finger on the pulse of the very contemporary this is a very interesting anthology, creating an intimate and intersesting portrait of Norway through the twentieth century. *Ray Keenoy*

'Worn out by pacing she sat down on a settee and leaned back against the wall, her arms crossed on her breast. The moon was full and the room was so bright that every object could be seen distinctly. If only her mother would come through the door just one time more; she would throw her arms around her neck and cry, cry until the frozen crust around her heart melted away. She would tell her she wasn't happy, that she never could be-no matter how much they tortured her — that she didn't feel, would never feel, that it was her duty and her calling to make this fat self-satisfied man happy this man who never asked about her feelings, who treated her like she didn't have a soul in her body — something to be cranked like a hurdy-gurdy.' Amalie Skram *Constance Ring* 35

'"Really, Egelien! The things you say. Of course there are quite a number of women who only marry in order to be taken care of. And I wouldn't exactly defend that. But there is a difference."

"That's just what I'm saying.There's a devil of a difference.The more expensive a commodity is, the more the buyer prizes it.An expensive lady is honored and respected — but a cheap tart... One of them is borne aloft by the whole of society; the other is trodden underfoot by the whole of society. The former has secured herself respect and protection. She can afford to preserve her virtue from all other men except her husband — if it doesn't amuse her to be unfaithful. If it does amuse her — very well. If she is unlucky and is found out, then she can arrange a new and advantageous deal, if she hasn't been entirely stupid and made an idiotic choice of a lover. She can make a big thing of everything she has sacrificed for his sake — husband, home, children, virtue and reputation —so that he is forced to enter into the contract, take over her maintenance and marry her. In other words a married kept woman from higher society has arranged things so that she is always safe.'
Sigrid Undset *The Charity Ball* 91

'When they get money they go to the public baths. They jump in from the slippery tile edge and swim in the pool. Mostly they are in the shower room looking at the grown-up ladies. They have strange heavy breasts and hair under their arms and hair under their stomachs. Afterwards they giggle in the changing booth and describe the big disgusting bodies with ugly words, choking with laughter . They look at their own smooth young bodies, they cannot imagine that their bodies will change and betray them in this way. They walk home with wet hair excited and noisy, they begin to quarrel and aren't friends by the time they get home.' Bjørg Vik *The Entryways* 194

ASKILDSEN
Kjell

A Sudden Liberating Thought [En plutselig frigjorende tanke]

Kjell Askildsen (born 1929) had the strange distinction of having his first published book burned publicly by his own father, sheriff and prominent citizen of a puritanical town (Mandal) in southern Norway, an action worthy of one of the more pharisaic burghers of Ibsen's plays. Hardly surprising, therefore, that the young Askildsen, a challenger of all narrow orthodoxies, religious, ethical and political, when sent on a lecture tour, chose as his subject the false thinking behind the Fourth Commandment: 'Honour thy father and mother'! His crime according to his father and those like him had been too frank a presentation of sexuality. The depiction of sex as physical and psychic need has been central to Askildsen's work; spare, concentrated and often deliberately simple in manner, it could scarcely be less sensationalist. His quest is always for the truth about people's lives, and to find for his expression of these 'a new way of seeing things'.

A Sudden Liberating Thought is a collection of short stories. The short story is Askildsen's preferred medium, partaking as it does of an 'epiphany' (to use Joyce's famous term), a moment in which an insight into self or existence is gained, however fleeting or partial. With Askildsen you have the feeling that — arrived at doubtless after much struggle and difficulty — there is no barrier of literary convention between him and his subject. The two finest — and in Norway the two most praised — stories in the volume are of his very essence: *Ingrid Landbakka* and *Carl Lange*. In the first a working-class woman extricates herself from a conventional, if often painful marriage, but does so instinctually rather than consciously, respecting and being guided by, almost despite herself, the revulsions and yearnings of her own body.

Carl Lange presents us with a respectable middle-class man accused of 'interfering with' a young girl. During his nervously defensive dealings with the police, it emerges that a similar and unsubstantiated charge has, in fact, been brought against him before. A sense of deep unease and guilt now begins to take him over, and to determine his outward behaviour. This is the kind of story often called 'Kafkaesque', and indeed Askildsen, a well-read intellectual, is a fervent admirer of Kafka. But there's a sense in which his work is the very opposite of that great writer's. Kafka shows our life in society as being but a part of an extraordinary unchartable metaphysical whole. Askildsen shows us that the bizarre, the violent, the mystical are all there in ordinary life and ordinary people, part and parcel of what is going on all round us all the time. He himself said in an interview with a critic: 'Most of the characters in my books lead humdrum lives. This is a truth that must be told. It is a part of reality, and a matter of concern to me.'

Behind the conflicts between our capacity for fantasy (in thought and in behaviour) and our often dull daily treadmill lie the physical laws that condition our being — our bodies, the effect on them of time — and Askildsen's art courageously faces up to these.

Appropriately many of Askildsen's later stories, as we can see here, deal with men in old age. Their stripped-down conditions, and Askildsen's unflinching, often distressing renderings of them, have elicited comparisons with Beckett, whom Askildsen has translated. But once again Askildsen's intention is not to create a metaphor for life, but to show what life towards its end, with all its pathetic delusions and physical degradations, can be like. From such scrutiny we can proceed to live more honestly. *A Sudden Liberating Thought* offers us the work of one of the (inevitably) few European writers who are of truly major stature, and the translator, Sverre Lyngstad, has contributed an exceptionally illuminating introduction.

'The world isn't what it used to be. For example, it takes more time to live now. I'm well into my eighties but it isn't enough. I'm far too healthy, though I have nothing much to be healthy for. But life won't let go of me. He who has nothing to live for has nothing to die for. Maybe that's why.

Long ago, before my legs became too infirm, I went to my brother one day. I hadn't seen him in over two years, but he lived in the same place where we'd last met. "You're alive," he said, though he was older than I. I'd brought a snack and he gave me a glass of water. "Life is hard," he said, "it's unbearable." I ate and didn't answer. I hadn't come to argue with him. So I finished eating and drank the water. He kept staring at a point above my head. If I'd stood up and he didn't move his eyes, he would have looked straight at me. But he would probably have moved them. He didn't enjoy my company. Or to be more precise, he didn't enjoy himself in my company. I believe he has a bad conscience, not a good one anyhow. He has written a score of thick novels, I just a few, and they are slim ones. He's considered to be quite good, but more than a bit smutty. He writes a lot about love, mostly physical, wherever he got it from.

He continued to stare over my head, thinking perhaps he should be free to do so sitting there on his well-padded behind and his twenty novels, and I almost felt like leaving without accomplishing my object, except that it would seem a bit silly after such a long trip, so I suggested we play a game of chess. "It takes so much time," he said, "I don't have much time left any more. You could have come before." That's when I should have gotten up and left, it would have served him right; but I'm too courteous and considerate, it's my great weakness, one of them. "It won't take more than an hour," I said. "the game itself, yes," he replied, "but the excitement afterward, or the vexation if I should lose. My heart, you know, isn't what it used to be. I suppose yours isn't either.".. I parried, "You're afraid to die, eh? Oh well." "Nonsense. It's only that my life's work isn't done yet."' 187

BJØRNEBOE
Jens

Moment of Freedom [Frihetens øyeblikk]

Jens BjØrneboe (1920-76) had one of the most incisive and adventurous intelligences of any European novelist of his times, and an anarchic vision much taken up with the subject of gratuitous cruelty and why, shocking enough in private life, it is imported into the public arena with the seeming acquiescence of the many. Profoundly affected by the Fascist regimes of Germany and Italy, and by the German occupation of Norway, he examined this question above all in a trilogy of novels of which *Moment of Freedom* is the first (and self-sufficient) volume. It purports to be the autobiography of a key bureaucrat in a nameless Alpine state, a Servant of Justice, daily present in the courtrooms whose proper orderliness he oversees. The man who occupies this post must be circumspect, even taciturn, and so it is with our narrator.

So far the novel may sound like one by Kafka or Robert Walser, and though Bjørnebue was, like his central character, an ardent Germanist — these writers may stand behind it, *Moments of Freedom* is a very different work from any of theirs, letting us into a complex and self-aware mentality, interested in ideas and their justification and capable of relating them to subjective episodes of the past. His narrator's by no means very sympathetic mind is wide-ranging in its references (he can remind us of authorial voices in Saul Bellow or Philip Roth, or — perhaps a greater temperamental affinity in the Austrian writer Thomas Bernhard); one feels the burden of contemporary history and of the Norwegian experience behind the holed-up Alpine position from which he speaks. Spending his spare time writing a *History of Bestiality* — for which he has ample material — the Servant of Justice reflects on his life as he expatiates on human behaviour with at times a quite disconcerting cold cynicism. He has scant regard for religion, most political systems seem to him culpably fallible, almost all famous men have heavy feet of clay. Yet, as with Bernhard, even when we recoil, we respect. The title of the novel, we are told, is taken from the Spanish bullfighter's term, *el momento de la verdad*, the moment of truth, when the matador prepares actually to kill the bull. But the book's excellent translator, Esther Greenleaf Mürer reminds us that the Norwegian word for 'moment' *Øyeblikk* has the same form for singular and plural, and also has the sense of 'in the twinkling of an eye'. Therefore the servant's memoirs could be called *Glimpses of Freedom* which casts perhaps a more benign light on this stark work.

'I stood there as a child in a street of brothels, knowing my verses of Walther von der Vogelweide — not to mention Nietzsche. He got his syphilis in a brothel, so far as I know - and at the same time began to smoke hashish as well. And what would Teutonia have been without her great, narcomaniacal syphilitics and paralytics? The concentration camps are descended not from Nietszche,

but from Wagner — and Nietzsche knew what was coming. He sensed it between the bordello and the madhouse, on that road where so many good thoughts are thought. Whatever would Germania have been without syphilis? Heine, Hugo Wolf... Or Europe, for that matter: Maupassant, Baudelaire... What on earth would our beloved, stinking, beautiful Europe have become without our dope fiends, drunkards, homosexuals, consumptives, madmen, syphilitics, bed-wetters, criminals, and epileptics? Our whole culture was created by invalids, lunatics and felons.

There isn't one normal person who has done a useful or a lasting thing: it was the normals ones who built the slave camps in both Germany and Russia.

I know what I'm talking about. To search for a meaning in this lemurian chaos is to look for a needle in a haystack.' 40

CARLING
Finn

Commission [Oppdrag]

Finn Carling (born 1925) has suffered all his life from cerebral palsy, a disability which he commemorates in his autobiographical work (written in English) *And Yet We Are Human* (1958). His childhood was of necessity isolated and severely beset by pain and difficulty; a fantasy world in his own bedroom, a toy town inhabited by toy animals (Animal Town) was his principal source of comfort, and was to prove a mine of inspiration for his many later writings. Later in life he was to marry, have a son, and contribute to Norwegian society. Nonetheless his predicament has led him to explore and empathise with the lot of the marginalised, those excluded from so-called 'normal' existence: gays, the elderly, the misfits, animals. (Finn Carling has a specially developed feeling for these last, for dogs in particular.) His translator and friend, Louis A. Muinzer, who believes the writer to have 'genius', relates: 'More than a quarter of a century ago when I first met Finn Carling, I was appalled by the man walking towards me with a friendly smile on his face. I had had some acquaintance with disabled people but I had never known a man so grievously crippled as the one then approaching me... My pity lasted for about five minutes. After that it was replaced by envy, and I have envied Finn Carling ever since [for] his strength, his lack of pity, his intellecut\al honesty and his boyish good humour.'

Commission is — in the English-speaking world at any rate — his most praised work. In form a detective story, the tale of a quest for the solution of a mysterious death, it proceeds elliptically, from one flash illuminating darkness to another, bypassing the route of logic. And the solution when it is reached appertains to the inner world of the seeker, rather than to the dangerous external territory through which he has been passing.

A lonely, creatively blocked nameless writer staying in Corsica is approached by members of the powerful English shipping family, the Wardens, to find out what happened to Sebastian, the enigmatic son, part jetsetting playboy, part Christ-like friend of the poor and downcast, consorter with tarts and drop-outs, pre-pubescent in body yet an ardent lover: whether he committed suicide or was murdered. The search entails an almost Gothic parade of solipsistic figures: a brother engaged on horrendous animal experiments, a young woman who has had a heart-transplant and believes the organ to have come from Sebastian who now possesses her soul, a drug-dependant Singapore prostitute, a dog who may be an embodiment of Sebastian himself. Yet because the primary journey is towards a broader and more solid identity for the writer himself, the novel seems less fantasy than a record of psychic realities.

A cautionary note: Throughout, until the memorable last page, the author employs the impersonal pronoun for the writer, rendered as 'one'. Unfortunately in English this has precious and self-consciously upper-class connotations which are best forgotten by the reader.

'[The dog the writer has befriended has been tormented by village boys.] The dog looks at one. Its eyes are dull, almost lifeless. As one kneels at its side, it slowly lifts its head and licks one's hand. But it doesn't try to get up. An uncontrollable hatred surges up in one. A hatred that makes the tears flow, and one cries out in the darkness, without words. A rage one has never felt before is almost bursting one apart. A rage against violence and injustice. In a world like ours, why hasn't one felt it before? Was it such feelings that drove Sebastian in his fight against oppression...?

While the tears flow, one lifts the dog carefully, carries it up the steep hill towards the children in Lebanon, in El Salvador, in Eritrea. Seen and leafed on in the newspaper. Hasn't wanted to see! Now one feels the slack body of the animal in one's arms and the blood from the wounds pressing through one's shirt. One sees a child's, a woman's, an old man's face resting against one's upper arm, distorted with pain. One closes one's eyes to shut these visions out. When one opens them again one sees the dog. Its dark muzzle hangs down. Its eyes are without focus. A horrible thought: Is the dog dead?' 98-9

CARLING
Finn

Diary for a Dead Husband

A middle-aged woman, whose husband has died from a heart attack, keeps a spasmodic diary throughout the year following his death, to address him, more boldly than she did in life, and to reconcile herself to the condition of non-existence, his and hers to come. Felicia has long lived in the shadow of her husband, and has always therefore been judged by inappropriate standards; Carling's feelings for the marginalised are apparent again, indeed the whole book is a plea for a social inclusiveness that will embrace an unremarkable elderly bourgeois widow like his diarist. At the same time he shows that marginalisation itself promotes insights from which society can benefit.

'Didn't see that I felt alone. Have done so all the months since your death. First time a tap began to leak or the car refused to start, I was helplessly alone. Not lonely. You took care of practical matters in the forty years we were married. You were married.

When on a rare occasion you suggested I do something like that myself, I thought: I can't do that! As if it were a law of nature. It never occurred to me to try, though I knew of women who both fixed taps and got cars to start. Just said: I'm not like that.

I have thought about that, too: Why I didn't try. Did I go rigid from fear of failing? Of not preserving my self-image? Or more accurately, the image you had of me? Or did I feel deep inside me that I had to take care of *your* image? The image of the man who does things? I don't know. But now that I have changed the washers on taps and managed to start the car when it wouldn't budge, I see before me how you struggled. That you were clumsy and could seem scared. I hadn't seen that when you were alive.' 47-8

FALDBAKKEN
Knut

Insect Summer [Insektsommer]

Knut Faldbakken (born 1941) has enjoyed enormous success, both in critical reputation and sales, not only in Norway and Scandinavia but elsewhere, including lately the United States. In Britain he has not so far managed to gain any sizeable readership, which is surprising considering the universality of his subject-matter and the tense, erotic and often exciting nature of his plots. His over-riding theme is sexuality — its omnipotence and omnipresence — and the machinations of society, endorsed by culture and significant institutions, to prevent acknowledgement of the fact — despite the daily evidence to the contrary — as well as of the phenomenon itself.

Insect Summer is an account of the rite of passage of a boy Peter, fifteen, going on sixteen (his birthday features in the novel) who has, owing to his physical development, suddenly (as it seems to him) acquired insight into the sexual forces dictating life. He has erections at the mere mention of matters sexual, often he is possessed by the urge to masturbate, his desire for actual sexual congress seems impossible to fight against. The summer of the novel he leaves his family home in the city — where he wonders about his parents (eg 'Do they..? When did they last...? Is everything all right between them?') — to spend holiday weeks on his uncle's farm up in the mountains, a place he has long loved. His uncle is his father's younger brother, he even looks like him and like Peter himself — which sets new trains of thought in motion. Uncle Kristen is married to Aunt Linn, and they have no children.

Everything of the tragedy to follow is for the careful reader established in the opening chapters of the novel, even though Peter isn't mature enough to trust to some of his impressions: the irritation Kristen and Linn manifest towards each other, Kristen's oscillation between a certain nervousness (displayed at the hillside hut where Peter is to sleep) and his jaunty matiness, the unease that the disappearance of young Marie, their live-in help, occasions. The novel ends with a climax to my mind far more horrifying and convincing than that which brings to a close the famous *Go-Between* of L.P.Hartley. Yet it could be said that the whole of Peter's story is contained between his father's holiday leaving present of a sheath-knife (too boyish) and his birthday present of a watch ('a sign from him to me that I was grown up'). There are no Hartley-like scars that will inhibit Peter for the rest of his life. He has learned that life, thanks to sexuality's unbrookable force, can't be tidied up — either in theory or in practice. The most casual observation of the natural world will bear that out.

'Hypnotized, night insects flew senselessly into the lantern, dropping on the table, where they lay in their death throes with torn, trembling wings. I closed the door, feeling worn out, longing for nothing but bed, to give myself up to the darkness and the whims of sleep, the turmoil of dreams. I unrolled the sleeping-bag on the bunk, undressed, blew out the lantern and slid down into the cool cocoon. I'd thought I might masturbate, make peace with everyone, rid myself of the seamy suspicions about the people I held in esteem and who were fond of me, Aunt Linn and Uncle Kristen, Mother and Dad back in town, to put an end to ceaseless imagining and conjecturing, which merely reflected my own over-sensual relation to all the things and people in my vicinity. Yet I dozed off as I was struggling to get going, dozed off as I lay there, picturing how good it would be to meet them tomorrow without any misgivings, all speculation and all seamy suspicions simply left behind in the hut, crumpled up under the bunk in a handkerchief of shame.' 31

FALDBAKKEN
Knut

The Sleeping Prince [Maude danser]

This controlled yet nerve-rasping novel may remind British readers of Brian Moore's *The Lonely Passion of Judith Hearne*, both novels dealing with the tragedy of sexual repression. Faldbakken takes the case of Maude, a woman of 47 who has had no sexual experience, and for whom, as she enters menopause, things do not go psychically well. How could they? When so much in her life — looking after her mother, presenting herself as dutiful, pure and unimportant — has been founded not just on self-denial but on denial of the very urges and forces that promote existence itself. Maude, after her mother's death, comes to live at a private hotel (richly rendered by Faldbakken). Here she maintains a regimen of impeccable chastity, but within her thoughts are not chaste. Perhaps for the first time in her life she begins making sexual connections, being inspired to sexual thoughts and fantasies by casual sights and occurrences — just as young Peter was to be in *Insect Summer* published the following year. We realise quite how rotten are the fruits of the years of denial by entering Maude's thoughts about an elderly and ill resident at the hotel, Mr Eldmann. Isn't he communicating with her over and above the other guests? Isn't his most inoffensive-seeming remark or gesture a veiled attempt to express his feelings — more, his desire — for her. Take the reference to 'the roguish Amor on a painting'? What could that be but a covert declaration of his love for her?

She is wrong, deluded, of course. Mr Eldmann retains his impenetrable mask — and dies. But there arrives at the guest-house a certain König who is, in stark reality, interested in her, who would like to seduce her. Him she must confront in her long-protected virginity.

Sexual repression is also a repression of membership of the

human family. By holding oneself aloof and immaculate one is stifling the need to get close, to be involved, and even its imperative nature throughout our kind — and beyond. No wonder that when practised as thoroughly as Maude has done, and for so many years, this need turns murderous, allies itself with Thanatos not Eros.

The end of *The Sleeping Prince* is shocking in the literal sense; the act of love becomes an act of cruelty, the super-ego has become a tyrannical death-dealing monster.

'The whole thing was so unreal: Mr Kønig in dressing-gown and slippers here in her room. Candlelight. And she herself — here she was sitting on her bed with her hair down in a night-dress and négligée, showing a leg, a knee! Her first impulse was to beg him to go. It was all impossible after all, she could not go through with it; his presence in the room, a shocking, offensive foreign body. But suddenly he was close to her, his hands were stroking the silken cocoon which she had spun round her body, and his voice was whispering how lovely she was, how deeply he loved her, what a happy man he was; and then things fell into place again, for this was also a part of it, the fact that she permitted a couple of small tender excesses was all part of a natural, sensual escalation that could not be omitted. She let it happen, she even made little concessions, squeezed, patted and pressed herself so close, as closely as she could, against his corpulence; she made small noises, did things she knew instinctively that he would like, for she had also become a little restless and impatient.' 202-203

GAARDER
Jostein

Sophie's World [Sofies Verden]

Sophie's World, which came out in Norway in 1991, has proved one of the sensational publishing successes of the Nineties, selling over a million copies, heading bestseller lists in over forty countries, and in Britain undergoing in its paperback edition no fewer than twenty-three impressions between 1996 and 1998. As with that other immensely popular Scandinavian book, *Miss Smilla's Feeling for Snow*, these facts are interesting and revealing in themselves. Why should 'A Novel about the History of Philosophy' (to use its subtitle) have met with so widely enthusiastic a reception?

Sophie's World is a novel in that it tells a (progressively more complicated and baffling) story, and in that our curiosity as to how this will work out is never allowed to abate. Sophie Amundsen, a fourteen-year-old girl soon about to celebrate, and on Midsummer's Day, her fifteenth birthday, receives in her mailbox two white envelopes; the first of these contains a slip of paper with the words 'Who are you?' on it, the second encloses one saying 'Where does the world come from?' The first attempts to answer these questions follow soon afterwards, in brown envelopes addressed to her and bearing on the back the written instruction: 'Course in Philosophy. Handle with Care.' Together with these mysterious missives — which have their sequels — come communications addressed to one Hilde Møller Knag c/o Sophie Amundsen, and Sophie soon realises that this Hilde (of whom she has never heard) bears uncanny resemblances to herself, even in age and date of birthday.

Eventually Sophie meets her philosophy instructor, and the lessons are made face to face rather than through paper. The teacher is an enigmatic individual with the odd polyglot name of Alberto Knox. Meanwhile the riddle of Hilde's identity becomes more and more pressing, not least because of the increasing similarities exposed between the two girls. Sophie's father, for instance, is away from home — his is that most Norwegian of occupations, the captain of an oil-tanker — and so is Hilde's; he in his absence also exhibits Norwegian characteristics, for he is a member of the United Nations peace-keeping force in the Lebanon. But what is Alberto's relation to the latter? He seems to have one. Both girls are eagerly looking forward to their birthdays as occasions when the unexpected can happen — and indeed it does.

Though carefully prepared, the unravelling of the mystery of Hilde will take most readers by surprise; it involves a dramatic standing of the story-so-far on its head, for this is meta-fiction, and what has passed as straightforward is shown to be a sort of *mise-en-abyme*. I suspect that the many readers of *Sophie's World* have responded more to the presentations of philosophy than to the post-modernist fairy-tale of the story of Sophie Amundsen herself. These, after all, make up the greater part of the book. I'm not sure that Alberto isn't better when writing letters than when talking (when Sophie has to make regular interjections:'I can see that.' 'That sounds logical.') But he is always clear and persuasive — even when in a subsequent lesson he has to refute what he has previously made convincing, even appetising. As with the plot, maybe the earlier part of his exposition is more interesting than the later; his heart, I would say, is with the pre-Socratics, with Plato and Aristotle and with the Neo-Platonists rather than with nineteenth or twentieth century thinkers (Wittgenstein, for example, is never even mentioned). But central to the plot — which mimics certain key philosophic ideas — is the eighteenth century Bishop Berkeley and his view of subjectivity.

A very Norwegian or Scandinavian aspect of the book is Gaarder's belief in the importance of ecophilosopy (or ecosophy) and its great exponent, the Norwegian Arne Naess, and of international cooperation particularly over world trouble-spots.

What has earned the book its numerous admirers is its author's unflinching belief in the value of the humanist activity of independent thinking, and its lively ability to run the gamut of ideas from primitive animism to post-Marxism with a continuous respect — and clarity of summary. And in his delineation of Sophie and Hilde Gaarder shows the same respect:

"'When you see a shadow, Sophie, you will assume that there must be something casting the shadow. You see the shadow of an animal. You think it must be a horse, but you are not quite sure. So you turn around and see the horse itself — which, of course is infinitely more beautiful and sharper in outline than the blurred "horse-shadow". *Plato believed similarly that all natural phenomena are merely shadows of the eternal forms or ideas.* But most people are content with a life among shadows. They give no thought to what is casting the shadows. they think shadows are all there are, never realizing even that they are, in fact, shadows. And thus they pay no heed to the immortality of their own soul.'" 75-6

HAMSUN
Knut

Growth of the Soil [Markens grode]

Upon hearing of Hitler's death in the spring of 1945 Knut Hamsun wrote: 'He was a warrior, a warrior for mankind and a prophet of the gospel of justice for all nations. He was a reformer of the highest rank, and his historical fate was that he flourished in a time of unexampled coarseness, which felled him at last.' Hamsun is perhaps the best example of why 'political correctness'— a simplistic critical strategy with its roots in Stalinist Russia, from where it made its way into Communist Parties around the world and eventually into the American New Left and then into contemporary feminism etc — is not the right way to evaluate literature. Despite his repulsive political choices Hamsun, like that other enthusiastic fascist Ezra Pound, was great and liberating in his writing.

Growth of the Soil is one of the finest books of a revered author, irresistible and elemental from the first splendid image of a man trudging through the uncultivated common lands to find himself a space to make a farm and dedicate himself to 'the growth of the soil'. This is in fact one of the dominant images of the Norwegian psyche; the sense that there is a place in the forest where you can make a life for yourself, relying on yourself. Hamsun's forest-clearer, Isak, is the classic 'simple man' who 'reads no books' but is absorbed by the tiring daily rhythms of his farming life and experiences life with the contentment of the fully-occupied; 'and they went to sleep. And wakened in the morning to another day, with things to look at, matters to see to, once again; aye, toil and pleasure, ups and downs, the way of life.'

Just as in his short masterpiece *Hunger* Hamsun manages so effectively to capture and transmit the painful intense life of a febrile, marginal urbanite so in this rural epic he makes us feel the beat of the slow and satisfiying repetition of natural and agricultural cycles. It really doesn't matter whether this is your particular dream or not, Hamsun taps into something we all share somewhere deep deep down.

While today in England or America 'agribusiness' with its sprays and machinery transforms farming into a toxic factory system, *Growth of the Soil* is a wonderful description of a process that must have happened all over Northern Europe and North America at some time — the original settlement of the land for agriculture.

This isn't a book however that refers only to a romantic rural idyll; the pull of the cities and their different rhythms and knowledges are present too; although largely presented in a hostile way as a corruption. In this one can detect perhaps the thread that led Hamsun to his Nazi sympathies and there is even a brief crack right at the end of the book; — 'he's the modern type, a man of our time; he believes honestly enough all the age has taught him, all the Jew and the Yankee have taught him' — which bears a false and ideological note against the dignity of the rest of the text.

Within the rural world itself there is (realistically) plenty of hostility, jealousy and competition; Hamsun's idyll is not one made of sublime 'communitarian' human bonds but stems rather from the relationship between a person's work and their world. The message, timely enough, is that we enjoy life and feel fulfilled when we work on and with nature, remembering that the human world is also ultimately part of 'nature'. A beautiful and inspiring book. *Ray Keenoy*

[The book's first image — ed]

'The long, long road over the moors and up into the forest — who trod it into being first of all? Man, a human being, the first that came here. There was no path before he came. Afterward, some beast or other, following the faint tracks over marsh and moorland, wearing them deeper; after these again some Lapp gained scent of the path, and took that way from field to field, looking to his reindeer. Thus was made the road through the great Almenning, the common tracts without an owner; no-man's-land.

The man comes, walking toward the north. He bears a sack, the first sack, carrying food and some few implements. A strong, coarse fellow, with a red iron beard, and little scars on face and hands; sites of old wounds — were they gained in toil or fight? Maybe the man has been in prison, and is looking for a place to hide; or a philosopher, maybe, in search of peace. This or that, he comes: the figure of a man in this great solitude.' 4

[After Isak has founded his farm]

'The wilderness was inhabited and unrecognizable, a blessing had come upon it, life had arisen there from a long dream, human creatures lived there, children played about the houses. And the forest stretched away, big and kindly, right up to the blue heights.' 114

HAMSUN
Knut

Hunger [Sult]

Vitalist and villain, Knut Hamsun (1859-1952) aroused often bitter controversy long before his Nazism of the 1930s and 1940s, and his concomitant public support of the German conquerors of his country. As a radical young writer, an autodidact from the north of Norway with knock-about years to draw on, he attacked the preeminence of Ibsen, and is in fact the ruthless representative of the new generation who stands behind Ibsen's great late play, *The Master Builder*.

Profoundly anti-bourgeois, defiant of conventions literary, political and social, Hamsun was perceived as having brought something fresh and demotic not only into Norwegian/Scandinavian literature but into that of the entire western world. His reputation in the late nineteenth and early twentieth centuries can best be compared with that of the Russian Gorky, and — two decades later — with D.H. Lawrence. His style is, particularly in the earlier works, urgent and physical and the perfect vehicle for his subject matter. He chose to present men alone, roughing it, scraping a living in the city, in slums and dockyards, or living close to the elements; his admiration, not lightly given, went out to peasants, foresters or seamen — and also to hobos, tramps, drunks and tarts, to the folk who inhabit Gorky's *The Lower Depths*.

Hamsun was a stupendous — and frank — egotist in and out of his work, and doubts about his achievement spring from this. *Hunger* (1890), a first-person account of a young man's wanderings round Oslo (then called Christiania), poor, lonely, hungry, yet full of energy and feeling, astonishingly anticipates later writers in its conveying of sensory impressions, and its reliance on these to create a whole picture of an individual and his relationship to the external world. We can see the Hamsun of its pages — fearless in what he sets down, impatient of those dicta that would make a writer draw back from the crude, the coarse, or even the merely tedious — as a precursor of Joyce and Lawrence, Camus and Beckett, as well as of Kerouac and the Beats. His adventurous prose is mimetic of the material on which it is working so that it leaps tenses, reproduces the sound of movement, of always having to move on, it is lively and generous with dialogue.

As critics have pointed out we do not learn much about the narrator apart from his immediate predicament — though at the end he gets himself a job as a deckhand on a ship bound for Leeds (!) in England. Not that he's gone to sea before, but '.. give me a job and I'll do it. I'm used to a little of everything.' *Hunger* is a very male creation (at times it's impossible to believe that at any given time Hamsun's very sizeable readership hasn't been made up almost exclusively of young men) — and it must be added a very male romanticism that informs it. And here the difficulties begin — Hamsun's narrator has little thought for anything apart from himself, his gratifications, his excitements, and what is more is proud not to have any. This is self-sufficiency raised to the level of an artistic and anti-moral gospel. (It's surely of enormous significance that Hamsun's hero is a writer, the new kind of emergent writer-hero.)

Behind the primitivism and the very real response to life in the raw goes an intellectual rejection of civilised standards, a worship of selfhood and freedom from all chains that goes not just with, say, Whitman, but with Nietzsche, the secret (or maybe not so secret) presence in Hamsun's fiction.

'"Well, I never!" I blurted out. "Just you wait and see!" And I flung my arms lustily around her shoulders. Was the girl out of her mind? Did she take me for a complete greenhorn? Haw-haw, wouldn't I, though, by the living... Noone should say about me that I was backward on that score. What a little devil! If it was just a matter of pushing on, then...

As though I was good for much of anything!

She sat quite still, her eyes closed as before; neither of us spoke. I pressed her hard to me, squeezing her body against my breast, and she didn't say a word. I could hear our heartbeats, both hers and mine; they sounded like hoofbeats.

I didn't know what I was doing anymore, said some nonsense that she laughed at, whispered endearments against her mouth, stroked her cheek and kissed her again and again. I opened a button or two in her bodice and glimpsed her breasts underneath, white, round breasts that peeked out like two sweet miracles behind her underlinen.

"May I see?" I say, trying some more buttons, eager to enlarge the opening. But I can't get anywhere with the lower buttons, my emotion is too strong and, besides, her bodice is tighter there. "May I see just a little... a little....?"

She winds her arm round my neck, quite slowly, tenderly; her breath blows directly on my face from her red, quivering nostrils. With the other she begins to undo the buttons herself, one by one.' 136-137

HAMSUN
Knut

Mysteries [Mysterier]

Published two years after *Hunger*, in 1892, *Mysteries* was proffered to the world, as an example of, a blueprint for, a totally new kind of literature. And certainly reading it is like reading no other novel — though one can safely surmise that the author was an admirer of Dostoeyevsky. In contrast to *Hunger, Mysteries* is written in a limpid style feigning objectivity; even the excursions into the central figure's mind employ this objective style. Both the subject-matter and the meaning of the subject are mysterious; not for nothing is the title a plural noun. All this is emphasized by Hamsun's narrative manner, as if actual history is being presented us. The novel opens: 'In the middle of the summer of 1891 the most extraordinary things began happening in a small Norwegian coastal town. A stranger by the name of Nagel appeared, a singular character who shook the town by his eccentric behaviour and then vanished as suddenly as he had come.'

Nagel is to act as a divining-rod for the mysteries that this small, outwardly unremarkable town harbours and is the catalyst responsible for eruptions of emotional forces which respectable life has tried to keep repressed. Shortly before his arrival a man has been found dead, dead it's thought because of his love for a beautiful girl, Dagny, who is getting married to another man. Yet this event is itself but the tip of an iceberg made up of pent-up feelings and unrealised relationships.

It is a fascinating story made the more compelling by the author's atttitude towards it; there is much in it that he too finds baffling. Who really is Nagel? And why does he destory himself in the terrible and disturbing last pages of the novel? Yet just as *Hunger* purports to be a realistic exposure of an outcast's lot and is in truth deeply romantic, so the apparent objectivity of Hamsun in *Mysteries* conceals a subjective creation; town and people and Nagel himself are all projections of the author's highly individual mind. One that is proud of its individuality too; *Mysteries* shows a certain contempt for ordinary people, though, to give the author his due, this contempt is also one of the novel's themes. The principal antagonist to Nagel — in the thematic sense; in a literal one he could not, for the greater part of the book, be less of one — is a weak, hideous man generally known as The Midget. He, it transpires at the close of the novel, represents the ugliness of the meek Sermon-on-the-Mount approach to life, in Hamsun's opinion, always cringing and hypocritical and concealing unpleasant desires. The embodiment of 'slave-mentality' (i.e. Christianity) in a misshapen body is not the only distasteful element of the novel. Hamsun/Nagel the vitalist asserts will and strength over the gentler virtues and rejoices in this, even if it means defying conventional notions of sanity and insanity.

Mysteries has been called one of the 'half-dozen truly great novels of the twentieth century'; Martin Seymour-Smith in his *Guide to Modern World Literature* (1985) said of this 'great' and 'marvellous' novel: 'He who remains unmoved by it need have nothing to do with modern literature again.' I believe these estimations to be wide of the mark; *Mysteries* is an absorbing work of the imagination vitiated by the dubious elements in that imagination, which are not under the author's control and which seem to me morally reprehensible.

Hamsun's career — which has interested many, most recently (1996) the Swedish writer P.O. Enquist who has authored a prizewinning filmscript based on his life — would testify, to say the least to some moral deficiency. He took a keen interest in Nazism before there was any question of having to surrender to it; he made enthusiastic speeches in support of the Nazis whose occupying presence in Norway he welcomed. After the War and a degree of punishment he justified himself; it is unlikely he really repented. Ostracised by the Norwegian reading public he seems now to have been reinstated. But his conduct and his imagination cannot be seen as at variance; the evidence is also there in his writings themselves.

'Again he thought ofThe Midget....though his suspicion of the wretched,crippled dwarf was as strong as ever. He thought of Mrs Stenersen, who, though sickly and asthmatic, deceived her husband right before his eyes without batting an eyelash; of Kamma, the greedy little golddigger who followed him around with her deceitful arms outstretched wherever he went and was always turning his pockets inside out for more,never satisfied. East and west,at home and abroad, he had always found people to be the same; the same vulgarity, the same hypocrisy — from the beggar, who bandaged up a perfectly good hand, to the blue, ozone-filled sky. And he, Nagel, was he any better than the rest? No better, but this was the end.' 292

PETTERSON
Per

To Siberia [Til Sibir]

Per Petterson (born 1952), when already an acclaimed writer of short stories, lost four members of his family, among them both his parents, in a terrible ferry fire. His shock and grief affected the course of his fiction in two ways. First, almost every paragraph of his poet's prose, spare, exact and evocative, is informed by awareness of life's precariousness. The woman narrator of *To Siberia*, recreating her Danish youth in northern Jutland, captures that unease which undercuts the adolescent's sense of expanding physical powers because of realisation of the indomitable reality of pain and death. Secondly, Petterson wanted to explore in fiction his dead parents' lives. *To Siberia* is his mother's story; his father's will follow.

The novel takes its title from the imaginative space the heroine has settled on to help her cope with her frustrations and yearnings. The daughter of a mother possessed by religious mania and a somewhat hopeless carpenter father, and spending the important years of her childhood in Denmark under Nazi occupation, she has found consolation and inspiration for the future in dreams of a journey on the Trans-Siberian railway, just as her brother Jesper has fixed on Morocco as his place of antithetical happiness. The Siberian dream has an ironic political significance: the narrator has absorbed her brother's Marxist-Leninism, strengthened by her experience of Soviet Russia's dedicated enemies, the Nazis. When the war is over, she embarks on a deliberately proletarian lifestyle, taking menial jobs in Copenhagen, Stockholm, Oslo (the great worker-state still awaits her arrival). When — in a scene of great poignancy — she hears of Jesper's death in *his* chosen dream-country, Morocco, she is awakened to a new and terrible understanding of the relation between the realms of longing and those of actuality. The pains of reality must also pervade one's dreams. At the same time this novel pays a sustained, timely and salutary tribute to the courage and humanity of the Old Left.

This is a novel of extraordinary distinction, moving and thoughtful.

'Jesper doesn't want to be [confirmed], but he must. He will have his first suit and the whole family will be invited. My father sits writing down numbers on paper, he only takes every other pull at his cigar. He should have had a house built of wood that would smell like the workshop from floor to ceiling and not of mould as it does here after the autumn and driving rain on the outer walls. Here everything is brickwork and cement. The water seeps in through the cracks and spreads in damp flowers through the wallpaper so it peels off and the kitchen floor is icy to the feet even in summer with the sun shining in. There is no glow in bricks. In Siberia the houses are built of timber that gives off the good smell of tar and warmth in summer, and when the long winter sets in the glow stays in the logs and never fades. The wood contracts and waits and stretches out when spring comes and drinks in the wind and the sun.

When no-one is listening my father grinds his teeth. But I listen all the same. I show him books with pictures of Siberia and the houses there, and he slowly holds it at a long-sighted distance and after a while he says:

"That's a good piece of craftsmanship. But it is cold outside, terribly cold."' 51

RYGG
Pernille

The Butterfly Effect [Sommerfugleffekten]

The Norwegian detective story has become a much sought-after commodity in recent years, the majority of its practitioners today (as is the case with detective stories elsewhere) being women. Pernille Rygg (born 1963) gained a following with this her first novel, partly because of the unusual voice and personality of the narrator, Igi Heitmann, a psychologist concerned with chaos theory and married to a transvestite who loves her but for the most part prefers a young man as bed-companion.

Igi is the daughter of an unsuccessful private detective, killed before the novel opens. The discovery of a butterfly medallion among his effects makes her think he was on to something serious before he died. And she in turn makes a discovery of her own — of the body of a young woman who turns out to have been estranged from her parents, and from society as a whole. The pace of the sleuthing is very fast, and the reader becomes caught up in it, and feels too a sense of kinship with the places of Igi's life and adventures: for the greater part the more prosperous suburbs of Oslo (which means VERY prosperous).

Inevitably in a first book that is striving to succeed in a particular (and popular) genre, there is derivative and modish stuff here: scenes that might have been suggested by *Miss Smilla's Feeling for Snow* (and the scientist-heroine could owe something to her too!), themes of cult religion and child abuse are also thrown in. But, in addition to the success of the purely whodunnit aspects of the novel, it is distinguished by a genuine imagination at work and an ability to endow scenes with a vivid particularity.

'I drive back to the church. By now the porch is on fire, tongues of flame licking towards the body of the church itself, which so far looks relatively undamaged. The small separate chapel is worse affected: the flames engulfing its side walls meet across the roof in desperate fists of flame, fumbling, importunate, like the hands of an insane lover.

It's a beautiful, savage spectacle. I stand numbed, witnessing an ancient drama. There are no lunatics I understand so well as pyromaniacs.

The sparks from the roof rise into the sky, a golden galaxy outshining the pale stars. the flames have now devoured the roof, and the timber frame inside looks like a stark black skeleton in a sea of fire. One of the beams slowly gives way, slips into the burning space and vanishes. The roar of the flames almost drowns the sound of approaching sirens.

Another beam comes loose from the wall, hangs there like a scorched body, before crashing down into the waiting jaws of flame. Then, as a fire engine screeches to a halt behind me and the screaming sirens subside in a sob, the whole roof collapses. Sparks explode into the sky and a shudder runs through the front wall as the shock wave hits it; for a moment it seems to sway, then it cracks in two and half of it topples backwards.

Revealed in the gaping wound in the wall is the figure of a woman. Her torso rises and turns towards me before she too disappears into the flames.' 24-25

SANDEL
Cora

Selected Short Stories

This is a beautiful collection from the liberating Cora Sandel whose key autobiographical short story *The Child Who Loved Roads*, alongside the story *A Mystery* is reviewed in the excellent anthology of Norwegian women writers *An Everyday Story*. A typically independent, not to say wild, Sandelian female character shows up in *The Ways of Love* which features the delightfully squalid rag-pickers moll, Severine. *The Ways of Love*, a story which helped establish Sandel's reputation is typical too in the way it swiftly changes in tone from *buffo* (funny) to *triste*.

Sandel was one of that fascinating generation of Bohemian feminists like Djuna Barnes, Katherine Mansfield, or Anais Nin who often spent time in Paris in the1920s and 30s. They brought a new sensuality and simplicity of focus to literature; a disarming, irreverent female bluffness, unagressive but tenderly subversive.

A great Sandel theme, unsurprisingly given her own experiences and sympathies, are the frustrations of marriage. In *Larsen's* she pulls off the trick of exposing a marriage, a whole life and its disappointments in just a few pages. If *Thank You, Doctor* is the sad story of a young couple's difficulties, *The Child* is that of an established unhappy couple; the tense situation of the man and woman is mediated very cleverly through their child's presence. The same technique is continued more intensely in *The Flight to America* which pictures a marriage that, rather than just disintegrating, is positively exploding and this is its awesome and fascinating record...

If marriage is pictured as bleak by a woman who, one suspects, was a bit too lively to be happily married for very long, then the situation of women having sexual relationships outside marriage is shown, in *The Art of Murder* or *Klara,* as even more awful in the highly moralistic Protestant Scandinavia of the recent past.

There are other stories here too very worthy of praise, like *The Sisters*, about an 'odd couple' and the trials of an artistic career or *The Mother* about the joys of living it up; in any case in this book we meet an uncomfortably good writer writing exceptionally good short stories that are well worth tracking down... *Ray Keenoy*

'My window faces out toward the little path. I see everyone who goes by. And everyone sees in. Some fleetingly and as if by accident, others long and curiously. But the path curves and I can also see the nearest neighbouring house. A low, white-painted country house, two-story with dormers. A garden around it with flowering cherry trees and a tiny silver ball. All of it pretty, well ordered, almost prosperous.

The pale, dark-haired boy from over there goes by. ... He never looks in; he's the only one who doesn't. His sisters, on the other hand — they stare. They're two small girls with black hair curling over their shoulders, with thin bare legs, bare arms and bracelets. They have difficulty moving on; they walk backwards over the path, while their eyes stay glued to my window, on my newly washed white shoes that sit in the sun. On everything that can in some way help identify me, the strange city dweller. And their stares are gaping, slightly loony.' *Mother* 22

STEEN
Thorvald

Don Carlos [Don Carlos]

The Don Carlos of the title is Charles Darwin, and the novel, written in epistolary form, gives a lively, disturbingly ambivalent account of the impact of the great naturalist-to-be on a young Italian man his own age; the two meet in Buenos Aires at a time (1833) when the city is riven with incipient civil war. Don Carlos cuts an enigmatic figure, withdrawn, stand-offish, yet given to sudden prolonged stories about his recent activities (up in the Andes, down in Tierra del Fuego). Giovanni — author of the rich, emotional, detailed letters to his brother, Roberto, back in Italy, that constitute the book — doesn't know how to take him, not least because of the moral complexities of his own predicament; at times he is repelled, at times responsive to some strange sureness, some as yet concealed power in him. Don Carlos is full of contradictions, and not especially attractive ones either: his boyish zeal for hunting is combined with reverence for natural life, his oscillations between callousness and concern, his conventional religion (contrasting with Giovanni's passionate rejection of it) and the scientific theories he is formulating which will do more than any one other factor to dethrone and destroy it.

Don Carlos is essentially a modernist novel, presenting its subject and concerns from a skilfully chosen oblique viewpoint. Despite its elliptical nature and the often recalcitrant consciousness through which material is presented, it adds up to a remarkably unified image of conflicting aspects of human history meeting at one unique (but representative) point: political revolutionism versus conservative stability, safe unquestioning faith versus the so frequently destabilising force of reason. It also abounds in scenes of both beauty and horror, and in its courage of facing up to both in the natural world manifests its Scandinavian provenance.

'The rain of the past few days had made the roads almost impassable.A water waggon pulled by two oxen had overturned. One of the oxen had drowned in the mud.The huge wheels were just about to disappear.The water seller was hauling for dear life at the horns of the second ox.We tried to help. Several others came running.The water seller wept with rage and despair.When there was no hope left we made out way to the Matador Slaughterhouse to borrow a horse and a cart from a man I know. The slaughterhouse yard contained several small enclosures belonging to various slaughtermen. Though it was evening and the weather was wet work was in progress.The beasts were driven through the city streets into the enclosure. The matador rode towards the steer. His lasso of metal wire tightened about its neck.The muscle between its thigh and knee was severed. One knife thrust into the jugular.The blood spurted straight up into the air, before splashing over the entrails of the previous animal, which had emitted the same gurgling noises. The steer was butchered with an axe, its head severed, its carcass cut into three pieces lengthways.The long, dismembered pieces were loaded into the wagon which would take them to market.A couple of pigs wandered the enclosure eating the left-overs.A carrion-crow, a bird not unlike a sea-gull, snatched a piece of gut. Don Carlos left. He still had a tooth-ache.' 71-2

UNDSET
Sigrid

Kristin Lavransdatter [Kristin Lavransdatter]

Sigrid Undset (1882-1949) is one of the major figures of Norwegian and Scandinavian literature, and a writer, selling well almost from the first, who broke all national boundaries with her fiction. Though it is her novels with medieval settings that established her fame — above all the three-volume *Kristin Lavransdatter* (1920-22) but also the tetralogy *The Master of Hestviken (Olav Audunsson)* (1925-27) — Undset's first published novels dealt with life in contemporary Oslo, in particular the emotional desires and experiences of ordinary city women. The understanding of feminine passion endeared her not just to many women readers and feminists of the day, though in fact Undset's (ever-increasing) belief in self-discipline and in the dangers of sacrificing a whole (a marriage, a family) for the sake of self, eventually put a considerable distance between her and more radical members of the women's movement.

Sigrid Undset was the daughter of an eminent archaeologist

who died when she was only eleven years old, though his influence was with her for life. Denied university education for economic reasons, she became nevertheless very learned on the Medieval period; while Kristin Lavransdatter perhaps works on us most because its remote setting in time (the fourteenth century) enables its author to remove her characters from the burden of contemporary mores, it is also a superb and satisfying rendering of a period — as seen in the Gudbrandsdal (the district Ibsen immortalised in *Peer Gynt*) and other parts of Norway.

After the success of her early books Undset was able to travel, and Rome was a magnet for her. Here she met her husband, the painter Anders Castus Svarstad, already married with a family. Though her eventual marriage to him brought her some realisation of her nature, as well as children, it was not deeply to satisfy her, and in 1919 she separated from Svarstad and made her home in Lillehammer in Gudbrandsdal. Almost at once she began on *Kristin Lavransdatter* endowing her medieval heroine (perfectly convincingly) with many of the emotional, sexual and spiritual problems that she herself as an early twentieth-century woman had been wrestling with. At the same time she embarked on her move towards Roman Catholicism, being received into this organisation in November 1924, an event perhaps more shocking than divorce in so ardently a Protestant country as Norway!

Though *Kristin Lavransdatter 's* enormous fame (aided by Sigrid Undset's being given the Nobel Prize for Literature in 1928) has declined somewhat, there are signs that both novel and author are currently being re-appraised and esteemed (for instance Liv Ulmann's 1995 film of its first part). It is perhaps time that the heavy, creaking 1930 translation of this novel of a passionate and complex woman — and of Erlend her husband — was replaced by something better and truer to Undset's style.

'But after a little time had gone by, she came to think 'twas not so sure after all she was with child. She understood not herself why she was not glad — it was as though she had lain and wept beneath a warm covering, and now must get up in the cold. A month went by — then two; now she was sure that she had been spared this ill-hap — and, empty and chill of soul, she felt yet unhappier than before. In her heart there dawned a little bitterness toward Erlend. Advent drew near, and she had heard neither from or of him; she knew not where he was.

And now she felt she could not bear this fear and doubt — it was as though a bond betwixt them had snapped; now she was afraid indeed — might it not so befall that she should never see him more?' 128-129

The Birds [Fuglane]

Tarjei Vesaas (1897-1970) is one of this century's greatest writers — in any language. Though his first noteworthy books appeared in the 1930s, it was during and after the Second World War that his reputation as Norway's most considerable novelist was firmly established. A recluse, whom a fulfilling marriage to the poet, Halldis Moren Vesaas, rescued from the abyss of depression and despair into which as a younger man he had so frequently fallen, Vesaas was a conscious and highly original modernist who developed a fictive technique perfectly suited to his subjects, in both their surface and their deeper, existential aspects. His work is that of a visionary, often quiet, intense, restrained but never shunning the violent or the transcendental epiphany, and capable of rising to heights of a mystic's joy. His insights into human nature and into the world in which it has to test and find itself cannot be divorced from his stories or the characters they contain — most often drawn from the inhabitants of remote Telemark province — or from his mode of literary presentation, at once concentratedly visual, focusing on people, natural phenomena, the play of light, and sharply if discriminatingly aural too, catching the uncertainties, the tentative moves within the dialogue of often unsophisticated people.

Vesaas had a particular feeling for the adolescent sensibility, as it gropes to discover meaning in random-seeming experience. His peers are Franz Kafka, Virginia Woolf, Isak Dinesen, Eudora Welty and Patrick White.

The Birds shows his art at its most intense, subtle and beautiful. Mattis is thirty-seven, simple, helpless though strong; he lives with and is looked after by his slightly older sister Hege. We see both the action of the book and the world in which they take place through his eyes — and yet Vesaas enables us to see beyond him too, to be able to put him into both a mundane context and *sub specie aeternitatis*. At times — unexpectedly — this entails real (and tender) humour. The account of Mattis' attempts to work on a nearby farm at turnip-thinning and his fascinated interest in a couple of 'sweethearts' who are carrying out the same task is funny, and also endears Mattis to us readers; we too want to be his protectors, to shield him from the pains of life which he can apprehend but not understand. We see how he can get on his sister's nerves, for all her good qualities and her resolutions not to let him do so, how she feels that she is letting life go by, frustrated, unloved, as she devotes herself day in, day out on their lonely smallholding to Mattis' welfare. Then there appears in the neighbourhood a woodcutter, Jørgen, who becomes their lodger; it doesn't take Mattis long to realise the excluding interest he and Hege take in each other, and, confused, hurt, he resorts to actions that inevitably bring about his own destruction.

Yet we feel that Mattis' life — for all its limitations (which rather pathetically with his talk of the 'clever ones' he recognises) and its sorrows — contains much of richness and even glory. This is nowhere more memorably shown than in the descriptions of his identification with a woodcock — which becomes a dominant symbol of the novel. Like the snowy heron in Eudora Welty's famous story *A Still Moment* the bird becomes a conductor into mysteries of life and death which pass beyond the nameable but which Vesaas' spare poetic prose can movingly approach. This is a novel which asks to be read many times, but just one reading will haunt the mind and reach the heart.

'But inwardly Mattis was bursting with song: him and the woodcock. He felt an urge to walk through the little wood, right underneath the invisible streaks in the sky. That was his path, a path full of joy. He wasn't disappointed this time, either. After a little while he had to stop.

You are you, a voice inside him seemed to be staying, at least that was what it sounded like to him.

It was spoken in the language of birds. Written in their writing.

He was standing by a dried-up patch of bog right underneath the woodcock's path, standing looking spell-bound, reading a message it was that had been left there for him.

In the smooth brown surface of the marshy soil were the faint imprints of a bird's feet. A number of tiny, deep round holes had been dug as well. The woodock had been there. The deep holes had been made by the woodcock's beak which it thrust down into the ground to dig up morsels of food, or sometimes just to prick out messages.

Mattis bent down and read what was written. Looked at the graceful dancing footprints. That's how fine and graceful the bird is, he thought. That's how gracefully my bird walks over the marshy ground when he's tired of the air.

You are you, that was what was written.

What a greeting to receive.' 75-6

The Ice Palace [Is-slottet]

The Ice Palace appeared late in Vesaas' career (published in 1963, when he was sixty-six) and is his best-known and most appaluded work. It won the coveted Nordic Council Award, and was described by its British publisher Peter Owen — truly a veteran connoisseur of world fiction — as 'the best novel I ever published'. The situation and the story which springs out of it are of the simplest, its layers of meaning inexhaustible. It must be considered a classic of modernism as well as having an idiosyncratic (and very Scandinavian) reverence for the Nature that holds us all in its power.

Two girls, both eleven years old, become friendly: Unn who is a newcomer to the rural district, and Siss. Siss is gregarious, a leader at school, Unn is shy and introverted; Siss comes from an ordinary enough family, Unn, who now lives with her aunt, is motherless, her mother having died in the spring, while her father (never married to her mother) has disappeared. Yet though Siss is central to many a school game, it is in fact Unn who is the more adventurous of the two, and who discovers the 'Ice Palace' which the ice in a huge waterfall has created. It is a discovery which leads her to death, itself another discovery which seems to beckon Siss.

The symbols — the wintertime freeze, the waterfall, ice — being so overt and dominant, it is perhaps mistaken to call *The Ice Palace* a symbolic novel. Rather the girls are the natural phenomena and subjects of the novelist's inquiry, rather as they might be in a poem, by Rilke, say, or Pasternak. It is tempting to see them as twin aspects of the *anima*, conducting us to the realm ofThanatos (death) and back.

'And what was this?

It must be the ice palace.

The sun had suddenly disappeared. There was a ravine with steep sides; the sun would perhaps reach into it later, but now it was in ice-cold shadow. Unn looked down into an enchanted world of small pinnacles, gables, frosted domes, soft curves and curved tracery. All of it was ice, and the water spurted between, building it up continually. Branches of the waterfall had been diverted and rushed into new channels, creating new forms. Everything shone. The sun had not yet come, but it shone ice-blue and green of itself, and deathly cold. The waterfall plunged into the middle of it as if diving into a black cellar.

Up on the edge of the rock the water spread out in stripes, the colour changing from black to green, from green to yellow and white, as the fall became wilder. A booming came from the cellar-hole where the water dashed itself into white foam against the stones on the bottom. Huge puffs of mist rose into the air.

Unn began to shout for joy. It was drowned in the surge and din, just as her warm clouds of breath were swallowed up by the cold spume.' 47-48

VESAAS
Tarjei

Spring Night [Varnatt]

This novel reveals Vesaas' uncanny ability to uncover the mysteries of quite ordinary-seeming lives, the secret histories and tangled hopes and fears that every one of us carries around. His method in this novel is akin to a film-maker's.

Presented from the point of view of a fourteen-year-old boy, Olaf, and taking place (as its title indicates) on one spring night — and the morning after — the novel moves from person to person, from group to group, pausing enough to let us observe with our eyes and listen with our ears to the currents at work but never forgetting our sense of being concerned with the intricate relationships between a handful of people.

Olaf and his older sister, Sissel, are left on their own by their parents for a night, during the course of which they have unexpected visitors. A car brings to their isolated house a young woman about to give birth, her husband Karl, disconcertingly stern of aspect (he has in fact been in the War which has left unhealable psychological scars), Karl's appealing sister Gudrun, and their father, Hjalmar, whose dithery ways, reflecting his truly indecisive personality, have earned him the names of 'The Flutterer' and 'The Butterfly'.

Meanwhile back in the car is Kristine, Hjalmar's psychotic wife. Each member of this family arouses Olaf's curiosity, makes an appeal to his burgeoning realisation of the power of human emotions, and brings forth from him a desire to please (as a boy; as an incipient adult). Birth and death are to occur during the night's long course — the light 'white' Northern night is marvellously evoked — yet there is no symbolic strain here. Rather, through the medium of Vesaas' spare yet highly-wrought modernist artistry, readers have the sense that things are unfolding exactly as they do in real life. But behind the action there is a sense of the transcendent, as ordinary reality's constant attendant. In its mastery of the interplay between people and between external and internal phenomena, this could be considered Vesaas' most inclusive and therefore satisfying novel.

'It was known as the wet glade.

Olaf had stopped in the middle of it.

The glade lay on the side of the mountain, but a vein of wetness ran through the steep slope. It kept the earth raw and dark, and certain types of plants grew there in wild profusion. The luxuriant growth made it smell different than other parts of the forest. Grass and trees, and the grass was full of bits of rock from forgotten slides. At the top was an overhanging ledge of rotten stone. In the open patches between the trees grew patches of angelica — and it was these large flowers more than anything else that had drawn Olaf to this spot so often throughout his boyhood. He would not have been able to explain what there was between him and them, but for him they were wonderful plants as they stood bristling grotesquely with their bursting wheels of blossom.' 14-15

WIESE
Jan

The Naked Madonna [Kvinnen som kledte seg naken for sin elskede]

Although — or perhaps because — its author is a distinguished Norwegian publisher this is no heavyweight book of Scandinavian angst but a very fast-moving mystery set in Italy. Not a cops-and-robbers or smart-detective-meets-local-colour mystery but a 'cultural' mystery story with a closed-off Ligurian valley, a miraculous variety of wine and an even more miraculous old painting of the Madonna and child.

In the first part of the book *Rome 1989* an eminent researcher in that most mysterious of archives the Vatican Library, is the conduit for the events of the novel and its hero. The necessary villains of the piece are various Bishops and Cardinals embroiled in age-old Vatican crimes and misdemeanours — or so its presumably Protestant author likes to imagine.

In the second and longest part of the book *The Forgotten Papers in the Vatican Library* a series of narrators takes us through tales-within-a-tale, with the main tale being the story of the creation of the miraculous painting, an altarpiece Madonna and child. A young painter, a disciple of a disciple of a disciple of the divine Giotto, is blessed with both artistic genius and considerable folly and falls in love with his model, a beautiful young woman with a troubled past. With their story as a starting point Wiese tells a series of stories of fortunate and unfortunate sexual encounters, ranging from paradisacal life-long unions to vengengeful emasculations. Perhaps the most interesting part of this section was its study of craftmanship at its highest, i.e. artistic, level, as Wiese depicts for us something of both the state of mind and the technical exigencies behind the creation of exceptional works, combined in the careful description of an artist's preparation of his canvas.

The short final section, also set in Rome in 1989, is the brief denouement of the book which could be summarized as an entertaining tribute to both Italian art and to the Italian art of living, things well appreciated by cultured Scandinavians. *Ray Keenoy*

'It is instilled in me how important preparations are, not only for painting, but also for achieving peace of mind.' 66

SAMI (LAPP)

GASKI
Harald

In the Shadow of the Midnight Sun; Contemporary Sami Prose and Poetry

Harald Gaski (born 1955) is Professor of Sami literature at the University ofTromsø in northern Norway, a distinguished writer, scholar and critic himself — and a lecturer who can make his own Saını culture, its ancient lore and its contemporary problems and challenges, come to life. *In the Shadow of the Sun* is the first wide-ranging anthology of Sami writing to be published in English (by the Norwegian publishing house Davvi Girji); fascinating in its range and in the artistic merits of its contents, it begins with an invaluable and informative essay on Sami matters by Professor Gaski himself, who has also written short explanatory critical and biographical introductions to all the pieces included.

Altogether the Sami (formerly known as Lapps) number about 50,000. They live in Norway, Sweden and Finland, mostly in the north of those countries, and in Russia (the Kola peninsula), the majority living in Norway, and the Norwegian dialect

(Northern Sami, with a new orthography dating from 1979) is that with the greatest official currency. The geographical region where Sami live is called Sapmi. Primarily their literature is oral or derived from oral tradition, central to all Sami culture being the sung poem called the *yoik* (see extract below) which is bestowed by composer/singer on another person and has shamanic properties. As long ago as the late seventeenth century a Sami theological student (Olaus Sirma) wrote down yoiks, to be published in a collection edited by Professor Johannes Schefferus called *Lapponia* (1673). However the Sami had to endure much the same cultural contempt and restrictions that other small nations in Europe have suffered (Basques, Welsh, Bretons, Irish, Jews etc). They have had their language banned at times, their religious artefacts burned, their grazing lands taken over (they are not entirely safe now!) and even their shamans killed.

Professor Gaski writes: 'The first book writen in the Sami language by a Sami and based on material from everyday Sami life, *Muitalus sâmiid birra (Turi's book of Lapland)* by Johan Turi (1854-1936), a reindeer herder, was published in 1910.' This book — from which a passage follows — was long a source-book for Sami lore and life, and inveighed against the exploitation ('opening-up') of Sapmi. But from the 1920s onwards novels and poems (and drama with folk-roots) have developed. In this anthology look out for pieces by Eino Guttorm (born 1941), by Kirsti Paltto (born 1947), the leading Sami woman writer, and also a fine writer of children's books, and John Erling Utsi (born 1952), a writer in many forms and associated with the great annual Lappish fair at Jokkmokk in northern Sweden. The Sami language is extraordinarily rich in words for plant and animal life and natural phenomena (more different words for snow, it's said, than even Peter Høeg's Miss Smilla knows) and therefore is peculiarly difficult to translate. Behind the writings there stands not only a little-known way of life but a beautiful and unique (and also too little-known) cosmology.

'The Sami way of singing is called 'yoiking'. It is an art form with which to remember other people. Some are remembered with hate, some with love, and others with sorrow. And the yoik works in such a way that when a talented yoiker sings, it is so good to hear that people are moved, but when the yoikers are the kind who swear and threaten to butcher the reindeer and even kill the owner, then it is terrible to listen to.

There are also yoiks dedicated to nature and to animals, to the wolf and the reindeer, both tame and wild....

Two young women are talking to each other. one of them says to the other: "Make a yoik for Niillas, the one you love!" All the girls think that Niillas is a handsome fellow, and all of them want him, and that's why they sing about him so often. A yoik of that kind is called a *luohti*. The girl then begins her Niillas-*luohti*.

"Voya voya nana nana
what a man, so stalwart,
so handsome to look at,
voya voya nana nana -
when he runs, it's as if he had wings
voya voya nana nana." 45-6

VALKEAPÄÄ
Nils-Aslak

The Sun, My Father [Beaivi, Áhcázan]

This book won the prestigious Nordic Council's Literature Award in 1991, and is almost impossible to define or categorise. Made up of poems (or yoiks), of lists of names, of personal apostrophes, it is in format mimetic of the Sami herding and driving of reindeer, one page, for example, giving us a reproduction of reindeer footprints, another citing animals typographically so that we get the impression of their movements over the snow-covered land. This book brings us, as no other publication yet has been able to, into not only the life-style, but the mind-set of Sami, even today. Life is hard, sometimes heart-breaking, but also full of wonder and numinous joy. Place-names proclaim the latent magic of the natural world; religion tells the Sami as they cope with harsh conditions that there will be *saivu* for them, a paradise after death.

Nils-Aslak Valkeapää (born 1943) is Finnish by nationality. Born into a reindeer-breeding family, he is an artist in many media, painter, photographer and graphic artist as well as writer. He opened the Winter Olympics in Lillehammer (Norway) with a series of yoiks that he had composed for the occasion, and has been the first cultural coordinator of the World Council of Indigenous People. He also, it seems to me, has broken new formal territory for books.

'we migrate
in our own land
to the summer lands
to the winter lands

in Sweden we were Swedish Sami
in Norway Norwegian
some with names in books
in both countries
others in none.'

SWEDEN

BERGMAN
Ingmar

The Best Intentions [Den goda viljan]

Not the least remarkable feature of Ingmar Bergman's remarkable career — and, born 1918, he must be the most famous and influential of all Sweden's post-war practitioners of the arts — is the fact that in his seventies he found a new medium for his genius: the novel. We have to assume that after completing his autobiography, *The Magic Lantern* (published in 1987) Bergman felt a need to explore in even greater depth and intimacy the tormented family from which he came, and felt that fiction would serve that need best. *The Best Intentions* is a recreation of the personalities and mutually destructive relationship of his mother and father. Later Bergman made a script from this his first excursion into the novel-form — for the prize-winning film directed by Bille August, and for a television serial. A fair proportion of the book is written out as if it were indeed a film-script (reminding us that the scripts Bergman wrote for his films are always worth reading in themselves), and in certain scenes we can very much feel Bergman, the supreme visualist, a movie-maker for over forty years, at work: the marvellous meeting in the coffee house between Anna (as Bergman calls his mother here) and the waitress with whom Henrik (his father, Erik) has been living for two years before his marriage; the arrival in the parsonage of the near-simple boy, Petrus. But what impresses most here is the richness of his specific novelist's touch: Henrik and Anna seem to have vast reserves of life behind what we are shown or told, relating them to the characters of the great nineteenth-century novelists, Balzac and Tolstoy, of whom Henrik is so fond.

At the close of *The Best Intentions* Ingmar himself is soon to be born. Therefore, except in a few authorial comments, he himself makes no appearance in the book, and, emotionally bound up in the drama though he is, he does his best to be fair to the complex people his parents were. He even succeeds in making us feel a certain splendour in his clergyman-father's Protestant faith, though he reveals all too amply its ultimate and crippling joylessness and guilt-inducing quality.

Henrik, introverted, proud yet passionate, is seen as the victim of his own heredity and early experiences. We can appreciate his inability to escape from himself in the very opening scenes, in which he refuses the olive branch his dying grandmother is offering via his distinguished father. Instead he prefers to cling on to the existence of poverty, obscurity and ignominy that his mother and he have made for themselves. Similarly later, working as a priest in the isolated and largely uncongenial rural parish of Forsbode, Henrik declines to admit his incompatibility with the people with whom he has to work and live. In his guilt-driven desire to serve them, he wrecks — or comes near to wrecking — not just his own life, but that of his vital young wife, and of his sons' (both the born and the about-to-be-born).

Henrik meets his wife, Anna Åkerblom, because she is the sister of his closest university friend, Ernst. Perhaps, as shown in two touching scenes, Ernst is the only person with whom he enjoys any ease of relationship. Daughter of prosperous, educated Uppsala bourgeoisie (the whole Akerblom family is richly evoked) Anna has a more open temperament than Henrik, and is better able to express emotion. She is however scarcely less of a victim — in her case, a victim of a spoilt child's expectations that blessings and treasures will ever flow onto her lap. Nor is she any less proud — or passionate — than her husband, as is revealed in her determination, in the face of others' judgement, to marry him. The reader is left thinking that there was no way in which the ensuing marriage could have been any happier than it was.

Inspecting the country parsonage that is to be their home, Henrik and Anna note the earth-cellar, and Anna observes: 'There'll be lots of wild strawberries on the top of it, I see.' There's a metaphor here. His parents' anguished life together was the earth-cellar that made possible such fruits of Ingmar Bergman's distinguished and original art as that masterpiece, *Wild Strawberries*.

'ERNST: Don't disappear, Henrik. We can have dinner at Cold Marta's at five, can't we? What about it?

HENRIK: I don't know. There's no point.

He has his pack in his arms and takes his student cap down from the hat shelf. Ernst opens the hall door and Henrik disappears down the stairs with great strides. Ernst closes the door and slowly goes in to his sister. She is still standing by the window showing all the signs of anger and pain.

ERNST: Anna, my cranberry-heart, how have you brought about all this?

Anna turns to Ernst and puts her arms round his neck, then cries very dramatically and possibly enjoyably for a few seconds.Then she falls silent and blows her nose on the proffered handkerchief.

ANNA: I'm sure I love him.

ERNST:And he?

ANNA: I'm sure he loves me.

ERNST:Why are you blubbing then, in that case? Listen,Anna?

ANNA: It HURTS so.

Ernst is told no more.he sits down on a chair and takes his sister on his lap,and there they sit in tender intimacy without saying another word.The rain stops and the sun draws hard white squares and rectangles on the protective curtain over the windows.The whole room appears to be floating.' 63-64

BERGMAN
Ingmar

The Magic Lantern [Laterna Magica]

Though this is straight autobiography (published in the year of Bergman's seventieth birthday), *The Magic Lantern* merits its place here, not only for its narrative power, but because it is the source-book for the three family-inspired novels Bergman has written in the Nineties — as well as, obviously, for his magnificent corpus of films. (And the film that Bergman made as his 'farewell', *Fanny and Alexander*, released in 1982, draws on family material.) It is perhaps too little appreciated by non-Swedes that inside his own country Bergman is almost as famous as a theatre-producer as he is as film-director; his work at the Malmö City Theatre, his productions of Strindberg, Ibsen, Buchner, Shakespeare, at 'Dramaten' (Royal Dramatic Theatre, Stockholm) are important chapters in the annals of Swedish theatre history. Reading this book should redress that imbalance in his reputation.

In addition to his artistic achievements Bergman has created his own legend which — especially as disseminated through those achievements — has done so much (perhaps too much!) to promote in the outside world ideas about Sweden and Swedish national identity — ideas which have, inside the country, been as much resented as cherished. The sensualist who has had to live with a legacy of Protestant guilt; the creative mind who finds more to feed on in breakdown and madness than in the stuff of ordinary Swedish life; the small boy trapped inside the mature man who still remembers the lashes of his upbringing; the man close to nature who is nonetheless obsessed by the fact that he has to die — these are predicaments of Ingmar Bergman the individual, it must be remembered, not the attached baggage of every Swedish contemporary of his.

Bergman has been tempestuously and famously involved with many women (a surprising number of them actually became wives!), and the women of his films — Harriet Andersson, Bibi Andersson, Liv Ullmann — were embodiments of the feminine for a whole generation.

Bergman doesn't always write frankly or honestly in this memoir — or, rather, he writes with as much frankness and honesty as he feels will not impair his own inner world or his own widely received image as a great illusionist, a magician (hence the title). He is evasive on the subject of the impact he has had on the women who have loved him, and strangely quiet about his children. A youthful admirer of the 'New Germany', he — like his father and older brother — was a Nazi. He admits: 'I loved (Hitler) too. For many years, I was on Hitler's side, delighted by his successes and saddened by his defeats,' leaving us wanting to know a great deal more about his partisanship, and not feeling that his later self-exculpation is quite enough. Even in the more sympathetic matters of his quarrel with Sweden as a result of arrest on an erroneous charge of tax-fraud, his subsequent breach with the Residenztheater in Munich and his reactions to Olaf Palme's death (the popular Swedish Prime Minister gunned down in the street by unknown assassins), he is highly selective in what he gives us.

Nevertheless this is a fascinating book, not least because, where his multi-faceted creative work is concerned, Bergman has been the very prince of honesty, faithful to his own vision, faithful to the laws of his various chosen means of expression. So perhaps it is only right that the passages one returns to most often in *The Magic Lantern* are those that bear on imagination and art.

'Film as dream, film as music. No form of art goes beyond ordinary consciousness as film does, straight to our emotions, deep into the twilight room of the soul. A little twitch in our optic nerve, a shock effect: twenty-four illuminated frames in a second, darkness in between, the optic nerve incapable of registering darkness. At the editing table, when I run the strip of film through, frame by frame, I still feel that dizzy sense of magic of my childhood: in the darkness of the wardrobe, I slowly wind on one frame after another, see the almost imperceptible changes, wind faster — a movement.

The mute or speaking shadows turn without evasion towards my most secret room. The smell of hot metal, the wavering flickering picture, the rattle of the Maltese cross, the handle against my hand.' 73-74

Sunday's Child [Söndagsbarn]

Private Conversations [Enskilda Samta]

Bergman continued his fictionalised prose autobiography with two other books, *Sunday's Child* (*Söndagsbarn*) (1993) — made into a film directed by Bergman's son, Daniel — and *Private Conversations* (*Enskilda Samtal*) (1996). The first is essentially concerned with his relationship with his father; he himself appears as a little boy of eight, universally known as Pu. Its story is of the significant journey Pu undertakes with his intimidating unpredictable father through the idyllic summer landscape of perhaps Sweden's most beautiful province, Dalarna. Though there are moments of pleasure (Pu is delighted to get away from his teasing brother, Dag), the novella is above all the tracing of the beginning of that deep unease which prevailed in Bergman's dealings with his father for the rest of the latter's life. The work is made the more imaginatively effective by its use of flash-forwards showing Bergman's father on his deathbed. *Private Conversations* presents the searing extra-marital affair of Ingmar's mother, Anna with a student-priest, Tomas, who is a friend of her husband. Constructed in the form of a sequence of conversations, reflecting film and stage techniques, this is in many ways — in its empathy and its pared concentrated artistry — the most remarkable of these three works, though its starkness and sombre presentation of desire's losing battle to conventions have earned it less admirers than its predecessors.

'It is true people often talk about "decisive moments". Dramatists in particular make much of this fiction. The truth is probably that such moments hardly exist, but it just looks as if they do. "Decisive moments" and "Fateful decisions".... they sound plausible. But if looked at carefully, the moment is not at all decisive: for a long time, emotions and thoughts have consciously or unconsciously been flowing in the same direction. The actual breakthrough is a fact far back in the past, far back in obscurity.

Anna starts moving. In her darkness, her anger and her suffoctaion, she is inexorably on her way to alter the lives of a great many people. At this moment of the breakthrough, real reality, a sense of mysterious desire is moving on the edge of her consciousness. Everything will collpase now. In this way I shall be annihilated. So it is *at last* at an end.' *Private Coversations* 35

DAGERMAN
Stig

A Burnt Child [Bränt Barn]

A Burnt Child is one of the greatest Swedish novels of the century, and the work which above all others places Stig Dagerman (1923-54) indisputably in the world literature class. Dagerman's penultimate completed novel — the humorous bucolic *Wedding Worries* (*Bröllopsbesvär*) followed a year later — *A Burnt Child*, deeply autobiographical, came out when the author was an amazing twenty-five years of age: it shows an astonishing mastery of different but harmonising styles and constitutes a rich and artistically satisfying expression of Dagerman's intense yet riven vision of life. Critics have from the first rightly praised the realism (the firm grasp of social detail, the ear for the speech of a particular working-class *milieu*) and the psychological penetration (the careful anatomy of the young man's states of mind, and the conflict between them and his sexual drive). Dagerman's development here surprised many after the rather Expressionistic manner of much of his earlier work, but in fact the novel is more than just a realistic/psychological study. It epitomises, in a very individual way, the angst-ridden mood of the 1940s, in Sweden and elsewhere, what was known in Swedish as *fyrtiotalismen* (the spirit of the Forties). Swedish writers, Dagerman eminently, learned much from pre-war 'hard-boiled' American writers, whose mentor was Hemingway, but intellectually they were closer to French existentialists; they shared their sense of the terrifying hollowness of civilisation after a war which had shown beyond doubt just what humans were capable of. For present-day readers *A Burnt Child* is surely *the* classic of Swedish existentialism.

Set in the working-class district of Stockholm called Söder (the South), *A Burnt Child* deals with the inter-relationships of four people, principally from the standpoint of one of them, twenty-year-old Bengt, a virtual self-portrait. (Bengt is, as the younger Stig had been, a student at Stockholm University, often cutting classes for personal, interior reasons.) The novel opens with the funeral of Bengt's mother; on that very same day, through hearing an unexpected voice on the other end of the telephone line, he is made to realise (even though he lacks the necessary corroborative information) that his father has a lover, whom he proceeds to track down: she is the cashier at a nearby cinema, her name is Gun. Bengt himself has a fiancée, Berit, a timid but not unsensual girl who has come to Stockholm from the North of Sweden. The father, whose combination of working-class reticence and male appetite is wonderfully and subtly brought to life, lets his mistress into his son's life, thinking him, for all his protests that friendship with her is disloyalty to his mother, experienced and mature enough to accept the situation. He even organises a holiday for the four of them, himself and Gun, Bengt and Berit, on an island in the Stockholm archipelago, days of light and sun and water during which many currents flowing within each person make themselves apparent. Bengt, though he for some while believes himself to dislike this woman in his father's life, feels a powerful sexual attraction to her, an attraction which is reciprocated, and converted into consumingly satisfying physical relations — and love. No convenient solution to the emotional tangle is to be found. Bengt makes an attempt at suicide which is surely a plea for recognition as a full adult; he recovers, his father and Gun marry, the anniversary of Bengt's mother's death is reached. But strong feelings continue.

The existentialist in Dagerman is shown by his vivid yet careful delineation of the bewildering discrepancy between our thoughts and our actions, between our actions and our feelings, and between our feelings and thoughts. This is emphasized by the ingenious form of the novel which interpolates into the third-person narrative letters by Bengt, mostly to himself, which often present events very differently, often markedly so. At variance with Bengt's own view of himself are his seizures of violence, his ill-treatment of Gun's little dog, his slitting of his own wrists and his strange subsequent feeling of joy, all surely reflecting deep disruptive compulsions from within Dagerman himself — and pointing forwards to Dagerman's personal dissolution.

But idealogue though Dagerman was, *A Burnt Child* mustn't be thought of principally in terms of philosophical issues, important though these are, but valued for its fearless — and warm-hearted — exploration of individual predicaments. These are brought to life with great attention to minutiae (at times the description of objects anticipates the French *nouveau roman* of the 1950s) and with a broad strong sense of what is truly important in our dealings with one another. One can't help feeling that Stig Dagerman almost knew *too* much to endure life alongside less sensitive others.

'The father rattled the glasses, and when the son sat down he had already poured out a nip. He had filled his own glass to the brim, but into the son's he had poured five drops too much so that it ran over. When they toasted each other the first time their hands were shaking slightly, but the second time they were steadier. The third time they met each other's eyes. Their eyes were beautiful then, and not until their eyes were beautiful did they dare begin discussing what they were afraid of discussing. They sat close to each other too, as though it felt safer like that. The father put his arm round the son's shoulder. His arm was soft and warm, so was the shoulder.

- Do you miss Mum very much, the father said.

- Yes, the son said, I do miss her.

The father noticed that the son had not said "very much". So he asked once again.

- It feels rather empty, doesn't it, he enquired.

- Yes, the son said, it feels rather empty all right.

- I would like to do something for you, my boy, the father said.

Because they were drunk and close to each other the son could not say what he wanted to say, so he said something else. When he had said it he noticed that it also was true.

- If I didn't have you, he said, it would feel very much emptier.

- My boy, the father said again.

He was suddenly moved, and saw by the son's face that he was moved too. To keep their emotion alive the father poured out another nip each. He didn't want to make the son drunk, he just wanted to make him beautiful. When someone is moved he is beautiful.' 76-77

DAGERMAN
Stig

The Games of Night [Nattens Lekar & Vårt Behov Av Tröst]

Insofar as it's possible to have a key to a mind and a literary output as complex, profound and tragically split as Stig Dagerman's, this collection of shorter writings (principally short stories) can be said to provide it. In the first story in the book, *A Child's Memoirs* Dagerman sets down his recollections of his early years in the country with his grandparents, in limpid prose in which the note of pain, of awareness of suffering as inseparable from the human lot, never ceases to be audible. Dagerman was the illegitimate child of a quarryman from the north Uppland village of Älvkarleby (about a hundred miles to the north of Stockholm) and a young girl from Härnösand (in Ångermanland) who vanished two months after his birth. Until he was twelve, he was brought up by his grandparents, stern, good-living people ('in their way the finest people I have ever met'). Dagerman experienced the harshness of country life first-hand, and the harshness was compounded when Sweden entered the Depression.

At twelve Stig moved to Stockholm, to the household that features in *A Burnt Child*; here, when he was 16, he learned the appalling news that his grandfather had been murdered, knifed by a maniac. His grandmother died from the shock some weeks later. Thus the only two people who had given Stig the love and security he so desperately needed were no more.

In this volume stories such as *The Surprise* and *Open the Door, Richard* (the second told from a woman's point of view) deal with the tensions between rural and urban life; Stig felt after his grandparents' death that he was cut off from life-giving roots. As a restorative he plunged into intellectual activity, political and literary, with great energy. Precociously, spectacularly gifted, he had by the age of twenty-six produced four novels, four plays, a travel-book, a book of stories and much journalism, including diary-poems (still inspiring today) for the anarcho-syndicalist newspaper for whom he worked. He married young, though this marriage foundered; later he fell in love with, and married, the well-known actress, Anita Björk. *The Games Of Night* carries a moving introduction by the English writer and expert on Ibsen and Strindberg, Michael Meyer, who was a close friend of Dagerman's, and of Anita's too, and who would discuss with him literature, sport (a passion of Stig's) and personal matters as well.

Meyer was aware of the paralysis that had overcome Stig after his amazingly productive mid-twenties. 'Block' is an inappropriate word for his condition; Stig teemed with ideas, to which publishers (understandably in the light of his fame and achievments) would respond — but to no avail. There were at least six projects on which he was nominally at work, though unable to produce more than a few pages. The indecisions and inability to persevere were in fact manifestations of schizophrenia. Several times, and by several different methods, he attempted suicide, but on November 4th 1954 he was found dead in his garage suffocated by exhaust fumes. The curious fantastic fragment with which this volume ends — *A ThousandYears with God*, to deal eventually with the strange visionary 19th-century Swedish writer, Carl Jonas Almquist — gives us some idea of the terrifying landscape that was Stig's imaginative world at the time of his suicide. Brilliant though it is, it is hard to see it as the opening of a work with enough objectivity to be assimilable by others. One turns back to the clarity of his remembrances of childhood to see how an indestructible darkness had entered Stig's mind, never to relinquish its cruel grasp.

'When (my grandparent's deaths) happened I was no longer there. I was at college in Stockholm, and I thought I should never be able to bear the loss of those from whom I had learnt most, and whom I most loved. The evening I heard about the murder I went to the City Library and tried to write a poem to the dead man's memory. Nothing came of it but a few pitiless lines which I tore up in shame. But out of that shame, out of that impotence and grief, something was born — something which I believe was the desire to become a writer: that is to say to be able to tell of what it is to mourn, to have been loved, to be left lonely.' 28

DAGERMAN
Stig

Island of the Doomed [De dömdas Ö]

This was Dagerman's second novel, but in my experience British readers should turn to it only after immersion in the writer's other work; its expressionist style, its omnipresent symbolism, its ideological debates are apt to prove barriers for those accustomed primarily to English writing. Laurie Thompson who has made a very powerful English version of this difficult work speaks of it, in *Aspects of Modern Swedish Literature:* Norvik Press 1999, as 'one of the few Swedish novels which can rank alongside the works of Kafka, Sartre and Camus as an aesthetically and intellectually stimulating statement on the human condition.'

Seven individuals are shipwrecked on a tropical island, uninhabited except by lizards and birds: each, while an autonomous being, represents a philosophy, a *Weltanschauung*, rather as do the characters in the laboratory situation of Thomas Mann's *The Magic Mountain*. The two who survive the others are — especially in the light of the *fyrtiotalismen* (this term is explained in the review of *A Burnt Child*) that informs the book — the two who engage the author's (and our) interest the most: anarcho-syndicalist Lucas Egmont and the *de facto* nazi, Captain Wilson. The rendering of the island has much of the nightmare about it, but it is difficult (as of course with dreams) to argue away its relationship to 'reality', to the ubiquitous destructive forces in Nature, or its correlative property for the destructive impulse inside ourselves and the culture we have (so precariously) built up.

'Then he paused again, gripped by a strong feeling of being watched by someone he couldn't see as yet. The penny dropped immediately, and he stepped back in irritation. It was the birds that were observing him as they sat clamped to the cliff, apparently guarding the way down to the beach, motionless and silent, without so much as a twitching of their wings: he could see now that they weren't in fact as big as he'd thought when they swooped down a short while ago. They were dangerous because of their numbers rather than their size, and their beaks were as sharp as talons; he couldn't make out their eyes, which seemed to be directed at him and yet failed to follow him when he backed off; they were grey as well, as if covered by a film. Without a sound, he broke off a blade of grass and moved stealthily towards the crevice, letting the grass blade swing to and fro all the way along the row of birds: but their eyes just kept on staring vacantly in the same direction.

'No doubt about it: the birds were blind, and that was why they brushed along the grass before landing. Dumb and blind, they led their lives on this island, and one could well ask why. Were they waiting for something? Were they intending to take advantage of a certain shipwreck? Was their sole purpose to wait for these seven people condemned to die?' 83

DAGERMAN
Stig

The Snake [Ormen]

Dealing with life in the Swedish army during World War Two — when the country, officially neutral, though hedging its bets, had to be prepared for a German invasion — this book is a sequence of related stories concentrating in the main on the inarticulate. Dagerman's characters live by the male code of barrack-room, bar and pick-up joint, one which affects even the unlikeliest. Gideon, for example, a clean-living mother's boy, very soon finds himself 'wanting to try out his body with somebody else's and later stand in front of the mirrors in the washroom in the evening and boast about it, like everybody else did.' This is a world of men without women, which means, of course, a world of men burning for women; it's pervaded by a certain cynical masculine romanticism, perhaps necessary to counteract the engulfing boredom of the army, and the great uncertainty beyond all the fatiguing routines: would or wouldn't Sweden be forced into military combat, and if so, what would the outcome be?

The snake of the title would seem to stand for what we cannot (and should not) control in existence. In the first story *Irene*, Bill discovers the reptile when he's out on a military exercise in the country; in an existential moment he decides to keep it. (*The Snake*, as a whole, demonstrates Dagerman's admiring kinship to Albert Camus.) Later the snake re-emerges in the Stockholm quarters of the conscript regiment, creating panic, confusion — and also welcome relief from tedium. The second section of the book, following on from the hot, airless summer's day of the first, and with an urban, nocturnal setting, is made up of six pieces of varying lengths, ingeniously inter-connected thematically. The second of these *The Mirror* recounts the visit of two drunken servicemen to the smart flat of the girls they've just picked up, a situation comically too much for them to handle. It's a small masterpiece of sad wry humour, and brings home just how many-sided was Dagerman's imagination. The last piece of the six, *The Flight that Didn't Come off* acts as a kind of 'envoi' to the whole, and introduces into the book an intellectual, a writer (suitably named Scriber), a stand-in for Dagerman himself — or rather for the tragic side of his complex personality.

The delineation of ordinary men in the daily round of army life is, in this final story, given a dark context, made part of a general human evasion of reality. To this are opposed the snake and the fear it brings. Dagerman himself, as Laurie Thompson relates in his perceptive introduction to the book, had a very deep fear of snakes, dating perhaps from a boyhood encounter with an adder in the woods. But fear is to be welcomed — since it is acknowledgement of the complexity and precariousness of life.

'(said Scriber) "It's the tragedy of modern man that he no longer dares to be afraid. That's disastrous, because the consequence is that he's forced to stop thinking. That's only logical because anybody who doesn't dare to be afraid has to stop doing things that make him feel uneasy and can let him through the back door into a situation where he's frightened. Isn't that why it's so easy for anti-intellectualism to become popular, isn't that why all kinds of blood mysticism and sex cults are taken up so eagerly by all those people whose cowardice leads them to blame all problems on guts and glands?.... I am a socialist but not in the sense you seem to think I am.... I'm striving for social justice all right, by which I mean a system in which there's no longer a slave market, in which people no longer feel gratitude as a matter of course towards their employers, a bank or a lottery for giving them the right to live. A system, then, where the right to live is taken for granted, and where you can provide toy shooting ranges and efficient popguns for all these war-mongers, who form the core of reactionary outlooks. On the other hand, I have absolutely no desire to see well-being as a part of this system. It has transpired, unfortunately, that quiet contentment has a certain tendency to degenerate into belching and super-satiety. In a world full of secure belchers it could be that the most essential elements of all are the possibility of being knocked about and the ability to feel fear.'" 236

Blackwater [Händelser vid Vatten]

Blackwater (1993) could quite legitimately already be called *the* Swedish novel of the Nineties. Critics and ordinary readers, inside Sweden and out of it, have responded to it with an enthusiasm which suggests that its appeal is to deep universal feelings, thoughts, fears and hopes. Awarded the Nordic Council's Literature Prize and the August Prize, it is an utterly compelling mystery novel (one feels one is being mistreated when forced to break off from reading it) in which the elaborations of the plot ('I am rather good at tension, I must say,' Kerstin Ekman admits) and the violence of the events in no way dwarf the psychological stature of both the principal and the subsidiary characters. On the contrary, much of the power of this book comes from one's sense of the ineluctable reality of the people concerned, and of the society of a remote part of northern Sweden (Jämtland, near the Norwegian border).

On Midsummer Eve 1974 a young woman, Annie, arrives at Blackwater, together with her little daughter, Mia, expecting to be met by her lover, Dan, who has joined a latterday hippy (or Green Wave) commune, Starhill, up on a mountain in the vicinity. He is not there to greet her. Bewildered and disappointed, she takes her daughter for a walk. Close to the edge of the lake she comes across a blue tent, a strange choice of site for campers, she thinks, since they would be unable to hear anyone approach.... And indeed these ones didn't. Annie discovers that the tent has been slashed and the couple within hacked to death. Just before she makes this horrendous find, she sees a young man of somewhat Asiatic appearance running fast along the path. She deduces later that he must be the murderer, and as, next day, he turns out to have fled the neighbourhood, where his father is an important man of property in the forestry business, there seems every reason for her deduction to be correct.

But it isn't; Kerstin Ekman gives readers access to the youth, Johan Brandberg, and what has been happening to him. Indeed he shares our sympathetic attentions during the course of this long and ramified novel with Annie herself. Johan, a strong, intelligent and sensitive boy, is bullied by his jealous half-brothers, who throw him down a well and leave him there (thus bringing to mind the treatment of Joseph by his half-brothers in the Bible).

Johan finds heaving himself out of the well a long and difficult business, especially as he decides to take with him an eel which he has come across at the bottom of it. He has only just emerged from the well when Annie catches sight of him; desperate not to go back to a home where such cruelties can be inflicted on him, he takes himself out of Blackwater as fast as he can, and thumbs a lift over the mountains, over the border to Norway, with a strange woman (a Finnish anthropologist as it turns out) who will act the part of an 'anti-mother' and initiate him into sex. Johan's mother is Sami (Lappish) — hence that Asiatic appearance — and hence too maybe a certain wildness in his gentle personality which the Finnish woman will bring out.

The paths of Annie and Johan diverge. Annie, after splitting up from her feckless lover and the sorry community of Starhill, stays on in Blackwater, becomes a teacher (and a very good and innovative one) and later has a sustaining relationship with the doctor. Johan is glad to stay out of Sweden, though he never in point of fact lives very far from his native home, and takes an interest in Sami matters; he trains as a meteorologist, and his great recreation is the traditional northern one of dog-sledding.

The opening and the closing sections of the book are set eighteen years after the discovery of the murdered bodies (an incident based on a real-life one in Gällivare, Lapland, in the 1970s.) The dark past asserts itself again, for Johan meets Mia, Annie's daughter, at a dog-sledding, and they become lovers, emboldening him to return to Blackwater again. Annie is horrified; she believes him to be a dangerous murderer. But as we know he isn't, and as we are aware of many secrets and evasions in the life of this isolated community, we ask ourselves: who did, so wantonly as it would seem, kill those outsider campers in the blue tent?

So richly worked is *Blackwater*, so intense is the exploration of lives that are either inter-related or else mysteriously touching on each other, that it yields treasures long after the answer to the dominant mystery is known. This is truly a novel for re-reading. The battle between different cultures is at stake as well as different values, yet, with its intense rendering of the wild forest-country of Jämtland, and of the forces of Nature behind it, which govern our intimate, as well as our external, beings, the novel has a metaphysical as well as a psychological and a social dimension. If the community of Blackwater can be seen as a metaphor for northern Scandinavia threatened from without and from within, it's also a metaphor for the uncertainties of life itself.

'What did she actually see? Afterwards, she didn't know. So many hideous descriptions appeared. She had probably read some of them. She couldn't remember later.

For a long time, there was a great empty space there. She saw her own hands under the water, white, even whitish green. She saw the spruces. They had knotted together to form a great nodule, grown together where one of them had been bent by a storm long ago. The wet jeans were hanging over a branch. The swampy patch of small birches on the other side of the river — always softer, greener and more secretive than the side you are on.

She wanted to run away. But she must have gone on a few steps more. She felt sick and her legs refused to carry her. Then it struck her with great violence. She fell to her knees, the palms of her hands propped against the swaying ground. When she got up, her hands were bloodstained. She rubbed and rubbed them against each other, then tried to wipe them on her skirt, but that wasn't much use. She staggered away, crawling the first bit, then dipping her hands into the water. It was cold. Strong current. Swift transparent water. Her hands were clean. She vomited into the water and the current took away the mess she had heaved out of herself. The water was soon clean again, clear and swift-running. With her head averted and without looking at the tent she went back up to Mia.

'They weren't there,' she said. Roughly she grabbed the girl's arm and hurried away towards the marsh. The sun was coming through the white woolly tufts now, floating, apparently hovering above the sedge. The tent was no longer visible. She saw the river and its swift water, dark, foaming in whirlpools. And the ground on the other side.

Afterwards she was no longer sure of the place. It was not marked, had no boundaries. It wandered like a sunspot between shadows of clouds. It was an event, an event by water. As everything is.' 58-59

EKMAN
Kerstin

The Forest of Hours [Rövarna i Skule Skogen]

This is the vast, ambitious novel that preceded *Blackwater* (in 1988), and it could be cited as the major Swedish excursion into Magic Realism, though this would be to underplay its consistency with Kerstin Ekman's imagination. Its central character is a troll, Skord, denizen of the wild, beautiful Skule Forest up in the Norrland province of Ångermanland. He is young when we first meet him — at some point in the Fourteenth century — and he is to live on for five centuries. At the time of his death the railway is being forged through the virginal forestland. Skord doesn't remain unchanged during his long life, however, though for the initial centuries he presents a constant-seeming boy's aspect to the world. Later on he obviously ages, at times disconcertingly fast. One man who hasn't seen him for seven months thinks that seven years (or even seventeen) could have passed, Skord looks so much older. By the time he comes to die, he is weary, feeling that he has indeed lived a very long time. But the last stage of his life is marked by love, for the strange but human Xenia, of a greater intensity and reality than any previous emotion he has known. 'Skord loves Xenia the way the salmon leaps in the waterfall.'

What is a troll? Skord can pass himself off as a human, is able to speak to humans, to have sex with them, and to fight alongside them. But much of what he does is acquired parrot-fashion, through mimicry. (He can also talk with animals and birds.) Essentially he is an outsider to our race, capable of both seeing through the elaborate devices we construct to protect ourselves from the obvious but frightening truths of existence (religion, art, scientific theories) and yet, chameleon-like, of exploiting these. In this, of course, he embodies in exaggerated form a trait of many humans who borrow or steal ideas and then use them to make gains over their fellows. It is no accident that Skule repeatedly feels at home among the bands of robbers — misfits, psychopaths, deformed persons — who haunt Skule Forest, battening on and terrifying those they come across.

For much of the action of the novel Skord is engaged in philosophic activity — travelling with a medieval Magister, working as an alchemist to produce 'Live Gold', and later practising as a mesmerist when this was fashionable. Kerstin Ekman enters fascinatedly into all these pursuits, but ultimately reveals them as illusory, destined to failure. Beyond all ideas there remains Nature — even if it too will ultimately perish — one of whose kingdoms is Skule Forest.

'No woodland is as wild as the forest of Skule. It lies between the coast and the high hills, starting in the arid, alien landscape below the treeline. Nowehere else is the Baltic sea so deep, nor do the islands have such precipitous peaks. The sea is a cold autumnal blue and the red granite glows unquenchably beneath the attacks of the waves against the rocky precipices. The forest grows on hilsides and on the steep sides of the dark river ravines. The slopes are covered with moorland and the streams leap from waterfall to waterfall. There are fields of scree and stones everywhere, deep clefts and heavy, sharp-edged rocks. Only the still, clear-water lochs are smooth-watered but their depths chill the eye.

Strands of time run through the forest. The high fields of scree are solidified waves of stone, long swells of unmoving time. Tall trees, once whispering in the wind, have sunk into the peat bogs, where time ferments in the marshy pools. Here and there, flowering woodland penetrates the darkness of the firs and the sea of stones, forming wedges of broad-leaved trees, fragrant night-flowering plants and humming frail-winged insects. There, the noble trees sing. The leaves of linden and hazel dance in a gentler wind and their roots send tendrils into a richer soil than the meagre ground under the firs. It is forgotten woodland, flowering in borrowed time.' 310

EKMAN
Kerstin

Under the Snow [De tre små mästerna]

As a young writer Kerstin Ekman earned herself the name 'Deckardrottning' ('Queen of the Detective Story'), and when she began work on *Blackwater*, she told her husband: 'I do believe, after all these years, I'm writing a detective novel again!' (though the book was to prove far more than that). *Under the Snow* is from 1961, when its author was only 28 and firmly dedicated to the detective genre. It remains a compelling mystery and whodunnit (the terms aren't quite interchangeable) but to us now it anticipates, in significant ways, some of the very aspects of the later masterpiece which have made it such an international success.

Under the Snow is set in the wilds of Norrbotten, north of the Arctic Circle, where tundra meets high, bare, inhospitable mountains, an exceedingly sparsely populated region, the naturally taciturn inhabitants of which speak Finnish or Sami rather than Swedish. (Its very place-names suggest this, as a glance at the map shows.) First through Torsson, a policeman originally from central Sweden, and secondly through David, a rather garrulous, line-shooting young painter from Stockholm who pals up with him, we are introduced to a Norrbotten community (Rakisjokk) — in a state of anxiety. As in *Blackwater* its very smallness and isolation intensify the emotions and relationships of its members — and all are perforce mindful of the awesome power of Nature (the long implacable winters, the unbroken light of the summer which does not preclude sudden treachery in the weather). The climate helps to nurture suspicion — and worse.

Both the policeman and the artist are drawn to Rakisjokk because of the death of one of its inhabitants, Matti, a painter. The former is called to the village one March day (at the height of the Arctic winter) to examine his body and pass official judgement as to why he died. Curious though the case is, Torsson has to record that Matti died as a result of a drunken fight with another man from the village, after which he just lay down in the snow in a half-stupour to die... He cannot rid himself however of the feeling that the whole village is conspiring to conceal information from him. Later on that year, in July, David Malm makes his way to Rakisjokk to look up Matti whom he'd met, and liked, in Stockholm earlier. On learning from a villager of Rakisjokk of his self-willed death, he is utterly incredulous. The man he knew would never have killed himself, even in the circumstances presented to him! David teams up with Torsson, and together — forming an unexpected yet almost affectionate duo — they set out to get to the bottom of what happened that March night — and before it, for they uncover a web of secrets.

As a detective story the novel contains a gallery of characters sufficiently strongly-drawn for the solution to the puzzle to be a satisfactory and interesting one, and the sense of mystery is increased by the use of the mah-jongg game, full of esoteric symbols and rituals, with which some of the main characters like to pass the long nights of northern winter. As a thriller the book contains two scenes that seem to become part of the reader's own experience: the discovery of a remote rift in the mountains where ancient cults have been practised, and the danger-fraught climax in a deserted village. But as in *Blackwater* what makes the novel a living work of art is its sense of a way of life, of a society both close-knit and fragmented, both representative (in the human emotions that animate it) and particular (true to the laws of its own curious geography and history). The use of the atavistic Sami religion and its sacrificial places (or 'Passesadje') is especially imaginative, complementing the arcana of mah-jongg, in its demonstration of the lore and tradition so important to most cultures.

'The valley looked long when seen from the opening, then disappeared through the magic of perspective into the dark mountainsides. The stone blocking the entrance had an overhang and in the shadow below it lay a collection of stones placed in a semicircle.

'So this is your actual... the actual "passesadje",' said Torsson in an unnecessarily loud voice as he pointed at the stones. He made a sweeping gesture with his arm and looked round like a tour guide at the dead landscape.

'Those bones...' David muttered vaguely.

'Of course,' cried Torsson. 'Reindeer bones. Sacrificed. Sure to be ancient. They're quite white. Look, they've had the sense to split them and suck out the marrow first. The gods can always put new flesh on bones and fill them with marrow.'

He added the last remark in an almost ingratiating tone which made David look round.

'Ridiculous!' David said suddenly. 'the whole thing is ridiculous.'

'Yes, isn't it?' Torsson agreed, and they both fell silent.

David lit his pipe. They moved away from the "passesadje" to take a look around them. Towards the valley was a large area of untrampled ground, here and there a ragged cairn of stones, impossible to say whether made by humans or not. Gradually their sense of insecurity faded. They adjusted to the stillness....' 106

EKMAN
Kerstin

Witches' Rings [Häxringarna]

For many years Kerstin Ekman's very considerable reputation rested principally on her great quartet of novels centring on women's lives as passed in and around her own native town of Katrineholm. *Witches' Rings* (1974) is the first of these, opening in the mid 1870s and closing in 1904; its successors are *Springkällen (The Spring)* (1976), *Änglahuset (The House of Angels)* (1979) and *En stad av lus (A City of Light)* (1983). These novels have as their foundation Ekman's massive research into a century of Swedish sociological history. "No history book has succeeded in documenting and bringing to life the growth of modern Sweden in the way your books have," said the then Social Democrat Prime Minister, Ingvar Carlsson to the novelist (quoted in *Literature in Sweden:* 1997), and one can see what he meant. But it is what Ekman has done novelistically with her material which makes *Witches' Rings* so impressive; for her purposes — presenting a history of a place not just through women but through officially *unimportant*, not to say marginalised women — traditional methods of presentation had to be discarded and new ways found, at once sharp and impressionistic, individualised yet representative of the different generations of women many of whom would not even make the records. In a sense the purpose of the quartet is contained on the gravestone epitaph quoted by Kerstin Ekman on the very first page of *Witches' Rings*:

'Soldier no. 27 for Skebo district
Johannes Lans

b.29 July 1833 d.12 June 1902
and his wife
R.I.P.'

The wife doesn't merit either dates or name, it would appear. Perhaps those putting up the stone didn't know these facts, and certainly didn't think it important to find them out. Ekman sets out to redress the gross imbalance. Soldier no 27's wife was Sara Sabina Lans, whom 'no-one called by her given name'; the novel is an account of her hard adult life during the course of which she was paid scant attention, and ends with her death in the presence of her granddaughter, Tora, who has always looked on her as her mother. 'A person has to cope. A person always does,' is Sara Sabina's last recorded utterance.

Witches' Rings concerns itself also with Sara Sabina's daughter, Edla, who dies giving birth to Tora. The portrait of her brief, tough, unfulfilled life and of the members of the community that impinge on it is exemplary in its combination of tautness and richness of suggestion. And if the men are exploiters and deniers of freedom, they are also themselves victims. The novel is a passionate indictment of a so-called traditional way of life, as later its successors will be of what is crassly put in its place, but it is free of bitterness, is a true humanist history of growth against all obstacles, and in such portraits as that of Mamsell Winlöf, keeper of the Railway Hotel, a humour by no means incompatible with charity is to be found.

'A thought struck him that would never have entered his mind with his wife Caroline. When he saw the fold in Mamsell Winlöf's neck, the soft recess that separated chin from neck, and which would probably separate one chin from the next in just a few years, he thought he would like to lay his sexual organ there. This was the way he would like to make love to her. It must have had something to do with her in particular that he was not overcome by an immediate sense of shame the moment he thought this. He had never taken a stand on all the gossip about her background and about the origins of her money.... Now his excited thoughts suddenly took a stand of their own.

When he embraced her it all happened so fast that he more or less came crashing down on her. She had leaned too far back in her chair, no longer sitting like a decent woman. As he came down on her, she bucked from the pelvis, a rough jolt that threw him off her and landed him on the rug in front of her chair. It was instantaneously perfectly clear to him that no virtuous woman would have built-in reflexes enabling her to buck so sharply and so effectively with her pelvis as to keep herself from being mounted when she did not wish to be. No, that had been an instinctive, depraved movement. His next manoeuvre came to him quickly, and he knew exactly what he would say when he had crawled back up. He could hardly be too bold.

But he never got up off the carpet. Mamsell Winlöf placed one hand, strong as man's, on his chest and pushed him down. She burst into words that could have been a serving girl's, but her voice was that of a cultivated woman.' 63

ENQUIST
Per Olov

Captain Nemo's Library [Kapten Nemos bibliotek]

With deep autobiographical roots, and reflecting the private mythology of his childhood past which Enquist has made use of in other works — notably the magnificent, agonising play, *The Hour Of The Lynx* (1988) — *Captain Nemo's Library* can be seen as (so far) its author's crowning achievement as a novelist. Interestingly, for a writer famous for his social conscience and political commitment — and some of whose earlier books, *HESS* (1966) and *The Legionnaires* (1969) have a documentary nature — *Captain Nemo* is an intensely personal and emotional work, though with far-reaching existential preoccupations.

To what extent do our secret desires determine what happens externally, both to ourselves and to others? Should we feel guilt for our wishes, our inner life? How, without violating our sense of responsibility or reality, can we find redemption for ourselves?

In fact this strange and baffling novel, in which we move in and out of the mentally disturbed narrator's subjective world, had its origins in a real event. In the author's native province of Västerbotten — Enquist shares with his virtual contemporaries, Kerstin Ekman and Torgny Lindgren, a deep attachment to Norrland, and an imaginative interest in the workings of remote, spiritually independent communities — a mix-up of two male babies took place. In Enquist's novel, in September 1934 (the month and year of his own birth), the midwife at the local hospital gives the wrong baby to the two mothers under her care. Six years later her mistake, long suspected, is proved — and rectified. The nameless narrator is taken away from the 'green' house he proudly thought of as his own home and from Josefina, the woman he'd thought of as his mother, and sent to live in a very different household nearby, with his real mother who is of tinker stock and deranged in her wits. Meanwhile Johannes has the benefit of the more prosperous home. The two boys become best friends, but there must inevitably be tension under the surface.

This potentially tragic situation is compounded by another, also involving a child of gipsy or tinker extraction: Josefina decides to adopt a daughter (an older girl) to be a sister to her true son. But a close bond grows up between the outcast narrator and this girl, Eeva-Lisa. Later he tries to help when, in her teens, she gives birth to a boy who then dies and has to be disposed of. The feelings that prompt him to help her are made more complex by his blaming Johannes, his best friend (and rival), for having failed Eeva-Lisa.

The climax of the novel and its terrible aftermath are presented elliptically, and though it is clear in stark fact what happens, the events are ultimately inseparable from the surges of emotion and the hallucinatory states of mind they inspire in the boy at the book's centre (as recalled by the older institutionalised man he has become). Here Enquist shows himself as at the height of his (very considerable) powers. I know little in contemporary literature to compare with the final scenes of this book — when the narrator, who has found an alternative life for himself in Jules Verne's stories of Captain Nemo and who, to a heightened degree, shares Enquist's empathy with the natural world, retreats, away from society and danger, to a place called the Cave of the Dead Cats. This, so it's said, is where the cats of the neighbourhood go to die. And it is here, imagining that Eeva-Lisa has come to him in the form of a cat, and that Johannes, his dear companion is missing not dead, that the boy experiences a kind of prolonged mystic communion with living and dead — to be shattered when authority apprehends him.

It is not too early, I believe, to think of *Captain Nemo's Library* as a great novel; it is certainly one that can — and should — be turned to again and again. It yields different meanings on each reading, both literally and spiritually. It is possible, for instance, to take the novel as a working-out by the traumatised, speechless, asylum-inmate narrator of psychoses the external causes of which cannot be found. In this interpretation the betrayed and drowned Johannes is but a projection of the hero's mind, an embodiment of who knows what tragedy; hence disturbing reverberations are set up in the reader's mind about the nature of reality, the otherness of other people, the creative faculties of the fractured self.

'Out there, above the water, hung a strange morning mist: the darkness had lifted, but there was still a hovering grey cloudiness, not white but somehow reflecting darkness; it hovered a few metres above the surface of the water which was absolutely still and shiny, like mercury. The birds slept, tightly wrapped in themselves and their dreams. Can it be that birds dream? The mist was so low that it left only water and birds to be seen, only a black unmoving surface of water, an endless sea. I could imagine myself on the outermost shore, and in front of me nothingness. An outermost boundary. And then the birds, wrapped tightly in their dreams. Suddenly a movement: a bird taking off. I heard no sound. I just saw it, beating the surface with the tips of its wings, free itself, rise at an angle, upwards: and it happened suddenly and so lightly, so weightlessly. I saw how it took off and rose and rose up towards the grey ceiling of mist, and vanished. And I heard not a single sound.' 246

ENQUIST
Per Olov

Downfall [Nedstörtad ängel]

Provocatively entitled 'A Love Story', this extraordinary book is unlike any other, and, coming out in 1985, heralded the significant move in Enquist towards the private and mystical. The question animating the interrelated narratives is: 'What *is* a human being, and what attributes and capacities does s/he have to possess to qualify?' Enquist forces us to realise how much we rely on unquestioned norms, on lazy definitions we have received from others, to answer this. *Downfall* insists that we confront what convention would term the freak or the misfit — and that we see these 'abnormal' beings as fully human, to the point of having passions every bit as strong and dominating as those of more ordinarily blessed folk.

Downfall can be viewed as, at the deepest level, the most uncompromisingly anti-Nazi book imaginable.

Here Enquist's skills as one of Sweden's leading journalists meet his gifts as a novelist. We encounter in the pages of this book the (true-life) Mexican, Pasqual Piñon, born with two heads, the larger male and the smaller — growing on top of it — female. A love existed between these two heads — and how, in the face of physically observable evidence — dare we deny its validity? *Downfall* is no less insistent that we accept the emotions of a young schizophrenic murderer (personally known to the author) and those of a figure from cultural history, the deranged Ruth Berlau who fancied that Bertolt Brecht had spurned her, and went around carrying a plaster-cast of his head in a hat-box. And through these stories of bizarre-seeming loves and destinies Enquist weaves recollections of his own life, casting his growing up in rural

Västerbotten in that mythological light he later develops in his *Captain Nemo's Library*, and expressed in poetic prose of extreme beauty.

'There were quiet white January nights when the moon was white and it was cold cold cold; the telephone wires were fastened to the wall of the house, the house was made of wood and Daddy had built it himself, it was like a gigantic resonating box, and the wires sang.

It was an enormous song brought from the stars, it came night after night when it was cold. It sang in the heavenly harp as if someone out there in the winter's night had drawn a giant's bow over the strings, it sang, a thousand years of sadness and forgiving, wordlessly and sadly, all night long, one end of the wires stuck to a wooden house in Västerbotten County, but the other end hung on far out in space, hung on to dead black stars. The song came from space and was wordless and was about the wordless. do not forget us, it sang, do not forget us.' 56

ENQUIST
Per Olov

The Magnetist's Fifth Winter [Magnetisörens femte vinter]

The Magnetist's Fifth Winter was Enquist's breakthrough novel, published n 1964 and set in a small German town, Seefond in autumn-winter 1793-1794. Its central figure is Friedrich Meisner, the magnetist of the title, who has fled there. Meisner is obviously based on Austrian quack Anton Mesmer (1734-1815) the father of 'mesmerism', exponent of the idea of 'animal magnetism' by which he is able to cure people. In his presentation of him — partly through a pseudo-documentary method such as Enquist was to employ in subsequent novels (eg *Hess* and *The Legionnaires*) — Enquist is able to discuss the human ability (and perhaps need) to surrender to figures of power, who can invade or dominate body and mind. There are clear parallels established between Meisner/Mesmer effecting miraculous cures and Christ; politically we are compelled too to think of the Fascist or Communist demagogues. Yet the novel raises an intriguing question. Townsman Claus Selinger, whose diary we read, has a blind daughter. Meisner makes her see again. Selinger later finds Meisner out in a deception which he makes public. But the fact remains that his daughter can now see. Every situation is more difficult than the interpretations made of it.

'Yesterday Maria saw the sky for the first time. At her own urgent request we led her out into the garden. Since it is autumn, many of the deciduous trees were bare; but the tall elm which stands beside the well had still not lost its leaves. Gently screwing up her eyes, she contemplated the scene. When I looked more closely at her, I saw she was weeping.

'You're crying, Maria,' I said.

'The wind is too strong for my eyes,' she explained.

At the time the wind was very slight. But afterwards she pointed at the great stone pool which gathers the water from the spring, and called it a soup plate. I corrected her gently.

For almost half an hour we stayed out in the garden. Then the wind really did begin to blow. Yet she said she wished to remain there and see the leaves blowing up against her bare wrists, having so often felt them but never having actually seen them. However I was anxious, and led her back indoors.

I must show great circumspection in teaching her to see. She can see now; but no one knows what she sees.' 103

ENQUIST
Per Olov

The March of the Musicians [Musikanternas uttåg]

This novel from 1978 can be seen as a watershed in Enquist's career. It continues the politico-cultural probings of its distinguished predecessors: *The Legionnaires* (1968) which examines a controversial episode of post-War Swedish history, and emphasizes the difficulty of making moral judgements without hindsight; *The Second* (1971), again founded on fact and intimately connecting the world of sport with the world of politics, more specifically with Swedish socialism; the collected short stories *Stories from the Time of the Cancelled Revolts* (1974) which deal with the collapsed revolutionary movements of the 1960s and 70s. *The March of the Musicians* arises out of an investigation of the history of Swedish Trades Unionism, of industrial conflicts up in Enquist's native Västerbotten, around the timber-mills of Bureå, in the early years of the twentieth century. Again defying cherished national self-images, Enquist depicts the workers as often (cruelly) opposed to Trades Unionist concern for their rights, treating agitator Johan Elmblad contemptuously, and showing him up as powerless in the face of other social and cultural forces. The family at the centre of the book, the Marklunds, embody the pietistic quietism of Enquist's own family, which prefers Christian-inspired resignation over socialist activism. The young man, Nicanor, a stand-in for Enquist himself, is however drawn to the movement and indeed to the agitator himself.

But by writing about Västerbotten, its timber business and

his family, Enquist — perhaps without knowing this — embarked on a presentation of a private myth, with its roots in familial and local history, and started on that inward turn, the finest fruit of which is *Captain Nemo's Library*. Already in *The March of the Musicians* the figures of the mythic tragedy are there, though they will later undergo transformation and development. Eva-Liisa (sic) here, for instance, based on Enquist's foster-sister, anticipates the Eeva-Lisa of *Captain Nemo*, her rape by Uncle Aron the seduction, pregnancy and death in the later book. Sombre, poetic and personal, the 1978 novel perhaps provides the best gateway into Enquist's work, more easily accessible than the subsequent novels, demanding less particular knowledge of Swedish history than *The Legionnaires* etc. The title of the novel comes from the Brothers Grimm story of the *Town Musicians of Bremen*: 'Come away with us.... There's always something better than death', the novel having begun as an inquiry as to why so many from early twentieth century Västerbotten ended up in Brazil.

'[Nicanor goes into Eva-Liisa's room] When he was back on her bed, she looked at him.

Her eyes dark, fixed on him steadily. By fixing her eyes on him, she seemed to be wanting to force out an answer, or to ask for something, but her eyes, watchful and swollen, did not surrender, and he no longer believed they were in Karelia looking at alpine flowers shimmering against the snow. Hair short, nails bitten, Lord in thy mercy see to it that the sin does not spread so that the boys do not become like her. For our blood's sake.

She scarcely seemed to be breathing, as if asleep, but her eyes were open.

He stretched out his hand, holding the lump of sugar towards her. She did not move. She did not take it. He waited for a long time. Outside, the aspen leaves moved softly, trembling gently, but all he saw was Eva-Liisa's eyes, very dark, watching him. He held the piece of sugar closer to her, right up against her mouth. Lips dry, slightly bitten; she was breathing. Close, close to her lips, he held it. And then, at last, he saw her lips part almost imperceptibly: and with the very tip of her tongue, she carefully touched the rough white surface of the sugar-lump.' 75

FREDRIKSSON
Marianne

Hanna's Daughters [Anna, Hanna och Johanna]

This is a history, covering 120 years, of three women, grandmother, mother and daughter, moving from 1870 — when Hanna is conceived — to the late 1980s, when Anna comes to terms with ageing and death. Hanna is Johanna's mother, Anna Johanna's daughter. The English title is not as misleading as this statement might suggest, however, since not only does Hanna survive to a great age, but her dour personality, forged in a hard school of life, determines to a considerable extent the emotional careers of her descendants.

Marianne Fredriksson surveys the three women's lives from the perspective of Anna. In doing so she gives us a social history of Sweden itself, as it progressed from being one of Europe's poorer nations, to its mid-century position of the continent's richest, Switzerland excepted. She is also charting the emancipation and liberation of women, a parallel upward movement without historical precedent.

Hanna, born of farming stock in remote Dalsland (bordering on Norway), is sent at the age of twelve to work for her aunt and uncle. Her cousin Rickard assaults her and makes her pregnant. For the next four years she is stigmatised as 'whore', and her son as 'bastard', an experience which, though she triumphs over it, is to leave her with an uncompromisingly dark vision of life. Whatever the dilemmas of her daughter Johanna — who identifies with the Swedish Social Democrat party which gained its extraordinary hegemony in the early Thirties — or her grand-daughter, Anna — whose life will be led with that hegemony effectively over — neither will ever undergo the degradations, the dismissals from humane considerations that Hanna and her sisters all too regularly knew. So, with qualifications, this is a story of progress.

But menstruation, sexual intercourse, pregnancy, giving birth, the menopause, ageing, dying — these will always impose themselves on women, bringing disruption and pain, and also — the last two not excluded — satisfaction. Johanna is a long time dying, dwelling on an unreachable plane of consciousness, and yet we feel that she is experiencing something with its own peculiar rewards. And ageing and dying are part of men's lives too, and Marianne Fredriksson portrays males with compassion and charity. They have been victims too. The portraits of Ragnar, Hann's bastard son who exerts so much charm on so many, and of Anna's selfish but feeling and morally principled husband are very sympathetic. A bestseller from 1994, not only in the Scandinavian countries but elsewhere, *Hanna's Daughters* is hypnotically readable, moving, authentic and rises to heights of poetry:

'Anna made a detour round by the shore and sat in the car for a while, looking out over at the headland where she'd learned to swim. Where hawkweed and sea campion, crane's bill and bird's-foot trefoil grew among the coarse grass there was a boatyard. Here there were simple once individually owned cottages now smartened up with Mexican tiles and such insensitive extensions that they were scarcely recognisable. Over towards the mountains where her childhood meadows had been, with their wild strawberries, cornflowers and cows, were now rows of terraced houses like horizontal high-rises.

Only the lake beyond was unchanged as were the islands, their low profiles outlined against the grey horizon.

Lost country, lost childhood.

We once walked hand in hand across that shore meadow with towels and a picnic, sandwiches, coffee for you, soft drinks for me. I'm growing up, she thought with grief. And anger. Why does it have to be so ugly, so barbaric?

Once upon a time her mother had been as beautiful as the landscape here. Now she's falling apart. I'm trying to learn to accept it. About time, for I'm old, too, soon will be.

Must go home.' 16

GUSTAFSSON
Lars

The Death of a Beekeeper [En biodlares död]

One of the most distinguished Swedish novels of the last half-century, *The Death of a Beekeeper* (1978) reflects Gustafsson's philosophical preoccupations (he is a professor of philosophy in Austin, Texas) and also — in its fragmented yet concentrated presentation of the central character's predicament — his (very considerable) achievement as a poet. Lars Lennart Vestin shares his creator's first name and birth-year (1936); he is dying of cancer of the spleen (with secondaries). The novel consists of extracts from his notebooks mostly made in the spring (his last one) of 1975: the Yellow Notebook in which this retired divorced schoolmaster recorded household expenditure, notes about bee-keeping, and reactions to certain external events, the Blue Notebook in which he placed newspaper cuttings, quotations from books he'd been reading, and stories which he'd tried to write, and — perhaps most importantly of all — the Damaged Notebook. It is in this last that he set down not only urgent notes to himself (as one might on a memo-pad) but his physical impressions of the disease that will so shortly kill him, the stabs of pain, the consuming searing work of that pain on the frail if stubborn body, the temporary retreat of pain, indeed of all external manifestations of the cancer, and its inevitable reassertion. Disjointed pages of the Damaged Notebook end the novel: 'Why am I of all people identical with this pain?/ Why am I of all people identical with someone who experiences this pain?' and (true not only of Lars himself but surely of many, many of us) 'I have wanted much too little. My whole life long. People never had the feeling that I had any need of them.' It's interesting to compare *The Death of a Beekeper* with one of the outstanding novels of the previous decade, Doris Lessing's *The Golden Notebook* (1962), in which the notebooks represent differing, contrasting strands of a personality. But Gustafsson subjects his chosen extracts to a peculiarly intense discipline of subordination to his theme — how should we, and do we face our end?

A bleak eschatological novel, not made the less bleak by the beautifully etched seasonal fluctuations between snowy winter and burgeoning spring against which it takes place. But the grimness of its situation is somehow transcended by the courage of the unremarkable, quietist notebook-writer; his feeling for Nature, his regard for his bees and his dog, his ability to rise above circumstances and see the life around him with a grateful objectivity: these, for all their apparent modesty, are deeply impressive. And from his existential decision not to open the truth-telling, death-sentence-pronouncing letter from the hospital forwards we find him sympathetic. His life hasn't really been very satisfactory — to himself or anyone else — but certain experiences, which he recaptures in his exercise-books, seem, as again surely is the case with each one of us, to be of a kind which renders that statement meaningless.

'In the summer as little boys, yes even as high school students, we often sat on the locks of Färmansbo and fished. The lazy, tough, no not tough, but melancholy Kolbäcks River forms a little waterfall there. At this point there was a small island with the remnants of an old ironworks. Earlier masses of umbrella mushrooms grew there.

On the southern end of the island is the Färmansbo lock. A path leads to it, which is shaded by such high trees that it is utterly tranformed into a green tunnel. Ancient algae move on the stone banks of the canal.

At the lock itself the water is deep, coal black — the Kolbäcks River does not bear this name by accident — and at high water it creates black whirlpools, which always fascinated us when we were boys.

As early as May we would spend whole afternoons there, the pike were very active around that time.... Naturally, now and again it would happen that we got a fish on the hook, dramatic episodes with giant pike, who tore the golden glittering lure and disappeared with the whole thing in their mouths, great pike who continued to writhe in their mouths, great pike who continued to writhe in the grass like snakes, and sometimes one of us would slip on a wet stone and fall into the black, always cold water.

But I don't think that fishing was the most important thing about this lock.

The black, flowing water was kin to the black darkness in our own pupils.

We would sit there, look down, and talk about strange things with one another.' 137

GUSTAFSSON
Lars

A Tiler's Afternoon (En Kakelsättares Eftermittag)

Gustafsson has the reputation, not only founded on his long residence in the United States, of being a non-Swedish (or even anti-Swedish) Swede, one who repudiates the materialism and denial of individuality that he sees as endemic in the egalitarian Welfare Culture of Sweden's *folkhem*. It isn't quite fair to call him right-wing, though at times he has seemed this. *A Tiler's Afternoon* — despite its appearing in 1991, when that culture was well into national retreat (and the centre-right Parties, led by the Conservatives, were the victors in the autumn election) — aims many a blow at an over-organised, bureaucratic society which puts so little emphasis on individual enterprise; indeed the very conception of Torsten Bergman, the tiler of the title, is, one might say, a swipe at a particular socialist view of people and occupations. Torsten is — as Russian Turgenev might have said in a very different context — a 'superfluous man'; the state no longer permits him to work. His skills as a tiler — he is a 'thin man with white hair', 65 years old and abandoned by his family — can only operate in the black economy; he has been robbed of the dignity that should be his, and his manner and behaviour are beginning to reflect this.

But this novel is a long way from being an anti-socialist tract. As in the earlier *Death of a Beekeeper* Gustafsson reveals a sensibility, an insight into the human condition more akin to Samuel Beckett's than to anybody else's, combined with a sharp intellectual penetration deriving from his philosophic studies and an ability to render place and social context that place him in a firm Swedish tradition. *A Tiler's Afternoon* is perhaps best described as a farce with tragic undertones. The tiling work on which Torsten embarks turns out to be unwanted for he has got the address where it's needed wrong. He meets during the course of the day a cousin of his whom he hasn't seen for years, the rather hopeless Stig who just can't be believed when he talks (as he does) about himself and his achievements. (The reaction of these elderly men to each other is superbly done.) The afternoon of the title is a wasted one, and yet.... memories, feelings, thoughts redeem it. As with Lars in *Death of a Beekeeper*, what has brought the central character comfort and pleasure (his early hobbies of crystal wireless sets and cameras, for example) has done nothing for him in the way of social standing or income. But this tells against those who would judge him not against Torsten himself.

'His first camera was a pin-hole camera that he'd made himself, the second was a Zeiss box camera. There was nothing or everything to photograph: the bare and empty street in winter with its snowdrifts, the leafless maple trees on Knektbacken Hill (where you could still see the wind-torn remnants of his kite), the stylish new Post and Telegraph Office. The really interesting and important part was not what pictures you took. The main thing was the developing.

In the glow of the red lamp up in the attic, in the gentle spray from the suspended watering can, just as the very first shadows began to emerge in the developing liquid, that was when he would feel something that must have been happiness. The transition from pale, vague shadows to pictures obviously took place as gradually and imperceptibly as plants growing. It was astonishing that the world could work like that. In a way he couldn't easily describe in words, it reminded him of himself.' 36-37

JERSILD
P. C.

Children's Island [Barnens Ö]

This could justly be thought *the* Swedish novel of the 1970s (year of publication 1976). The account of a boy of almost eleven at large in Stockholm one summer is impressive in both its actuality — we enter with ease Reine Larsson's being in its physical and mental totality, while Stockholm is brought to life as a virtual character in the novel by a multiplicity of intimate details — and its metaphoric quality. Reine, vivid in his individuality though he is, and still deep in a boyhood of junk-food eating, private code-making, and fact-collecting, partakes of Everyman, while

Stockholm — from Reine's home of Sollentuna, sprawling suburban satellite to the inlets of the Baltic — stands not only for Sweden itself but for any western society, prosperous but with an underbelly, confident-seeming but in truth plagued by doubts and worries, desirous of happiness above everything else but rarely attaining it.

Reine, who lives with his divorced mother, is supposed to go away to summer camp — on the rather disquietingly named Children's Island. He doesn't want to go. Other kinds of activity and enterprise call him, and besides he has much he wants to find out about. The problem of death and its relationship to life nags at him; he can't understand why there are so many catastrophic happenings outside Sweden (the first half of the 1970s was, after all, overshadowed by the Vietnam War, against which Sweden's Prime Minister Palme protested); sex baffles him — though he is aware of his mother's physical relationship with Stig — love even more so. When will his own pubic hair arrive? (He examines his groin every day.) And who really *was* his father? Could it by any chance have been that most famous of Swedes, Dag Hammarskjöld (in reality not interested in women)?

So he decides to deceive his mother into thinking that he has gone to Camp when in fact he has remained in Sollentuna with all Stockholm stretching itself before him, demanding exploration (and visits to McDonald's?) He doesn't realise how much life *costs* — nor that as a ten-year-old he lacks proper social identity and is therefore at the mercy of individuals and social forces. He works — with old women putting letters on the ribbons of funeral wreaths, for example; he tries to enjoy himself; he puts himself at the mercy of his mother's slob of a boyfriend; he even captivates a woman, Nora, a salesgirl. But there remains loneliness...

This is a profound and richly worked book, dealing with existential themes and applying keen intellectual analysis to mid-century culture. But no description of it would be adequate that did not stress its sheer delightfulness and energy — and the warmth with which Reine is brought to life.

'Hunger struck Reine a blow in the solar plexus. He abandoned television cables and fled out into the kitchen. What was there to eat? Unfortunately, almost nothing. The icebox was as empty and as defrosted as before, but there was another pack of Finnish melba toast in the oven. There were seven boxes of spaghetti in the cupboard, all opened and all practically empty. Also a few cans of soup, a plastic jar of rice, sugar, salt and other spices, jars of peeled tomatoes, another of snails, but — thank goodness — a can of corned beef and a can of pineapple. He quickly opened the last two, thrust a fork into the meat and slid a spoon carefully into the fruit. Together with the Finnish toast, he took them back to bed. A man must have some comforts.

Before he started eating, he switched on the television, and a clock against a green background said five minutes to the news. He managed to get all the food inside him except the toast before the clock reached half-past seven and faded out. Reine turned swiftly over in bed and lay on his back with his feet on the pillow. If you watched television lying upside down, it wasn't so horrible. Because it could be horrible, burning children in Vietnam, or when the police chief in Saigon shot a prisoner through the head right in front of the camera. If there must be executions, they were best watched upside down. And another thing: he had learned at school that people realy see the world upside down; that was how their eyes functioned. But very early on in life you learned to turn the picture right side up in your head. It sounded a bit odd, but it was true. Reine didn't want to have anything to do with that kind of trick; he wanted to see the world as it really was, just as you'd seen it from the start when you were born, upside down.' 20-21

JERSILD
P.C.

House of Babel [Babels Hus]

P.C. Jersild (born 1935) was a physician who became medical adviser to the National Government Administration Board before devoting himself full-time to writing. He was therefore peculiarly well-equipped to be the author of a novel which has at its centre a large hospital (the House of Babel of the title, employing as it does people of many nationalities). The book takes us to numerous departments, makes us privy to all manner of intricately related decisions and activities, and confronts us with doctors, nurses, anciliary staff, administrators, patients. But Jersild is a committed socialist (he has contributed regular articles on politico-social matters to the Swedish daily, *Dagens Nyheter*) a 'humanist socialist' as he himself emphasizes; *House of Babel*, opening with pages which give us the main annual causes of death in contemporary Sweden, presents illness and those experiencing it from an intensely moralistic socialist perspective. How does modern society regard health and the lack of it? What powers are they prepared to give those concerned with the care or cure of the ill, and what moral judgement are we prepared to exercise on them? In the late capitalist world how far have we surrendered our critical faculties and ethical proprieties to big business — even in that most sensitive area, the well-being of our own bodies and those of people we love?

Jersild unites his comprehensive accounts of the multi-faceted Enskede Hospital in 'the northwest part of southern Greater Stockholm' through the person of Primus Svensson. Primus is an elderly man, a retired printer, taken ill while tending to his beloved allotment. He is suffering from arteriosclerosis; later he is found to have cancer. We meet the nurses who tend him, the hospital worker who brings him books, the consultants who diagnose him, and we see and hear much that he doesn't — and couldn't. Yet he remains — even after his death — the central (and sympathetic) focal point. Long separated from his wife, Ellen (now dead) he is estranged from his son, who works for the giant pharmaceutical company, Luna — and in fact, unbeknown to him has dealings with the very hospital in which he himself now is. Their coming together brings a harmony to the novel at least as satisfactory as the relationship between the two cousins in Thomas Mann's *Magic Mountain*.

Jersild has said he divided himself into three during the writing of the novel — he became the young intern, Martina Bosson, morally scrupulous and inquisitive; the successful doctor who wants to give up his work, Gustaf Nyström, and Primus' middle-aged son, Bernt, a tormented alcoholic. The human dramas in this novel of the creations of civilised man versus the ills all flesh is heir to are so intimately and vividly rendered that in themselves alone they expose the coldness of bureaucratic politicking and the immoral greed of the pharmaceutical giants.

'Now they [intern and patient] had come to the most awkward questions of all, the ones you were supposed to squeeze in between other things so that it seemed natural. But she'd not done that. She was tired. They had had four hours of lectures, the professor's round, and she'd already done one case history on a Finnish woman, with the help of an interpreter.

"Have you ever been to sea?" she said, feeling her way again.

"National service?"

"Yes, or been in the Navy?"

"Yes, I was at Oscar Fredriksborg. And was in the Coastal Artillery."

She couldn't ask the shameful question that way, then. She was tired, so asked straight out: "Have you ever had venereal disease?"

He picked up his spectacle case, opened it, closed it, then put it into the drawer in the locker. Then he looked straight at her.

"I've not had either gonorrhea or syphilis."

She breathed out. Now the case history was practically done and she could dictate it. No, hell! She'd almost forgotten the form. Every infarct patient was to be interviewed according to a special stress form. It was part of a research project the head of the unit was doing. He was going to write a dissertation on it. She hadn't the energy to ask any more questions, so she decided to do the form after the physical examination.

She went into the examination room and fetched the little cart with the examination tray on it.

When she returned, he had fallen asleep. But she had to wake him and start on the laborious exploration from head to foot.' 31

JERSILD
P.C.

A Living Soul [En levande själ]

An audacious tour-de-force, *A Living Soul* (the title of which begs the difficult question governing the entire novel) has as its protagonist a human brain (known as Ypsilon) placed in an aquarium filled with nutrient fluids. This brain of course once controlled an entire body; now it is relieved of the business of directing limbs; also a brain can feel no literal pain, that terrible normal concomitant of being alive. One eye is attached to it, so Ypsilon can see (and catching sight of the reflection of 'himself' in the tank's glass is deeply unpleasant for him). Not only has the brain been stripped of control-functions, it obviously has no sex, and all memories were removed (with his knowledge and seeming consent) in the last operation it endured so it has none of the past which conditions and directs other humans.

Therefore — can we call Ypsilon human at all? Where does humanity begin and end? A major theme of all Jersild's work is our moral obligation to extend sympathy to all living beings, whatever definition 'living' is accorded. Ypsilon may not feel in a physical way but it does in a mental way — fear, worry, jealously, competition, even love. This is both a brilliant and a deeply felt book — perhaps the most terrifying aspect of it being the dependence of a complex organism on other beings more powerful (for Ypsilon is but an ingredient in an ambitious labortaory project) — and one even more troublingly germane to our period than to 1980 when it first appeared.

'With a brutal splash, I'm heaved over to one side and begin to list to starboard. Outside the laboratory inclines precariously. I have company in the aquarium. I feel the lash of a whip over one of my ears, and in the next moment a rat comes swimming over me, with its belly hanging down. Its tail beats. The rat seems confused, scrapes the glass, turns, and dives. With its cheeks puffed out and its nostrils pinched together, it glowers straight into my eye.

I must not be afraid! I must not.... Yes I must!!! I violently let go of all my feelings. Through the turbulent water I see the three oscilloscopes directly opposite; they're fluttering this way and that, as if seen in a curved mirror. Scared! Scared! I have to become even more scared, SCARED, S-C-A-R-E-D!!! At last the instrumentation reacts: when all the curves threaten to derail, the alarm goes off.' 39

JÖNSSON
Reidar

My Life as a Dog [Mitt liv som hund]

One of the most delightful and poignant of Swedish novels from the past quarter-century, *My Life as a Dog* (1983) is the recreation by his adult self of two significant years, 1958 and 1959, in the boy Ingemar's life as he stands awkwardly and truculently poised on the threshold of puberty. The construction of the book, sandwiching memories of the earlier year between recollections of the subsequent one, sometimes leads to unnecessary obfuscation, but it is atoned for by the moving revelations of the novel's last section.

Ingemar and his elder brother are members of a dysfunctional family; their labourer father is erratic and unreliable, while their mother dying of tuberculosis is — as the novel eventually makes plain — not only a woman tragically (and sufferingly) cut off in her prime, but a manipulative and somewhat irresponsible one as well. Authority, in the form of the Swedish welfare state (with its foster-homes and district visitors) has to step in to see that the children are being adequately provided for, but both boys — and especially the adventurous, day-dreaming, fantasizing Ingemar — defy the best-made plans. Ingemar's love and loyalty go to such people as his ne'er-do-well uncle with his boyish ways and coarse jokes and only occasionally to those who can adequately guide him towards some form of maturity. The novel can be seen as a metaphor for the relationship between a public system (shown as fundamentally benevolent) and the individual (full of vagaries, inconsistencies and anarchic promptings); what makes it so agreeable is the refusal to condemn either side, though obviously the author's sympathies are with the unfettered human spirit.

The novel's Swedish title is difficult to translate; it really means My Life *like* a Dog which isn't very English. Now petted, now neglected, now fending for himself, now showered with attention and concern for his health, now grumbled at and dismissed, Ingemar's lot in boyhood has all too many parallels with a dog's in a western community. In fact there is a real dog in Ingemar's life, his beloved Sickan, the discovery of whose fate provides one half of the novel's moving double climax. As in *The Catcher in the Rye* and P.C. Jersild's *Children's Island* much of the book's force comes from the narrator's digressions on life, sometimes impressive because he sees so clearly, so ruthlessly, sometimes because his vision is still restricted by innocence and misplaced trust. The characters other than Ingemar are drawn with sharpness, and, particularly in the case of the brother, with an observant sympathy.

My Life as a Dog was made into a memorable film by Lasse Hallström, who went on to direct (in English) the not dissimilar *What's Eating Gilbert Grape*?

'Every day my body rushed away from the past. I was split into two people. The person I recognized as me was pushed further and further away into a desolate landscape that became more and more unattainable as time went by. In front of the mirror where Mr Holdst [an older man who's befriended Ingemar] was staring at himself with a glazed look I saw one single big eye which became everybody's eye. And that eye only wanted to see the me wiped clean of memories, that eye was my uncle and my aunt, it was everyone who pretended that life went on regardless. Nobody wanted to say anything about the people who were missing. Time heals all wounds.

I lied like a faithful dog to Mr Holdst and wondered what he'd say if I told him the truth. What would he have done if I had shown him that I felt sorry for him?

I wallowed in kids' lies. In a few years' time I would be able to advance to a senior level. My shining armour was just a shell waiting to be filled with dung and excrement. And I could even kid myself that it was possible to skip life right up to the comfort of Death's door.' 135-6

LAGERLÖF
Selma

Gösta Berling's Saga [Gösta Berlings saga]

Selma Lagerlöf (1858-1949) has proved one of the most widely read of Swedish writers, for many years a representative of Swedish culture, and the first Swede (as well as the first woman) to win the Nobel Prize for Literature (in 1909). She was born and raised in the family home of Mârbacka, in Värmland, a province of singular beauty and richness of folklore — which she was to mine continually in her work. Teacher and educationalist, writer in several different genres, humanitarian and resolute anti-Fascist, Selma Lagerlöf would superficially appear to have been almost from the first a member of the 'great and good'. In fact she was a far more unconventional person than the above would suggest. Her father to whose memory she was devoted was feckless and went bankrupt; she herself was lame and grew up apart from other children, very much living in the world of fantasy and folklore, and later in life she knew passionately reciprocated lesbian love. Moreover in her work itself a wild vein is present, above all in *Gösta Berling's Saga*, the book that made her world-famous, one of the best-loved Swedish novels, and the basis of a very successful film (directed by Mauritz Stiller and featuring Greta Garbo as Ebba Donna).

The story is of Gösta Berling, a defrocked priest, who, throwing himself into debauchery, becomes involved with different women. Yet the relationships also add up to a victorious pilgrimage towards virtue and peace. The book makes much use of inlaid stories; Selma Lagerlöf loved the 'tale', its universality of reference as well as its particularity, its shapeliness, and she was to use the device of tales told to an audience in *The Wonderful Adventures of Nils*. A work of widely acknowledged freshness, Lagerlöf herself, it would seem, stated debts to Thomas Carlyle and to Icelandic sagas.

'Before her knelt Gösta Berling. He had a face compassionate as a poet's and bold as a soldier's. His eyes were deep, glowing with wit and genius; they invited. He was supple and full of strength, fiery and intriguing. While the curtain rose and fell, the two remained in the same position. Gösta's eyes held the lovely Marianne: they invited; they implored. ... Then the beautiful Marianne bent down and kissed Gösta Berling. She did not now why — she had to. He stretched his arms up about her head and held her firmly. She kissed him again and again.' 65

LAGERLÖF
Selma

The Wonderful Adventures of Nils

The Further Adventures of Nils [Nils Holgerssons Underbara Resa genom Sverige]

When the Japanese novelist Oe went to Stockholm to receive the Nobel Prize for Literature in 1996, he said that he felt he knew

Sweden already because he had read *Nils Holgersson* (as the Swedes usually refer to the work) so many times when young. Many others could speak similarly (including myself), and not only non-Swedes. For the best part of a century Selma Lagerlöf's great two-part book has been the best means of knowing more about Sweden, the land, its real past, its mythological past, its lore, its natural history. Perhaps it is only fitting that Selma Lagerlöf, already an internationally famous author, should have written it at the request of education authorities to provide something that would make Swedish children more familiar with the geopgraphy of their own country. But right from the beginning, as she began work on it, *Nils Holgersson* spectacularly transcended its genre. It is part of all Swedes' awareness, has entered the national psyche, has acted as a literary ambassador for their country all over the world. Understanding of Sweden should begin here.

What started off as the machinery for the revealing of Sweden was nothing less than a stroke of sheer genius. Nils, a truculent boy of fourteen, living on a farm in Skåne (the southernmost part of Sweden) is metamorphosed into an elf-sized version of himself. It is a spring day when the wild geese are flying overhead bound for their summer quarters in Lapland. Nils, forgetting how small he is, jumps on the back of the farm's white gander who is tempted to join one of the flocks — to stop him. But of course he is too small to be able to do this. Instead he finds himself flying with the geese on their northward migration. In his present form he can understand the talk of animals and birds. Not a kind or admirable boy, he gradually becomes deeply attached to the geese themsleves, in particular the wise, if sharp-tongued leader, old Akka from Kebnekaise, and his own 'charger', Morten Gander. He learns unselfishness from them, indeed, and is able to deliver them from certain predators, human and animal — notably Smirre the fox. Conversation with the denizens of the forests over which he is flying teaches him the legends every different Swedish province has engendered. Sometimes — as off the coast of Gotland — he actually participates in the legends' actions himself (e.g. in the visit to the submerged medieval city).

Lapland and the Arctic summer are attained; then the homeward journey begins, following the west of the country whereas on the upward flight the eastern side was kept to. On the whole the second part of the book (*The Further Adventures* in English) lacks the inspirational intensity of the first, but it makes up for this in the very moving last chapters. Nils must return to Skåne; the geese must go on south to Africa. Nils feels desolate — but when he is returned to ordinary human life he will do so as someone with a different conception of Nature (as well of his whole vast country) than before. He has been educated by the creature-world — and the plea for humans to respect the habitat of birds and animals is as relevant and needed today as when it was written.

Readers today will note many ambiguities in the whole story that it is possible escaped the author herself. Why was Nils so 'bad' at the beginning when only a little kindness from the geese could bring out such amiable qualities in him? Is it that conventional pious Swedish families struck Selma Lagerlöf as having less to give a growing mind than the denizens of the wild? But what will not fail to excite — at whatever age, in whatever decade — is the feeling of Sweden revealing its wild but various land for the attentive, responsive traveller, and the feeling too that this should stand for our whole approach to our own lives' course.

'Nils had grown so giddy that it was a long time before he came to himself. the winds howled and beat against him, and the rustle of feathers and swaying of wings sounded like a great storm. Thirteen geese flew around him, flapping their wings and honking. They danced before his eyes and they buzzed in his ears. He didn't know whether they were flying high or low or in what direction they were travelling...

At last Nils just made himself cast one glance down to earth. Then he thought that a great big rug lay spread beneath him, which was made up of an incredible number of large and small checks.

"Where in the world am I now?" he wondered.

He saw nothing but check after check. Some ran crosswise, and some were long and narrow, but everywhere there were straight lines. Nothing was round, and nothing was twisting.

"What kind of big checked cloth is this that I'm looking down on?" said Nils to himself, without expecting any one to answer him.

But instantly the wild geese who flew about him called out: "Fields and meadows. Fields and meadows."

Then he realized that the big checked cloth that he was travelling over was the flat land of southern Sweden.' 19-20

LAGERKVIST
Pär

Guest of Reality [Gäst hos verligheten]

Perhaps Lagerkvist's most durable as well as most accessible work, *Guest of Reality* (1925) is a recreation (in the form of a novella) of the world of the author's early years; it is therefore invaluable for its illumination of his career and *oeuvre*. A member of the Swedish Academy and winner of the Nobel Prize for Literature 1951, Lagerkvist, who enjoyed the greatest esteem in his lifetime, was very reticent about his private life, and indeed removed personal material to Stockholm's Kungliga Biblioteket, not to be read until he was dead.

Here though we are taken to a Småland town at the turn of the nineteenth century (in point of fact Växjö), to its station restaurant in a few rooms of which grand building a large family are making their home — the cirumstances of Lagerkvist's own growing up. Like Anders in the novella he was the youngest member of a railwayman's family, an imaginative, curious child with an early propensity for exploring the metaphysical dimension of life: why do we have to die? Do we have to die at all? How can we know that we are alive? No answer satisfies the boy, but the very act of questioning assists his development.

Anders' parents are devoutly religious, as were Lagerkvist's own, regular readers of the Bible, possessing indeed no other books but the Bible, the Psalmbook and Arndt's *Sermons*, (or any picture other than a portrait of Luther) and believing literature in general to be a sinful activity better shunned. Lagerkvist, of course, broke away from this, and the breaking away must have been a very difficult process, but in *Guest of Reality* he accords his parents an admirable and moving dignity. Lagerkvist was to say in a private notebook that he felt grateful for the non-literary atmosphere of his home. Certainly it must have assisted what could be termed his agnostic spirituality, present in him even when very young and fortified by his feeling for Nature. Again reflecting Lagerkvist's own experience, Anders has a very strong relationship with his grandparents, smallholders living outside the town who have preserved old rural ways. As Robin Fulton, the novella's sensitive translator, says, *Guest of Reality*, forsaking conventional structure, is a sequence of epiphanies, each marking an intensification of the central figure's awareness of life's mysteries.

[Anders and his father are riding along the railway-line, on a trolley, towards his grandparents' house in the country.] 'Father drew in the pole, held it ready to use as a brake on one of the wheels if necessary. The air whistled round their ears. The little wheel at Ander's feet span so fast the spokes were invisible, it hopped and skipped with joy. It was like a young foal in the morning just when it's been set free. The rail was a straight line, ox-eye daisies, buttercups, cowslips also became straight lines, the telephone wires glittered tautly up against the sun, the sparrows sitting on them suddenly scattered in terror into the forest where trees and bushes grew together into a smooth wall, a squirrel, startled out of its wits, scampered up the fence as if it couldn't get through.

It was over in a few minutes, all of the long slope. Then the countryside opened around them in every direction, with marshlands, little lakes, all sorts of waters, with tiled strips, grazing lands, countless ploughed squares, with fenced pastures, boglands and woodlands and farmsteads scattered among the oats and the rye out in the sun. The light was so friendly and open everything could be seen, and in the distance Grandfather's place was in sight, sheltered in a group of maples. The speed slackened. They rolled peacefully over a broad river edged with reeds and water-lily pads, in the current they could see shoals of bleak stirring in the glitter. Finally they reached a bumpy track that crossed the line, where they braked and jumped off and there they were, they'd arrived.' 27-28

LARSSON
Björn

Long John Silver [Long John Silver]

Long John Silver, said to be founded on Robert Louis Stevenson's friend, the lame poet W.E. Henley, has long been thought of as the most ambiguous figure of *Treasure Island*, at once morally fearsome and curiously heroic. Björn Larsson has given us the imaginary autobiography of this mysterious haunting and haunted man, telling us of both his earlier and his later days, and trying to answer some of the most teasing riddles of Stevenson's story.

Silver worked as a cross-Channel smuggler, and made the shackled passage on a slave ship from West Africa to the Caribbean. He was a pirate even before he was quartermaster to Captain Flint. He has inspired fear wherever he goes, is addicted to rum and has ended up on Madagascar. Yet he is not incapable of reflection and even of a degree of self-analysis.

Björn Larsson is a university lecturer in French and readers may note a kinship to the French master, Michel Tournier, in his combination of pastiche and imaginative re-creation. He is also learned in both British maritime matters and in the sea itself, having lived for six years aboard a sailing yacht.

'The year is 1742. I have lived a long life. No-one can take that away from me. Everyone I have known is dead. Some of them I have myself despatched to the next world, if there be one — but why should there be? In any case my fervent hope is that there is not, for we would meet again in Hell, Blind Pew, Israel Hands, Billy Bones, that dolt Morgan who dared to tip me the black spot, and all the others, even Flint, God preserve him, if there be a God. And they would bid me welcome, bowing and scraping, telling me that everything would be like the old days. But at the same time they would be radiating fear like a burning sun on a calm sea. Fear of what? I ask myself. In Hell they can hardly be in fear of death.

'No, they were never afraid of death, for by and large it was all one to them whether they lived or died. But even in Hell they would be in fear of me. Why? I ask. All of them, even Flint, who in every other respect was the most courageous man I ever saw or met, were afraid of me.' 3

LIDMAN
Sara

Naboth's Stone [Nabots sten]

Sara Lidman's has been a major voice in Swedish literature and culture ever since her novels of the early 1950s, written in the dialect of the Norrland province of Västerbotten. Her work is *engagé*, somewhat experimental and dealing to a great measure with the 'unloved' and the socially neglected. *Hjortronlandet* (*Cloudberry Land*) (1955) and *Regnspiran* (*The Rain Bird*) (1958) are famous productions of this period. In the 1960s Sara Lidman (born 1923) was, as a committed socialist writer, intensely involved with Africa and Vietnam and explored the moral dilemmas presented by these places in both fiction and overtly political polemic. She did not neglect northern Sweden and its problems however; *Gruva* (*The Mine*) (1968) is a report on the conditions for workers in a Norrland mine. Then in the late 1970s she began a novel sequence linked by the railway being built through the intractable Norrland countryside in the later nineteenth century. *Naboth's Stone* is the third volume from this sequence.

It is hard in so short a space to do justice to this profound, beautiful and moving novel. Its remarkable qualities owe enormously to Sara Lidman's original style and fictive methods. She is essentially a modernist who will break up conventional narrative to give us, often in disjointed form (or set down as poems or chants) and delivered in dialect, the thoughts, inconsequential-seeming yet also urgent, forcing their way up, of her characters; these, as in her early books tend to come from the inarticulate classes whom education has passed by, though the central recurrent figure of the sequence, Didrik Mårtensson, is a clever, enterprising and not unsuccessful man. As we read Lidman, we realise we are being given fragments of a northern Swedish epic, in which the epic is as concerned with the inner beings and the biological men or women as well as with external doings. (The account of Didrik's wife, Anna-Stava's childbed spring to mind here as illustrating Lidman's powers in making vivid all three aspects of life.) Further Sara Lidman has a very Swedish rapport with the natural world; the landscape is an active participant, and Didrik's horse, usually referred to simply as Horse, a real dramatis persona.

As in the novels of P.O. Enquist and Torgny Lindgren the community depicted for us is deeply, passionately religious, starkly Protestant or Puritan yet not without a certain animism springing from the closeness to Nature of its daily existence. This is as much a Bible-soaked culture as the not dissimilar rural American South (William Faulkner, Flannery O'Connor, Cormac McCarthy). The very plot of *Naboth's Stone* suggests the levels of Biblical consciousness on which the characters live. Anna-Stava, Didrik's beloved wife, at last, after several daughters, gives birth to a son (or 'Son', like 'Horse'). But she cannot breast-feed him, and so a wet-nurse has to be engaged. This woman with her own child and her concealed past becomes Abraham's bond-woman, the Hagar of *Genesis*, (she is known to us by this name) and so an inherited story enters and acts upon ordinary nineteenth-century rural life, rendered with countless felicities of detail and empathy.

'Seven miles up in the world, not a cottage, not a soul on the way, neither sun nor moon, no visible road

The only thing in sight snow-covered pines and spruces coming towards you eternally
until you're seized with terror and a deepening respect for Horse
who manages to make his way
so that you aren't buried under snow and pine-needles
the way the creature finds the way and keeps to it
it is a miracle
the most insignificant travelling companion becomes valuable
his voice, his breath, his movements
all his memories that come with him
crowded into one stubborn figure
maintaining the difference between him
and these monotonous almighty branches of trees.' 51

Ronia, the Robber's Daughter [Ronja Röverdotter]

It would be an unbalanced selection of Swedish books that didn't include something by the most-translated writer Sweden has ever produced, eclipsing even August Strindberg and Selma Lagerlöf, and who — she celebrated her 90th birthday on November 14, 1997 — has become a national institution, read by everybody, quoted and deferred to by politicians, and with a law named after her, the Lex Astrid, on the humane treatment of farm animals. But then she is a *children's* writer, though there are many who feel that, even so, the Nobel Prize for Literature should have been hers.

Like Ingmar Bergman her range of genres — all of which she informs with her own individual artistic personality — is truly Shakespearean. Happily the last full-length book she wrote, *Ronia, The Robber's Daughter* can be — and has been, widely — read as a novel. The eminent feminist and socio-political critic, Maria-Pia Boethius, whose standing in Swedish society is of the highest, sees *Ronia* as a seminal feminist and Green work, consistent with its author's thinking over the years but reflecting the healthiest strands of its decade, the 1980s.

Ronia has grown up in a robbers' lonely forest fortress, knowing 'that she was not the only child in the world', but experientially feeling herself to be this. Her home is in fact only one part of a castle which, on the night of her birth, was split in two by a wild storm, with a great chasm between the halves. As she moves into puberty, Ronia becomes aware that in the forbidden part of the fortress, on the opposite side of the chasm, another young human lives, but male: Birk son of her father's greatest rival.

In their first bemused encounter, Ronia and Birk, after exchanging childish questions with boasts and taunts, dare one another to cross the fathoms'-deep chasm between them. And though it is Birk who first has the idea, it is Ronia who first accomplishes the crossing. Then 'neither of them spoke any more, they simply jumped. Frantically and furiously, they jumped to and fro across Hell's Gap.' Everything that occurs afterwards is only an amplification of this. The attraction of the boy and the girl to each other is deeply disturbing to both bands of robbers, who live by a code inimical to tenderness. Ronia and Birk go to live together, in defiant friendship, in a cave in the forest, a dangerous place. The couple's life there is doomed, it's somehow mere escaping. And yet...

This 'and yet' is at the heart of the novel. For the young people's immersion in the forest is a 'participation mystique' with Nature, giving them the strength to deal with their bellicose inheritance and to see to the long-overdue restoration of sanity. It is a very Swedish paradox that it is out of the untrammeled wilderness that at last a truly civilised code emerges. Akin to the wisdom from the forest is the Wolf Music that Ronia's mother knows how to make, and the cry (a primal scream) with which she herself greets the spring. In the book it is the older men who have the most difficulty after the climactic events in re-learning how most deeply and satisfyingly to lead their lives; women of all ages and the younger men, represented here by Birk, attend to Nature more readily. The chasm breached is susceptible to many readings — the divide in Cold War Europe, the barriers imposed by creed and class, and, especially, by gender. Birk can stand as an admirable role-model for male readers. It is when he's at his gentlest that he appears also at his most masculine; the sexuality he discovers in the forest-cave is inextricable from tenderness and giving.

'And then spring came like a shout of joy to the woods around Matt's Fort. The snow melted, streaming down all the cliff faces and finding its way to the river. And the river roared and foamed in the frenzy of spring and sang with all its waterfalls a wild spring song that never died. The long, terrible winter was over....And at last Ronia was going to her woods, which she had missed so much. The moment the snow melted and all the ice thawed away, she should have been there to see what was happening in her domain...

And there was Birk, as he had promised. He was stretched out on a flat rock in the sunshine. Ronia did not know if he was asleep or awake, so she picked up a stone and tossed it into the water to see if he heard the splash. He did, and he sprang up and came toward her...

"I have to scream a spring scream or I'll burst," she explained to Birk. "Listen! You can hear the spring, can't you?"

They stood silently, listening to the twittering and rushing and buzzing and singing and murmuring in their woods. There was life in every tree and watercourse and every green thicket; the bright, wild song of spring rang out everywhere.' 76-78

LINDGREN
Torgny

In Praise of Truth [Till Sanningens Lov]

Narrated by a picture-framer, Marklund (born, we are told, in 1964), this is an elaborate and fast-paced story of forgery in competition with the genuine, and of the genuine in perpetual danger of being outdone by the counterfeit. Lindgren has in this novel of 1991 broken free from his near-mythical excursions to the northern Sweden of former centuries or to Biblical times, to turn illusionless eyes on the contemporary world, ones mocking and pitying by turns, and recalling those of such fellow-Catholics writers as the late Shusaku Endo (of whom he's an admirer), Walker Percy and Muriel Spark. Like them, while his story may traffic in the up-to-date — in this case in the world of art-galleries and their criminal, as well as legitimate, hangers-on, of tax-inspectors, the pop music industry and plastic surgery — he does not eschew the plot extravagances or the weird coincidences of the medieval fable (of the fabulous in other words) to make his points.

Marklund discovers in a provincial salesroom a painting, 'Madonna with Dagger', by the great Swedish artist (in some opinions the greatest Swedish painter ever), Nils von Dardel. Both subject and texture proclaim the great master, whom the narrator has always revered. But then the `same' painting turns up elsewhere, and the question as to which of the two is the true one and which the forgery raises its head, casting into doubt as it does the authenticity of so much in Marklund's life. Take for example Ingela, the girl he has been intimate with since childhood. 'No other child in Sweden has had such success. She was not even twelve years old when the whole thing began with that family show on TV one Saturday in November. When she later withdrew from her career, and thus also from her childhood, she was fifteen.' And now she has re-launched her career as Paula, a phenomenal success. But what with the media creation of her image, and her plastic surgeon and lover's creation of her face, she is perhaps every bit as much a forgery as the von Dardel painting into which Marklund has put all his savings, and the fortunes of which her own history parallels. Marklund is to realise that the border line between illusion and reality is a very blurry one.

Von Dardel is an apt figure to have evoked in this fictional examination of the real and the imitation. The very model of a *peintre maudit* with his bohemian French life, a friend of Cocteau, a lover of both men and women, alcoholic, and yet the creator of pictures with bright enamel-like surfaces, there's something — as all but his greatest admirers would admit — artificial in his very genius. And yet who is worthier of acclaim? *In Praise Of Truth* is a teasing and challenging book.

"'Forgeries!" he yelled. "Have you seen a single forgery on my walls?"

"No!" I said. "Absolutely not!"

He began to lecture me then at length; his voice was shrill, almost threatening.

"Of all the work that an artist produces, only half at most is genuine. Not even Picasso was able to paint a genuine Picasso every time. But I have never had a failure, a Klee by me is a genuine Klee, there isn't the slightest little weakness or flaw in my Dalís and Matisses and Chagalls. It's a question of the transubstantiation of paint: the paint must be transformed and turned into something higher and more wonderful than itself."

I had to agree. It was true.

"Authenticity is a quality of the work of art, it has nothing to do with who created it,' he went on. "No artist has to apply himself so rigorously to the question of authenticity as one who creates the paintings of others. He has to be up to the standard he's painting at. I have to be not just Lèger and Braque and La Fresnaye, I have to be the whole of the art of painting. It's a matter of empathy. Empathy and technique. Do you understand?'" 120

LINDGREN
Torgny

Light [Ljuset]

Remote in both place and time — the place specified (Kadis, in the province of Västerbotten), the time the Fourteenth century — *Light* is a terrifying parable of a stricken community that recalls Albert Camus' *The Plague*. Lindgren (born 1938), however, unlike the sceptical Camus, is a convert to Roman Catholicism. His concern is not only with how we cope with the kind of large scale suffering which can see the virtual elimination of the inhabitants of an area, but how we can grow through these ghastly experiences.

Light, an enthralling novel (Lindgren's storytelling powers are formidable, magical), contains scenes of horror that bring to mind the canvases of Brueghel or Hieronymus Bosch, but it also offers hope — hope in humanity, however badly it can behave when things start going wrong, and hope in some force beyond the human.

A man, Jasper, leaves Kadis for the town of Nordingrå, to

find himself a woman. Strangely he knows exactly what she'll look like, and the name he will call her by. But he doesn't find her. So he goes to another town further up the coast, Umeå, and here he buys a large doe-rabbit, pregnant (it's said) by a hare, whom he calls Maria, the unfound woman's name. Unknown to him the doe has a pestiferous flea in her fur, and that is how the Great Sickness comes to Kadis.

Great it certainly is: in a comparatively short time, the illness has run so rapid and so horrible a course, often sending its victims out of their minds before they die in agony, that only seven people are left in the community. Meanwhile the rabbits (as is their way) have multiplied and can be seen, healthy enough, everywhere. There are other animals as well, in particular Blasius, a pig of vast proportions, who is a character in this drama of survival almost as important as the humans themselves. Survival brings its own problems: guilt, unease, and tensions come to the fore, especially between two men who have been friends ever since early boyhood, Könik the carpenter and Önde the smallholder. Some of these tensions result in explosions of violence and cruelty, but strangely underneath runs, if sometimes so deeply it can't be seen, a current of benevolence. The novel closes with scenes of peace, for which the protagonists are profoundly grateful — though there's a suggestion that the cycle of suffering and redemption may conceivably be about to begin again. The novel abounds in ingenious coincidences and correspondences, reminiscent perhaps of all the interweavings of medieval art, and also — offsetting its starkness of theme and setting — in lively, at times pawky humour.

'Something remarkable was happening to Blasius [the pig]. Eira had always tried to keep him clean, every day she'd poured a bucket or two of water over him, but now he'd got really filthy again. He never remembered that he ought to scrub himself against the palings of his sty. Now that Eira was fully occupied..., Könik had often thought that he ought to make Blasius clean and tidy again. But he didn't get round to it. There were such a frightful lot of things that were wrong. So why should he bother particularly with Blasius?

He had a thick layer of all kinds of filth over his whole body, dung and straw and bits of food, and the food was mostly fish. The thick crust of muck and waste had begun to ferment, or rather to glow. It was the result of his extraordinary body-heat. Blasius became luminous. Late in the evenings he would begin to give off a glimmering blue-green iridescence. And they would all come and stand looking at him, they were convinced they were seeing a miracle. But Könik thought that this was just what might have been expected. When the world breaks up and disintegrates, miracles are only right and proper. If someone thinks up a fiction or a tall story in which he entraps both animals and men, one or another of them is bound to be afflicted like this. It would have been more inexplicable if Blasius had not become luminous, a pig of light.

But Eira, who'd noticed before how rubbish and old fish could glow, just said that they should scrub him clean, and when Onde did so, Blasius became himself again. But then Könik was almost frantic, he wanted to see the truth, he didn't want it washed away with water and a scraper.' 132

LINDGREN
Torgny

Merab's Beauty [Merabs Skönhet]

This volume of short stories provides the best introduction to Lindgren's work and his distinctive fictional universe. Set in remote Västerbotten, they show us remote tight-knit rural communities at no specifically stated time: beliefs are not just medieval but reach back into the pre-Christian past, though these men and women think of themselves — in the main — as devout Christians. Their lives are hard, elemental, heavy with superstition, yet at times touched by the glories, the otherworldliness of their faith. Lindgren gives us what could be termed imagined (or imaginary) folk-tales. His own compositions, they reflect the folk fable, the popular tall story and the Biblical parable, in style and narrative procedure; they have about them something of salty peasant wit and acceptance of difficulties, and often include events and epiphanies impossible to explain rationally — but which accord with the many-layered faith by which the characters live: farmers, preachers, well-makers, tailors, and the tramps and tricksters who bother them. In many ways the stories are reminiscent of those of Isaac Bashevis Singer, though some students of English Literature will think of that Christian bucolic master, T.F. Powys.

'This you shall know, all created things are unfathomable.

We all have the same spirit, yet most remarkable of all are the cows. No other living things are so filled with spirit and life, their udder that is weighed down by its sap and fruitfulness, and their bellies which compass four stomachs, and within all four there is life; and their eyes that understand and forgive almost everything, and their hides that tremble with happiness. Cows, they have been clothed with spiritual power.' 73

The Way of a Serpent [Ormens Väg På Halleberget]

Set once again in rural Västerbotten and in the past (this time in the late nineteenth century), and in length scarcely more than a 'novella', this is perhaps Torgny Lindgren's most perfect production, and, coming out as it did in 1982, it marked a turning-point in his career. The inspiration for it was, one assumes, 'The Book of Job'; throughout the book the narrator Johan addresses God as Job did, wondering at (and inveighing against) the arbitrariness as well as the injustice and cruelty of His decisions. The language is rich in echoes of the Swedish Bible and Protestant hymnals. Johan's particular complaint is that God permitted the local shopkeeper, Karl Orsa, to exercise power over others in the most sadistic way and for a long period of time, never stepping in to prevent the gratuitous suffering he caused. Why was this man able to inflict such misery, both in the way of sexual humiliation and of deaths, on the innocent?

Eventually Johan decides to take the law into his own hands. If God can't deal with this moral monster, then he, ordinary mortal though he is, will. But now it seems God finally does intervene in a human action. He brings about a landslide which destroys not only Karl Orsa himself, (as Johan would have wished) but Johan's dearly loved wife and children. And yet — according to Lindgren's Catholic vision — in the very ability of Johan to feel and rage as he does, the workings of God's grace are evident.

'You know that I was born defiant, you created me defiant. And you've always spoken to me and said: Do not be defiant, Bragging Johnny. You are strange like that, you form us in a very particular way, boastful or pig-headed or whatever, and then you use up our lives telling us that is exactly what we should not be, we're not to be the particular way you created us.

But on the other hand, you were fair in not giving me very much to vent my defiance on. If you'd made me the son of a shopkeeper or a big farmer, then I might have become a dangerous man with all that stubbornness and obstinacy built into me, I could have been a difficult master; but in the circumstances you put me in, my defiance was so slight and ineffectual that it seemed no more than a wasting disease within me. Lord, to whom shall we go?' 10

PLEIJEL
Agneta

The Dog Star [Hundstjärnan]

Distinguished as dramatist, poet, novelist and cultural critic, Agneta Pleijel (born 1940) has produced in this short novel of 1989 a beautiful and very haunting metaphor for the shattering effect on innocence (ignorance?) of knowledge — so often sought when the seeker is so unaware as not to be able even to guess at the consequences.

Ingert is the daughter of Lamek, a man from the plains countryside of southern Sweden — in which *The Dog Star* is set — and Finnish Siiri, whom he met in Stockholm when she was an evacuee from the Winter War in her country. One day, as she's returning home from school, Ingert is confronted by an older (to all intents and purposes grown-up) girl who tells her that she's her sister (half-sister). She has traced Lamek, her father, through the town's register. The arrival of Adele into Ingert's life means psychological anguish — and she herself is pubescent, on the threshold of coming of age sexually. Lamek, confronted with this result of a love-making that he has forgotten about and which meant scarcely anything to him even at the time, falls in love with his new-found daughter — and she with him. This infatuation, as Ingert begins to understand, is itself a reenactment of an earlier emotional drama. As a youth Lamek was popular with the opposite sex, with many admirers; he had, though, to deal with the jealousy of his young proud lonely mother (Ingert's Grandmother), who exerting all the charms in her unhappy being, made him her lover. From this situation he had to break away — to Stockholm where he contracted the unhappy relationship with Ingert's mother, Siiri.

Lamek's affair with his 'natural' daughter is too much for Siiri. She goes insane, is put in an institution, and escapes only to be killed in a car-crash. And their gentle son, Hugo, with an inner world he can only express in drawings, has to face institutionalisation too. But Ingert herself will survive.... The very seriousness of her feelings and of those of her kin bring about in her an awe towards existence, for which the Dog Star (Sirius) is a fitting symbol ('its absolute strength twenty-six times as great as that of the sun').

Stark though its subject-matter is, this is a novel of exceptional radiance, illuminating, like the star of its title, land and lives, a work both brave and life-enhancing.

'At first (Siiri, our dead mother) was a crane. Hugo and I stood in the wind out on the field and waved to her. But then she was so high up she was scattered into stardust.

I've read about that at the library and I told Hugo about it. The stardust radiates out into space and is carried to distant celestial bodies and forms new constellations, then is visible as a brilliant light in space. That's what happened to Siiri. Towards the winter we would just see her in the light from Sirius, the Dog Star, the brightest star in the whole sky. She would make the journey there and after that she would have forgotten us.

Hugo listened attentively, his eyes scarcely moving at all. And I knew that whatever happened about everything else, what I was saying about Siiri was true.' 120

SÖDERBERG
Hjalmar

Short Stories [Historietter]

Hajlmar Söderberg (1869-1941) is one of the very greatest Swedish writers, disgracefully little-known in the English-speaking world. Translations of his two finest novels, *Martin Birck's Youth* (1901) and the dark, extraordinary *Doctor Glas* (1905) have long been out of print. However his short stories — the earliest from 1897, the last from 1931 — are an excellent introduction to his powerful, original mind and art, and in common with everything else he wrote have a remarkable literary independence.

Very short, often ironic, not to say sardonic, in tone, they nevertheless encompass a wide range of human experience, and in their two or three pages hint at profound existential problems in an altogether provoking and stirring way.

Söderberg said that his great interest was religion, which might seem a strange remark from a declared and proselytising atheist, but is a true one even so. Söderberg — influenced by Ibsen, Zola and Nietzsche — in positing a world without God describes the difficulties concomitant with acknowledgement of this. His people — often ordinary and unintellectual — are caught between belief and unbelief: the young nightclub-goer in *A Dream of Eternity* who perceives in a nightmare just what an appalling idea everlasting life is, the parson who marries a gril from a strict religious sect who has inadvertently seen him naked in *The Parson's Cows*.

Sex makes the idea of a rational, judging God even harder to take — and Söderberg can write of sexual relations with a delightful lightness of touch — as of course can prolonged gratuitous suffering. (See *The History Teacher* sadistically tormented by his pupils, or *The Fur Coat* where the ill but well-meaning doctor is cuckolded by his best friend, or the marvellous poignant *The Chinese* with its delicate delineation of loneliness and ostracism.)

Söderberg was a Stockholmer who wrote about his city and its inhabitants with liveliness and intimacy. A Café Söderberg stands near the Opera where, as in his time, you can watch a whole diversity of citizens go by. His passionate belief in human rights led Söderberg to take, from the firtst, a bold and courageous stance against Nazism or any dealings with it, and he spent his last years in Denmark, dying indeed during the German Occupation.

For all his urbanity Söderberg, like many intellectuals of his time, had a keen interest in the natural world, particularly in animals. Often, for example, he writes of dogs as sharers in the human condition. His beautiful story *A Dog without a Master* is however not just an animal-tale but a meditation on existence itself:

'The dog, whose master died and was buried without the dog's knowing where, mourned him for a long time; but as the days went by and nothing happened that might remind him of his master, he forgot him. [One] year followed closely on the heels of another, and he grew old without noticing it.

It was a dark cloudy evening, wet and cold, and there was a shower now and then. The old dog had been down town all day on an expedition. He went up the street slowly, limping a little. He stopped a few times to shake his black coat, which with the years had become flecked with grey around the head and neck. As usual he went and sniffed first to the right, then to the left; and he made a detour into a gateway, and when he came out he had another dog with him. The next moment a third joined them. They were young dogs and frisky, and they wanted him to play with him; but he was in a bad mood, and it was also starting to rain very heavily. Then a whistle pierced the air, a long, sharp whistle. the old dog looked at the two young ones, but they did not react: it was not one of their masters that was whistling. The old dog without a master pricked up his ears; he felt suddenly so strange. There was another whistle, and the old dog jumped in bewilderment first one way and the other. It was his master that was whistling, and he must follow. For the third time somebody whistled, just as sharply and persistently as before. Where is he, then, which direction? How did I come to be parted from my master? And when did it happen, yesterday, ot the day before, or perhaps just a little while ago? And what did my master look like, and what sort of scent did he have, and where is he, where is he?' 57-8

By the Open Sea [I havsbandet]

In the 1890s Strindberg produced a series of wonderful seascape paintings, rivalled in the sense they impart of an ineluctable element only by Turner. Strindberg the painter has been, belatedly, recongised in Britain; the many sides of his genius are daunting indeed. The novel *By the Open Sea* (1890) is perhaps the nearest literary equivalent in Strindberg's oeuvre of those mighty works in oil.

Strindberg (1849-1912) is the colossus with whom every Swedish writer must come to terms. P.O. Enquist has written a play and a television serial about him; the as yet untranslated Björn Ranelid (born 1949) is very conscious of Strindberg's example and even notes parallels between the master's and his own life. It is as if Shakespeare had existed and written within living memory (and at the time of writing a daughter of Strindberg's is alive). Dramatist, diarist, novelist, essayist, political polemicist and activist, painter and even composer (!), he had imaginative and intellectual energy to a degree rarely equaled; he taught himself Chinese, he was a serious student of alchemy, he was an active friend to the Trades Union movement, which gave him an alternative Nobel Prize (he having shamefully been denied the real one). And his achievements don't stop with that list. For inside every genre he attempted he made radical changes, some of which have meant uneradicable changes in world literature itself. His earlier dramatic masterpieces, challenging Ibsen as it then seemed, are in their emotional atmosphere and sexual frankness very different from the plays of the great Norwegian. His later works for the theatre are innovative and extraordinary, anticipating Expressionism and the French and German cinemas, and indeed that of his compatriot Ingmar Bergman who has also shown himself a great Strindberg director (*A Dream Play*, *The Ghost Sonata*). His journals — eg *From an Occult Diary* — make journeys to domains of the psyche few have dared to explore, linking mental adventures with the metaphysical. And *By the Open Sea* is one of the essential Swedish novels.

It is set in the Stockholm archipelago, so beautiful and so dear to him, and which he had paid fictional tribute to in earlier work — in *The People of Hemsö*, for instance. But whereas his earlier writings had been lyrical, inspired by love, *By the Open Sea* is different in tone altogether. His reverence for Nature, for the sea is undiminished, but his attitude to the inhabitants of the skerries themselves has darkened. The novel deals with the fortunes of an intelligent, thoughtful man, an Inspector of Fisheries who comes to the fictionally named island of Östearskär and is ground down by the human life he finds there. Borg, the Inspector, is something of a Nietzschean, and a keen and thoughtful student of natural history. Though we are surely to think of his end as tragic and himself as the book's hero, with a relationship to Strindberg himself, we are also to consider it a critical portrait; Strindberg's mind was too complex and probing to encourage simple views of any situation. The novel is as redolent of the fascination the sea held for Strindberg as the author's paintings themselves.

'A dark cliff came into view on the headland of the last island. It was coal-black, made of the volcanic rock diorite, and as he drew near it he became depressed. The black crystallised mass seemed to have been spewed up from the bottom of the sea and then, as it had begun to petrify, had been involved in a fearful struggle with the water or some thunder-cloud. It had been split into eight parts and the rubble caried away by sea and ice or dragged into the deeps. The gleaming walls stood steep and straight as a die alongside the tiny harbour, and when the boat was anchored under them he felt as if he were in a coal-mine, or a sooty smithy.' 56

Background to Scandinavian and Baltic Fiction

This is a guide to fiction, in English translation, from the Scandinavian countries (Norway, Sweden and Denmark), their fellow-members of the Nordic Union (Iceland and Finland), and the newly independent and democratised Baltic States (Estonia, Latvia and Lithuania) the culture of which has often been influenced by Scandinavian examples. What the novels recommended here depict above all else is life in a prosperous, sophisticated, egalitarian society, one unequalled in its respect and provision for human rights, which has nevertheless maintained a sense of the atavistic, a relationship with a Nature largely innocent of mankind. This of course reflects a major feature of the Nordic Union countries themselves; an hour's drive out of those living testimonies to modern urban thinking, Oslo, Stockholm, Helsinki, and you are in vast, stubborn, ancient forest — emerging from which bears have recently been sighted in the comfortable Stockholm suburbs. Even in the more domestic Denmark, charming, easygoing Copenhagen is continually redolent of the sea and its power.

Key works of Scandinavian culture have long manifested this union. Ibsen's plays were initially greeted for their penetrating social insights — into women's rights even against the institution of marriage (*A Doll's House*), into the hypocrisy of the sexual double standard (*Ghosts*) — but his work, and increasingly so as we move through his oeuvre, brings Nature in all its force and strangeness into human lives: the very titles of *The Wild Duck* and *The Lady from the Sea* tell us as much. The people in the later Ibsen can't be redeemed without confrontation on its own terms with the wild.

The Finnish composer Sibelius was widely praised for development of the symphonic form unprecedented since the death of Beethoven, but we also revere his music for its admission of the sounds and texture of Nature — and not only in the tone-poems but in the actual symphonies themselves (consider the first movement of the Third Symphony in which the inspiring domain of wood and water seems to establish itself in our heads). In painting Edvard Munch's *The Scream* has become an icon of modern humanity's existential doubts, yet his art would not work on us as it does were it not for the painter's almost hallucinatory sense of the Norwegian landscape, particularly the coastline in the vicinity of Oslo. In fact the more we look at his canvases the more indissoluble do human beings seem from the rest of the created world.

So 'Scandinavia' to both the insider and the outsider means both thoroughgoing welfare systems with high standards of living, and characteristic landscapes which compel the people of the country to honour, love, safeguard and surrender to them: the treeless, volcanic, lunar interior of Iceland, the fjord districts of Norway with the North Sea cutting into great granite mountains, the seemingly endless forests of Sweden, the 55,000 lakes of Finland. There is therefore in the Scandinavian psyche an unflagging double awareness, a dual set of obligations, and its art expresses this.

I cannot think of any other culture, western or otherwise, in which this duality is so conspicuous and yet so well balanced. It can be explained. Scandinavia was industrialised late; for most of the nineteenth century these were poor countries, with an increasingly depressed rural population which emigrated in great numbers to America. With the technological advances of the late nineteenth and early twentieth centuries — hydroelectric power, Norway and Sweden's 'white coal'— the transformation of society became more than a possibility. As the century advanced, the Scandinavian societies grew not just prosperous but rich. They could organise themselves into 'new' societies owing little to the past but grateful to the Nature which, awesome and indomitable though it is, had also proved a friend. The Scandinavian societies had to deal with neither the fruits of many decades of complex and largely unregulated industrial life (the fates of Belgium, Britain and northern France) nor of elaborate and riven pre-industrial systems (the challenges to unified Italy and Germany). Modernity and progress, these constituted the 'good', and could be pursued without significant betrayal of the Nature so close to which the bulk of the Scandinavian and Baltic peoples had lived for so long. At times the Scandinavian societies' repudiation of the past — something both socialistic planners and business entrepreneurs agreed on — became something too like a fierce article of faith and could have an almost fanatical quality. (It still defies belief that the pulling down of Stockholm's ravishingly beautiful Old Town — Gamla Stan — was seriously debated in the mid-century; weren't its buildings, medieval to eighteenth century, a reminder of a sick unwanted bygone civilisation?) All this, in the changed climate of the 1980s and 90s has considerably diminished, but one can still be aware of such thinking; it still has to be heeded.

Of course the Scandinavian societies have ancient roots, and, especially in a rural context, long and continuous traditions of living. Another but related paradox of Scandinavia is that these new, modern societies are singularly dedicated to keeping up customs, preserving venerable ceremonies of living. It isn't so long back that members of the family now ensconced in the seamless ease of Copenhagen, Stockholm or Gothenburg suburbs were living close to the elements on a windswept island or in a hamlet enclosed by forest (Marianne Fredriksson's *Hanna's Daughters* brings this home to us particularly vividly) while it is only in the last two decades (it's said) that Oslo contains significant numbers of people who think of the city as their real, their true home. If knowledge of the past has played a comparatively small part until of late in Scandinavian society, consciousness of the immeasurable long span of tradition reaching back into life almost *outside* history is very strong indeed.

Iceland officially recognises the pagan religion, is mindful of elves when constructing new roads or housing-blocks, even incorporates addresses to trolls and other mythical beings into Christian and civic services. This is an extreme expression of a large-scale Scandinavian tendency. All Scandinavians and Balts would agree on the beauty, the inner necessity of this maintenance of a relationship with ancestors as enthusiastically as they would on the paramount importance of regular dealings with Nature. These agreements are surely endorsed by the comparative weakness of institutional religion, and of absolutist political creeds everywhere in this region except in (Roman Catholic) Lithuania.

The interconnectedness of the Nordic countries becomes the clearer when their languages are considered. Iceland was colonised by Norwegian Vikings in the ninth century CE; the geographical isolation of the island being what it is, its present-day language bears marked resemblance to Old Norse, and over the centuries has been affected by comparatively slight external factors — with the happy result that the wonderful Icelandic medieval literature (the sagas and eddas) are accessible to today's young. Close kin to Icelandic is Faeroese, the language of the 30,000 inhabitants of the Danish protectorate, though speakers of the one cannot follow speakers of the other.

The Scandinavian languages form a distinct and distinctive

branch of the Germanic group of the Indo-European family, and thus are kin to English, Dutch and German. But Finnish, the language of Finland, is not an Indo-European language at all but a highly and elaborately inflected language of the Finno-Ugrian family, and distant cousin to Hungarian. Among its nearer relations are Estonian (comprehensible to most Finns) and Sami (formerly called Lappish); this last was most probably borrowed or adopted from the Finns by the Sami people after they had settled in northern Scandinavia and was thus imposed on an older, independent, unrelated language. Finnish is spoken by about 4,000,000 Finns, that is roughly 90% of the population; about 10% speak Swedish, a reminder of the years when Finland was under Swedish domination and of the strength of the Swedish-speaking community, above all in professional circles, even after this had come to an end. Throughout the nineteenth century Finland was governed by Russia with Independence declared in 1917.

Finnish Swedes have a long tradition of articulate creativity in the arts, and this combines with the fact that many more people outside Finland know Swedish than Finnish to create an enormous imbalance in their literary representation abroad. The great majority of Finnish novels recommended in this book are Finland-wedish — and this despite the fact that some of the finest translato s into English today from any foreign language the poets, An elm Hollo, Herbert Lomas and Keith Bosley, render from 'Finn sh' Finnish. One can only hope that this situation will change and hat to familiarity with the Finland Swedish writers Tove J nsson, Bo Carpelan and Monica Fagerholm familiarity with such writers s Hannu Salama (born 1936) and Antti Tuuri (born 1944) will e added, writers who have a toughness and democratic spirit that would surely have wide appeal.

Meanwhile no understanding of the development of Scandinavian — or for that matter European — literature (of the whole complex relationship between nationalism, democracy and tradition) is complete without a reading of the great Finnish epic the *Kalevala*, wrought according to venerable metric laws and in Finnish by the dedicated scholar, Elias Lönnrot (1802-84) from a huge mass of orally transmitted poetry and legend. From its haunting stories composer Sibelius and painter Gallen-Kallela made many of their most durable and memorable works (the tone-poem *The Swan of Tuonela*; the great picture *Lemminkäinen's*

Mother). Keith Bosley's English version (1987) of this huge work is in itself a major contribution to English poetry.

If Estonians and Finns can converse with each other, the languages of the other two Baltic States, Latvian and Lithuanian, closely related though not mutually intelligible, constitute an independent Indo-European branch, the archaic grammars of which have long fascinated philologists as bringing us closer to the original Ur-IndoEuropean speech than any other extant language. (Lithuanian nouns have seven cases and singular, dual and plural forms.) The Baltic mythology, which Latvian and Lithuanian folk-poetry and theatre draw on, is a peculiarly rich and fascinating one, far too little known in the rest of Europe; it can stand up to any comparison with the better disseminated Norse and Finnish mythologies and has attractive bucolic and cosmological features all its own.

The repressive political past predicaments of Latvia and Lithuania, as of Estonia, have impaired the cultural developments that one feels that these societies were entitled to, though their post-*perestroika* history has been artistically galvanising. Estonia has in Jaan Kross and Jaan Kaplinski a novelist and a poet respectively of indisputable world stature. In both writers the proximity of the other Scandinavian societies — particularly Sweden to which so many Balts emigrated in the war years and even after — is palpable. The culturally important Jewish element in the Baltic lands, especially in Lithuania and in the city sometimes Lithuanian, sometimes Polish of Vilna or Vilnius, is not considered in this book which focuses primarily on post-World War Two literature. The writers in Yiddish from this area are dealt with in the *Babel Guide to Yiddish Fiction in Translation* (London: 2000).

In the early 1990s much energy went into the intensification of the centuries-old bonds between the Baltic and Scandinavian societies: there was the Saltsjöbaden agreement of 1993 of cooperation between Baltic Sea nations, and the establishment of an institution for Baltic studies on the island of Gotland.

The arts of peace and the promotion of peace have been of central concern and importance to the Nordic cultures and preeminent in their self-presentation. With nineteenth century beginnings - the work of Bishop Grundtvig in Denmark, the growth of cooperative movements and adult education centres (Folk High Schools) everywhere — the Scandinavian countries, less gravely affected by the Depression than most other developed societies, accomplished in the 1930s a popular embrace of a social ideal and programme that was not only for home consumption but for example and even export. Perhaps the official Swedish term for it, *folkhem* ('people's home') sums it up better than any other: a good society is where as many members feel as fully 'at home, 'at ease' as possible. In the post-Second World War years, the Nordic nations — perhaps most conspicuously the extremely affluent Swedes unburdened by war debts (in fact the country, as a neutral, sold strategic material and arms to both Nazi Germany and the allies) devoted themselves to a humane communitarianism that became the envy of the civilised world (hence the double-meaning of the term 'Swedish Model') and the admiration of the Third World to which they were oustandingly generous in money, time and manpower.

All too often the new and innovative, after getting taken up (mostly belatedly) elsewhere, become accepted so that credit for them doesn't go where it should. The Scandinavian societies (partly because of their relaxed laws on what the rest of the world called pornography) became, in the 1950s and earlier 1960s, almost synonymous with sex. With the sexual revolution of the later 1960s, the humane and inclusive Nordic sexual ethic, founded on humanist acknowledgment of the desires and needs of the human body and psyche, has too often gone unsaluted. How refreshing and how challenging it was in those years to meet, for example, in serious yet popularly addressed publications or films from Sweden and Denmark presentation of masturbation, contrasting with the fear-laden medieval rubbish so often doled out else, as a necessary release for an individual, or of orgasmic satisfaction as every bit as important for the woman as for the man. Commonplace enough views now, but not then.

With provisos Scandinavian culture — which can be, I believe, legitimately viewed as an entity — should be praised as one of the great accomplishments of the century now ending. And also surely as one of the most exemplary. Home, the community, the Nature that lies beyond these — how individuals find themselves in their relationship to these are surely matters of supreme importance to everybody. In keeping with its egalitarianism Scandinavian culture is not exclusive, does not only apply to those living in Norway, Sweden, Denmark or Finland, but is concerned with how most amply to be human and a part too of a great created whole.

PB

Database of Scandinavian & Baltic fiction available in English

This database is a resource for anyone who wants to read Scandinavian and Baltic writers in English. Its main goal is to let you know what's been translated. The reviews section of the guide contains many books that are currently in print and that you can find or order at your bookshop now but this section includes the majority of the contemporary (written after 1900) fiction translated from Danish, Estonian, Faroese, Finnish, Icelandic, Latvian, Lithuanian, Norwegian, Sami and Swedish and and published in the UK and the USA since 1945.

Please note that there may be discrepancies in the spelling of names and titles in foreign languages and that the *Babel Guide* is primarily a guide to reading in English.

Price and availability of books changes from day to day as publishers withdraw, re-price and reprint. This database is a handy guide but for the latest information on a particular book ask your bookseller or librarian. A few prices are included, but again please check with your bookseller.

Abbreviations:
HB = hard cover edition
PB = paperback edition
OP = out of print

Record details:
Author (surname)
Author (first name)
English title
Year this edition was published in the USA/Scandinavia/Canada
Original language title
Year published in the original language
Translator's name
US etc. Publisher
Pages
Hardback or paperback
Price in $
UK Publisher
Year this edition was published in the UK
Pages
Hardback or paperback
Price in £

SCANDINAVIA & THE BALTICS (GENERAL)

ANTHOLOGY
Hallmundsson, Hallberg (Ed)
Anthology Of Scandinavian Literature, An. From The Viking Period To The 20Th Century
Collier Books: NY
1965
362

ANTHOLOGY
Michael March (Ed)
Description Of A Struggle. The Picador Book Of Contemporary East European Prose
Picador: London
1994
404

ANTHOLOGY
Moseley, Christopher (Ed)
From Baltic Shores
Norvik: Norwich
1994
264
9.95

ANTHOLOGY
Sperry, Margaret (Ed)
Scandinavian Stories
Sperry, Margaret
F. Watts: New York, NY
1971
287

DENMARK & FAROES

ABELL
Kjeld
Three From Minikoi
De tre fra minikoi
Roughton
Secker: London
1960
319

ALLEN
Johannes
Young Love
Ung leg
Walford, Naomi
Knopf : NY
1959
215

ANDERSEN
Benny
Pillows
Puderne
Curbstone: CT
1983
184
8.95

ANDERSEN
Benny
Selected Stories
Curbstone: CT
1982
96
7.95

ANDERSEN
Maria
Howlin' Marie
Lene bourgeat
Elgaard, Elin
Moonbeam, Ont., Penumbra Press
1985
140

ANTHOLOGY
Bredsdorff, Elias
Contemporary Danish Prose; An Anthology
Bredsdorff, Elias
Greenwood P.: Westport, CT
1974,1958
375

ANTHOLOGY
Brask,Per K. (Ed)
Double Danish: Contemporary Short Stories From Denmark.
Dunvegan Ont., Cormorant Books
1991
120
Cormorant Books
1991.

ANTHOLOGY
Brønner, Hedin(Ed)
Faroese Short Stories
Brønner, Hedin
Twayne Publishers: New York, NY
1972
hb
267

ANTHOLOGY
Heepe, Evelyn & Heltberg, Niels
Modern Danish Authors
Heepe, Evelyn
R. West : Philadelphia
1978
222

ANTHOLOGY
Heepe, Evelyn & Heltberg, Niels (Ed)
Modern Danish Authors
Heepe, Evelyn
Folcroft Library Editions: Folcroft, PA
1974,1946
222

ANTHOLOGY
Holm, Sven
Devil's Instrument, The & Other Stories
Hestrup-Jensen, Paula
P.Owen: London
1971
hb
266

ANTHOLOGY
Jansen, Frederik J.B. & Mitchell, Phillip M.
Anthology Of Danish Literature
Southern Illinois U.P.: Carbondale, IL

1972
606
ANTHOLOGY
Heitmann, Annegret
No Man's Land. An Anthology Of Modern Danish Women Writers.
Norvik: Norwich
1987
211
9.95
BALLE
Solvej
According To The Law: Four Accounts Of Mankind
Ifølge loven
Barbara Haveland
Harvill: London
1996
89
9.99
BANG
Herman
Katinka
Ved vejen
Nunnally, Tiina
Seattle, Fjord Press
1990
174
1990
hb
BANG
Herman
Tina
Tina
Athlone: London
1984
hb
224
14
BJARNHOF
Karl
Good Light, The
Det gode lys
1957
Walford, Naomi
Knopf : NY
1962
272
Methuen: London
1960
264
BJARNHOF
Karl
Stars Grow Pale, The
Stjernerne blegner
1956
Walford, Naomi
1959
Methuen: London
1958
hb
262
BJARNHOF
Karl
Stars Grow Pale, The
Stjernerne blegner
1956
Walford, Naomi
Penguin: Middx.
1960
hb
267
BLICHER
Steen S.
Twelve Stories
Larsen, Hanna Astrup
Kraus Reprint: New York, NY
1972
305
BLICHER
Steen Steensen
Diary Of A Parish Clerk, The
Mermaid P: Seattle
1991
BLICHER
Steen Steensen
Diary Of A Parish Clerk, The
Paula Hostrup-Jessen
Athlone P: London
1996
hb
185
18
BLIXEN
Karen
Anecdotes Of Destiny
Penguin: Middx.
1986 (1958
pb
244
3.95
BLIXEN
Karen
Anecdotes Of Destiny
Books for Libraries Press: Freeport, NY
1971
313
Penguin: Middx.
1986
pb
244
3.95
BLIXEN
Karen
Anecdotes Of Destiny
Michael Joseph: London
1958
hb
BLIXEN
Karen
Angelic Avengers, The
Gengældelsens veje
Penguin: Middx.
1986
pb
304
3.95
BLIXEN
Karen
Angelic Avengers, The
Gengældelsens veje
University of Chicago Press, Chicago, IL
1975
304
University of Chicago Press, London
1976

hb
304
3.95
BLIXEN
Karen
Carnival
Entertainments And
Posthumous Tales.
Grafton: London
1987,1977
pb
315
BLIXEN
Karen
Carnival
Grafton
1987
pb
315
3.50
BLIXEN
Karen
Carnival
Efterladte fortaellinger
Heinemann
1977
338
BLIXEN
Karen
Dreaming Child And
Other Stories, The
Penguin: Middx.
1995
pb
86
0.60
BLIXEN
Karen
Ehrengard
Penguin: Middx.
1986
pb
2.95
BLIXEN
Karen
Ehrengard
Penguin: Middx.
1998
pb
111
6.99
BLIXEN
Karen
Last Tales
Sidste fortellinger
New York, Vintage Books
1991
341
Penguin: Middx.
1986 (1957)
pb
341
3.95
BLIXEN
Karen
Last Tales
Sidste fortællinger
Vintage Books: New York,
NY
1975
341
Penguin: Middx.
1986
pb
341
3.95
BLIXEN
Karen
Letters From Africa,
1914-31.
Breve fra afrika
Born, Anne
Pan
1986
pb
473
3.99
BLIXEN
Karen
Letters From Africa
Breve fra afrika
Anne Born
Penguin: Middx.
1986
pb
473
3.95
BLIXEN
Karen
Letters From Africa
Breve fra afrika
Anne Born
Weidenfeld
1981
hb
BLIXEN
Karen
Winter's Tales
New York, Vintage
1993
313
Penguin: Middx.
1983
pb
BODELSEN
Anders
Freezing Point
Frysepunktet
Joan Tate
Michael Joseph: London
1971
174
BODELSEN
Anders
Hit And Run, Run,
Run
Hoendelight uheld
C.Bly
Penguin: Middx.
1971
pb
219
BODELSEN
Anders
Operation Cobra
Operation cobra
Joan Tate
Pelham: London
1976
pb
141
BODELSEN
Anders
Silent Partner, The
Toenk pa et tal
David Hohnen
Penguin: Middx.
1978
pb
222

BODELSEN
Anders
Straus
Christensen, Nadia &
Taylor, Alexander
Harper & Row: New York, NY
1974
147
BORBERG
Svend
Sinner And Saint
Snyder og helgen
Tolman, Rosco N.
San Francisco, EM Text
1992
127
BRANNER
Hans Christian
No Man Knows The Night
Ingen kender natten
1955
Roughton, A.I.
Secker
1958
hb
301
BRANNER
Hans Christian
No Man Knows The Night
Ingen kender natten
1955
Roughton, A.I.
Brown & Watson
1966
318
BRANNER
Hans Christian
Riding Master, The
Rytteren
1949
Roughton, A.I.
British Book Centre: New York, NY
1952
159
BRANNER
Hans Christian
Story Of Börge, The
Historien om börge
Planck, Kristi
Twayne Publishers: New York, NY
1973
196
BRANNER
Hans Christian
Two Minutes Of Silence ; Selected Short Stories
Dan
Vance, Vera L.
U. of Wisconsin P. : Madison
1966
211
BRÖGGER
Suzanne
Fighting Pig's Too Tough To Eat, A
Norvik: Norwich
1997
pb
282
10.95
BØDKER,
Cecil
Leopard, The
Poulsen, Gunnar
Atheneum: New York, NY
1975
186
CHRISTENSEN
Lars Saaybe
Herman
Steven Michael Nordby
White Pine P. USA
1992
pb
186
12.00
DAVIDSEN
Leif
Russian Singer. The
Russike sangerinde, den
Schiott, Jorgen
Andre Deutsch: London
1991
hb
277
12.99
DAVIDSEN
Leif
Russian Singer. The
Random House
1991
DAVIDSEN
Leif
Sardine Deception, The
Uhellige alliancer
Nunnally, Tiina
Fjord Press: Seattle
1986
199
DAVIDSEN
Leif
Sardine Deception, The
Fjord Press: Seattle
1986
DAVIDSEN
Leif
Unholy Alliances. The
Uhellige alliancer
Nunnally, Tiina
Hale: London
1988
hb
196
10.95
DINESEN
Isak; *SEE* under
BLIXEN, Karen
DITLEVSEN
Tove
Complete Freedom, And Other Stories
Brondum, Jack
Williamantic, CT., Curbstone Press
1982
87
DITLEVSEN
Tove
Early Spring

Der tidlige forår
Nunnally, Tiina
Seattle WA, Seal Press
1985
227
London, Women's Press
1986
227
DITLEVSEN
Tove
Faces, The
Fjord Press
1991
19.95
EWALD
Carl
Battle Of The Bees And Other Stories, The
Sperry, Margaret
Crane, Russak : NY
1977
114
FREUCHEN
Peter
Law Of Larion, The
Ramsden, Evelyn
McGraw-Hill: New York, NY
1952
313
FALK-RONNE
Arne
Back To Tristan
Tilbage til tristan
Allen & Unwin: London
1967
151
GARUP
Olaf Baun
Crime In Fiction: 12 Short Stories
Ravn, Ole
Systime: Herning, Denmark
1994
208
GJEDDE
Georg
I, A Man
Jeg en mand
Granada Pub: NY
1978
223
GOLDSCHMIDT
Meir
Jew, A
En jøde
Ober, Kenneth H
Garland: NY
1990
hb
328
GRESS
Elsa
Simurg, The
Simurghen.
Tr. by Author
Quartet: London
1989
hb
265
11.95
GUNNARSSEN
Gunnar
Black Cliffs
Wisconsin UP
14.95
HANSEN
Eva Hemmer
Scandal In Troy
Skandale i troja
Grimm, Dorothy F.&
Karrel, Sven O.
Popular Library : NY
1959
126
HANSEN
Eva Hemmer
Scandal In Troy
Grimm, Dorothy F. &
Karell, Sven O.
Random House: New York, NY
1958
177
HANSEN
Martin A
Liar, The
Egglishaw, John Jepson
Quartet: London
1986
pb
205
4.95
HANSEN
Martin Alfred
Against The Wind: Stories
Schow, H. Wayne
F. Ungar Pub. Co. : NY
1979
276
HANSEN
Martin Alfred
Lucky Kristoffer
Lykkelige kristoffer
Egglishaw, John Jepson
Twayne Publishers: New York, NY
1974
377
HASSEL
Sven
Assignment Gestapo
Corgi: London
1977
pb
347
HASSEL
Sven
Blitzfreeze
Corgi: London
pb
3.5
HASSEL
Sven
Blitzfreeze
Jeg sa dem do
London, Severn House
1981
HASSEL
Sven
Bloody Road To Death
Corgi: London
1977
pb
317
HASSEL

Sven
Bloody Road To Death
Bowie, Tim
London, Alison & Busby
1979
pb
317
3.5
HASSEL
Sven
Commissar, The
Bowie, Tim
Corgi: London
1982
pb
367
3.5
HASSEL
Sven
Commissar, The
Bowie, Tim
London, Severn House
1985
368
HASSEL
Sven
Comrades Of War
Frontkammerater
Lyngstad, Sverre
Fawcett : Greenwich, Conn.
1963
304
Transworld
1968
316
HASSEL
Sven
Comrades Of War
Frontkammerater
Lyngstad, Sverre
London, Severn House
1983
316
HASSEL
Sven
Court Martial
Corgi: London
1979
pb
319
HASSEL
Sven
Legion Of The Damned
De fordomtes legion
Michael, Maurice
Allen & Unwin: London
1980
hb
297
HASSEL
Sven
Legion Of The Damned, The
De fordomtes legion
Michael, Maurice
Farrar, Straus, Cudahy : NY
1959
277
HASSEL
Sven
Liquidate Paris
Corgi: London
1991
pb
HASSEL
Sven
Liquidate Paris
Likvider Paris!
London, Severn House
1980
288
HASSEL
Sven
March Battalion
Marchbataillon
Transworld
1970
pb
220
HASSEL
Sven
Monte Cassino
London, Severn House
1980
252
HASSEL
Sven
Monte Cassino
London, Severn House
1984
252
HASSEL
Sven
Ogpu Prison
Gpu-faengslet
Corgi
1982
pb
3.5
HASSEL
Sven
Reign Of Hell
Corgi: London
pb
2.99
HASSEL
Sven
Reign Of Hell
London, Allison & Busby
1979
270
HASSEL
Sven
S.S. General
Ss-generalen
Bantam Books: NY
1972
281
Corgi: London
1972
pb
286
HASSEL
Sven
Ss General
Corgi: London
1979
pb
1.25
HEIBERG
Johan Ludvig
Soul After Death, A
Mermaid P: Seattle
1991

HEINESEN
William
Black Cauldron, The
Den sorte gryde
1949
W.Glyn Jones
Hippocrene
14.95
Dedalus: Sawtry, Cambs.
1992
pb
363
8.95
HEINESEN
William
Kingdom Of The Earth, The
Moder syvstjerne
Brønner, Hedin
Twayne Publishers: New York, NY
1974
171
HEINESEN
William
Laterna Magica
Laterna magica
Nunnally, Tiina
Seattle, Fjord Press
1987
159
Dedalus: Sawtry, Cambs.
1990
pb
6.99
HEINESEN
William
Lost Musicians, The
Dedalus: Sawtry, Cambs.
1990
pb
6.99
HEINESEN
William
Lost Musicians, The
De fortabte spillemænd
Friis, Erik J.
Twayne Publishers: New York, NY
1971
364
HEINESEN
William
Winged Darkness And Other Stories. The
Bronner, Hedin
New York, Irvington
1983
220
Wilfion Bks
hb
9.95
HOFFMANN
Poul
Brazen Serpent, The
Fortress : Philadelphia
1963
288
HOLBERG
Ludvig
Peder Paars
U. of Nebraska P. : Lincoln
1962
HOLK
Agnele
Strange Friends
Pyramid : NY
1963
190
HOLK
Agnete
Strange Friends
Hinton, Anthony
Pyramid Books: New York, NY
1955
190
HOLM
Morgen
I A Sailor
Jeg en-somand
Mayflower: UK
1970
pb
204
HOLM
Siv
I Am A Woman
Jeg, en kvinde
Brown, J W
Mayflower-Dell
1967
pb
220
HOLM
Siv
I Am A Woman
Jeg, en kvinde
Brown, J W
New English Library
1970
pb
125
HOLM
Susanne
I, Susanne
Jeg en elsekerinde
Mayflower
1974
pb
125
HOLM
Sven
Termush
Sylvia Clayton
Faber: London
1969
110
HOLM
Sverre
I A Man
Jeg en mand
Mayflower
1978
223
HOLM
Tine
I, A Teenager
Jeg - en pige
Mayflower
1971
pb
126
HØEG
Peter
Borderliners
Harvill: London
1995

hb
251
HØEG
Peter
Borderliners
De mƒske egnede
Doubleday; Toronto
1994
Harvill: London
1995
pb
251
9.95
HØEG
Peter
History Of Danish Dreams, The
Forestilling om det tyvende århundrede
Harvill: London
1996
hb
339
14.99
HØEG
Peter
Miss Smilla's Feeling For Snow
Frøken smillas fornemmelse for sne
Nunnally, Tiina
HarperCollins: London
1994 (1993
pb
410
4.99
HØEG
Peter
Miss Smilla's Feeling For Snow
Frøken smillas fornemmelse for sne
Nunnally, Tiina
Windsor Large Print: Bath
1996
hb
586
15.99
HØEG
Peter
Smilla's Sense Of Snow.
Nunnally, Tiina
Farrar: NY
1993
453
Harvill: London
1993
HØEG
Peter
Tales Of The Night
Fortallinger on natten
Harvill: London
1997
hb
308
14.99
HØEG
Peter
Woman And The Ape, The
1996
Q
Haveland, Barbara
Harvill: London
1996
hb
229
15.99
HØEG
Peter
Woman And The Ape, The
Kvinden og aben
Haveland, Barbara
Harvill: London
1997
pb
228
6.99
JACOBSEN
Jens P.
Marie Grubbe, A Lady Of The Seventeenth Century
Larsen, Hanna Astrup & Raphael, Robert
Twayne Publishers: New York, NY
1975
261
JACOBSEN
Jens Peter
Marie Grubbe
Fru marie grubbe
Larsen, Hanna Astrup
American-Scandinavian Foundation: New York, NY
1952
276
JACOBSEN
Jens P.
Mogens, And Other Stories
Grabow, Anna
Books for Libraries P.: Freeport, NY
1972
150
JACOBSEN
Jens Peter
Mogens & Other Stories
1882
Nunnally, Tilna
12.00
Fjord: Seattle
1994
pb
157
JACOBSEN
Jens-Peter
Niels Lyhne
Niels lyhne
Nunnally, Tiina
Fjord Press
1990
212
Fjord Press
1990
JACOBSEN
Jorgen-Frantz
Barbara
Barbara
Johnston, George
Norvik: Norwich
1993
pb
230

9.95
JACOBSEN
Jorgen-Frantz
Barbara
Bannister, E
Penguin: Middx.
1948
pb
246
JENSEN
Carsten
Earth In The Mouth
Jorden i munden
Anne Born
McClelland & Stewart: Toronto
1994
pb
Picador: London
1994
pb
108
4.99
JENSEN
Johannes Vilhelm
Fall Of The King, The
Bower, Alan G.
Seattle Wash., Mermaid Press
1992
287
JENSEN
Niels
Days Of Courage: A Medieval Adventure
Stallybrass, Oliver
Harcourt Brace Jovanovich: NY
1973
188
JENSEN
Virginia Allen
Catching
Collins: London
1986
KNUDSEN
Poul E.
Challenge, The
Vaeddemålet
Kingsland, L. W.
Macmillan : NY
1963
264
LARSEN
Michael
Uncertainty
Uden sikker viden
Lone Thygesen Blecher and George Blecher
Harcourt: NY
1996
Sceptre: London
1997
hb
260
10
LINDEMANN
Kelvin
Red Umbrellas, The
En aften i kolera-aaret
Greenwood P.: Westport, CT
1975
214
LUNDBERG
Knud
Olympic Hope, The
Det olympiske håb
Hansen, Eiler & Luscombe, William
Sportshelf : New Rochelle, NY
1958
171
Stanley Paul
1958
171
MADSEN
Svend Åge
Days With Diam
Norvik: Norwich
1994
pb
245
9.95
MADSEN
Svend Åge
Virtue And Vice In The Middle Time
Tugt og utugt i mellemtiden
Ogier, James M.
New York, Garland Pub.
1992
hb
573
Norvik: Norwich
1994
pb
245
MATHIESON
Egon
Blue-Eyed Pussy, The
Mis med de blå øjne
Rye, Karen
Doubleday: Garden City, NY
1951
111
MEYER
Niels
Revolt From The Centre
Boyars: London
1983
hb
9.95
MEYER
Niels
Revolt From The Centre
Boyars
1983
pb
5.95
MICHAELIS
Karin
Dangerous Age, The : Letters And Fragments From A Woman's Diary
Evanston Ill., Northwestern University
1991
215
MIELCHE
Hakon
Amazon, The
Hodge: Edinburgh
1949

hb
304
MOLLER
Kris
Shadow Man. The
A.S.P, Benfleet
1989
pb
4.5
MØRCH
Dea Trier
Evening Star
Aftenstjernen
Joan Tate
Lincoln, University of Nebraska Press
1988
268
Serpent's Tail
1988
pb
6.95
MØRCH
Dea Trier
Winter's Child
Serpent's Tail
1986
hb
9.95
MØRCH
Dea Trier
Winter's Child
Vinterborn
Serpent's Tail
1986
pb
6.95
NEXO
Martin Anderson
Pelle The Conqueror. Vol. 2 Apprenticeship
Fjord P
1991
NEXØ
Martin Andersen
Pelle The Conqueror
Pelle erobreren
1906-10
Murray, Steven T.
Seattle, Fjord Press
1991
NIELSEN
Torben
Unsuccessful Man, An
Galgesangen
Helweg, Marianne
Harper & Row: New York, NY
1976
147
OPPENHEIM
Ralph
Barbarian In India, A
En barbar i indien
John, Katherine
Nelson : NY
1957?
160
OPPENHEIM
Ralph
Door Of Death, The
Tufton, Joyce
Harvill: London
1948
hb
239
ØRUM
Poul
Nothing But The Truth
Kun sandheden
Barclay, Kenneth
Pantheon Books: New York, NY
1976
253
Gollancz: London
1976
254
ØRUM
Poul
Scapegoat: A Mystery
Syndebuk
Barclay, Kenneth
Pantheon Books: New York, NY
1975
255
ØRUM
Poul
Whipping Boy, The
Syndebuk
Gollancz: London
1975
hb
256
PALUDAN
Jacob
Jorgen Stein
Malmberg, Carl
U. of Wisconsin P. : Madison
1966
727
PANDURO
Leif
Kick Me In The Traditions
Malmberg, Carl
Eriksson - Taplinger : NY
1961
217
PONTOPPIDAN ET AL.
Royal Guest And Other Classical Danish Narrative, The
Mitchell, P. M. & Ober, Kenneth H.
University of Chicago Press: Chicago
1977
242
RASMUSSEN
Gerhard
No Leave For The Captain
Kaptajnen behover ingen orlov
1956
Savill, Mervin
Crowell : NY
1958
160
Kimber
1958

160
RIFBJERG
Klaus
Anna
Curbstone P. CT
RIFBJERG
Klaus
Witness To The Future
De hellige aber
Nunnally, T & Murray, Steve
Fjord P
1987
214
RYTTER
JøRgen
Autumn Crocus
Høst tidløs
Michael, Maurice
Chatto: London
1963
153
SCHERFIG
Hans
Idealists, The
Walford, Naomi
Elek
1949
hb
224
SCHERFIG
Hans
Idealists, The
Idealister
Hugus, Frank
Seattle Wash., Fjord Press
1991
270
SCHERFIG
Hans
Missing Bureaucrat, The
Forsvundne fuldmegtig
Hugus, Frank
Seattle Wash., Fjord Press
1988
207
SCHERFIG
Hans
Stolen Spring
Hugus, Frank
Seattle Wash., Fjord Press
1986
195
SCHMIDT
Ane
In The Flesh
Anne Born
Overlook P
1996
hb
17.95
SEEBERG
Peter
Impostor, The
Fugls fode
University of Nebraska Press
1990
113
SKOU-HANSEN
Tage
Naked Trees, The
De nøgne træer
1957
John, Katherine
Cape
1958
222
SOYA
Carl E.
Bedroom Mazurka: Seven Erotic Stories
Tilegnet boccaccio
Sphere
1973
pb
156
SOYA
Carl E.
Seventeen (1)
Sytten: erindringer og reflesioner
Carl Malmberg
Sphere
1974
pb
163
SOYA
Carl E.
Seventeen (2)
Sytten: erindringer og reflesioner (2-3)
Carl Malmberg
Sphere
1974
pb
187
STANGERUP
Henrik
Man Who Wanted To Be Guilty, The
Manden der ville vaere skyldig
Gress-Wright, David
M. Boyars: London
1982
124
STANGERUP
Henrik
Road To Lagoa Santa, The
Vejen til lag
Bluestone, Barbara
New York, M. Boyars
1984
284
London, Paladin
1988
pb
STANGERUP
Henrik
Road To Lagoa Santa, The
Vejen til lag
Bluestone, Barbara
M. Boyars: London
1983
288
STANGERUP
Henrik
Seducer, The It Is Hard To Die In Dieppe
Det er svert at do i dieppe
Martin, Sean
New York, M. Boyars
1990
288

SØRENSEN
Villy
Downfall Of The Gods, The
Ragnarok
Hostrup-Jersen, Paula
Nebraska UP: Lincoln, Ne
1989
123
SØRENSEN
Villy
Harmless Tales
Ufarhige historier
Hostrup-Jersen, Paula
Norvik: Norwich
1991
137
7.95
SØRENSEN
Villy
Tutelary Tales
Hostrup-Jersen, Paula
Lincoln, University of Nebraska Press
1988
244
Norvik: Norwich
1991
137
THOMSEN
Richard BøRge
Tyrants, The
De stærke viljer
1952
Walford, Naomi
Putnam
1957
hb
245
John Lane
1957
192
THORUP
Kirsten
Baby
Baby
Christensen, Nadia
Baton Rouge, Louisiana State University Press
1980
208
WILLUMSEN
Dorrit
If It Really Were A Film
Hvis det virkelig var en film
Rasmussen, Anne Marie
Willimantic, CT,
Curbstone Press
1982
126
WILLUMSEN
Dorrit
Marie, A Novel About The Life Of Madame Tussaud
Crampton, Patricia
London, Bodley Head
1986
hb
213

ESTONIA

ANTHOLOGY
A. Eelmäe (ed)
Sailor's Guardian, The. A Selection Of Estonian Short Stories
Hea meremeeste hoidja
T. Onu, E. Mannermaa, I. Anvelt. Tallinn
Tallinn, Perioodika
1984
160
ANTHOLOGY
E. Mallene (Ed)
Play, The. Short Stories Of Young Estonian Authors
Mäng (?)
A. Jõgi, I. Anvelt, E. Sillamägi and others
Tallinn, Perioodika
1984
176
ANTHOLOGY
E. Moroz (Ed)
Love That Was, The... Stories Of Estonian Writers
H.Smith, J. Robinson, R. Daglish and others
Moscow, Progress
1982
422
ANTHOLOGY
K.Pruul (Ed)
Estonian Short Stories. Writings From An Unbound Europe. J.Kross, A.Valton, M.Unt,M.Saat, M.Berg, T.Raudam,T.Vint, Ü.Mattheus, J.Ehlvest
R. Poom
Northwestern University Press, Evanston
1996
pb
277
14.95
ANTHOLOGY
Oras, A (ed)
Estonian Literary Reader
Bloomington, Indiana University, 1963. 387 pp.Bloomington, Indiana University
1963
387
ANTHOLOGY
Pranspill, Andres
Estonian Anthology; Intimate Stories Of Life, Love, Labor, And War, Of
Pranspill, Andres
The Compiler: Milford, CT
1958
320
BEEKMAN
Vladimir
Pilots In The Night

Aru, Mart
Tallin, Periodika
1988
151
BEEKMAN
Vladimir
Year Of The Donkey, The
God osla
Tudge, Liv
Moskva, Progress
1987
216
FREUCHEN
Peter
Ivalu, The Eskimo Wife
Ivalu
Jusztis, Janos & Ehrich, Edward Price
AMS Press: New York, NY
1975
332
HINT
Aadu
Windswept Shore, The
Tuuline rand
M. Rauk
Tallinn, Perioodika
1980
360
JOGI
Aino Et Al
Piper, The
Tallin, Periodika
1987
199
KALLAS
Aino
Eros The Slayer
A. Matson (from Finnish)
London
1927
KALLAS
Aino
White Ship, The
Valge laev
A. Matson
New York
1924
256
London
1924
KALLAS
Aino
Wolf's Bride, The
Hundimõrsja
A. Matson (from Finnish)
London
1930
114
KALLAS
Teet
So Much Sunshine
Nii palju päikest
I. Anvelt
Tallinn, Perioodika
1984
144
KROSS
Jaan
Conspiracy And Other Stories, The
Vandenôu ja teisi jutte
Dickens, E.
Harvill: London
1995
224
KROSS
Jaan
Czar's Madman, The
Keisri hull
Hollo, Anselm (from Finnish)
New York, Pantheon Books
1993
hb
362
Harvill: London
1992
352
KROSS
Jaan
Professor Martens' Departure
Professor martensi ärasôit
Hollo, Anselm
New York, New Press
1994
hb
295
Harvill: London
1994
295
KROSS
Jaan
Rock From The Sky, The
Taevakivi
Costello-Jones, Barry from Russian
Moskva, Raduga
1983
hb
341
KUUSBERG
Paul
Raindrops
Mutt, Oleg
Tallin, Eesti raamat
1988
364
LUTS
Oskar
Spring
Kevade
A. Jõgi and M. Rauk
Tallin, Periodika
1983
306
PEETS
Leonora
Women Of Marrakech : Record Of A Secret Sharer, 1930-1970
Taagepera, Rein
Durham N.C., Duke University Press
1988
215
PROMET
Lilli
Summer's Painting, A. and Other Stories
F. Glagoleva et al
Moscow, Raduga

1984
424
RANNAP
Jaan
Maari's Summer
Maari suvi
Jogi, Aino
Tallin, Periodika
1987
159
RAUD
Eno
Three Jolly Fellows
Naksitrallid
E. Mannermaa
Perioodika, Tallinn
1982-5
4v.s
SMUUL
Juhan
Antarctica Ahoy! The Ice Book
Jäine raamat
D. Skvirsky (from Rus.)
Moscow, Foreign Languages Publishing House
1963
311
TAMMSAARE
A.H.
Miniatures
Miniatuurid
M. Rauk
Tallinn, Eesti Raamat
1977
48
TAMMSAARE
A.H.
Misadventures Of The New Satan, The
B. Põrgupõhja uus vanapagan
O. Shartze
Moscow, Progress
1978
312
TRAAT
Mats
Inger
Inger
Tillemann, Helmi
Tallinn, Periodika
1989
232
TUGLAS
Friedebert
Riders In The Sky. Selection Of Short Stories
Taevased ratsanikud
Mutt, Oleg
Tallin, Periodika
1982
173
UNT
Mati
Autumn Ball, The. Scenes Of City Life.
Sügisball
M. Aru
Tallinn, Perioodika
1985
192
VETEMAA
Enn
Three Small Novels
R. Daglish
Tallinn, Eesti Raamat
1976
196
VILDE
Eduard
Milkman Of The Manor
M. Rauk
Tallinn, Eesti Raamat
1976
196

FINLAND

ANTHOLOGY
Dauenhauer, R (Ed)
Snow In May: An Anthology Of Finnish Writing, 1945 - 1972
Fairleigh Dickinson University Press: Rutherford, NJ
1978
389
ANTHOLOGY
Hawkins, H &
Lehtonen, S (eds)
On The Border: An Anthology Of Finnish Writing
Carcanet: Manchester
1995
pb
164
9.95
ANTHOLOGY
Carpelan, Bo et al (eds)
A Way to Measure Time
Finnish Literary Society: Helsinki (Finland)
1992
435
ANTHOLOGY
Jarvenpa, Aili Et Al
Sampo, The Magic Mill: A Collection Of Finnish-American Writing
Minneapolis MN, New Rivers Press
1989
406
ANTHOLOGY
Väänänen-Jensen, Inkeri
Finnish Short Stories
Iowa City Iowa, Penfield Press
1991
238
JOENPELTO
Eeva
Maiden Walks Upon The Water, The
Neito kulkee vetten päällä.
Nelson, Therese Allen
Porvoo, WSOY Finland.
1991
460

JOENSUU
Matti Yrjänä
Stone Murders, The (Harjunpaa And The Stone Murders In UK)
Harjunpää ja poliisin poika
Taylor, Raili
New York, St. Martin's Press
1986
185
Gollancz: London
1986
hb
156
KIVI
Aleksis
Seven Brothers
Seitsemän veljestä
Matson, Alex
American - Scandinavian Foundation : NY
1962
347
KOKKO
Yrjö
Way Of The Four Winds, The
Walford, Naomi
Putnam: New York, NY
1956
286
KORPELA
Kaarlo
Money Maker, The; Or, The Sins Of The Fathers. Raggedy Maija
Rahan tekija. Renttu maija
Dahlbacka, Mildred Korpela
Dahlbacka: Waukegan, IL
1975
136
LINNA
Väinö
Unknown Soldier, The
Tuntematon sotilas
Putnam : NY
1959
316
Collins
1959
384
LINNA
Väinö
Unknown Soldier, The
Tuntematon sotilas
WSOY, Porvoo: Finland
1982
311
OTAVA
Merja
Priska
Portch, Elizabeth
Van Nostrand : Princeton
1964
176
Benn: London
1964
176
OTAVA
Merja
Priska
Priska kesästä kesääno
Portch, Elizabeth
Heinemann: London
1967
176
RINTALA
Paavo
Long Distance Patrol, The
Sissiluutnantti
Michael, M
Allen & Unwin: London
1967
183
SARIOLA
Mauri
Helsinki Affiar, The
Lavean tien laki, oikeudenkayntiromanni
Blair, Alan
Curtis Books: NY
1973
192
SARIOLA
Mauri
Torvick Affair, The
Blair, Alan
Walker: NY
1973
176
SILLANPÄÄ
Frans E.
Maid Silja, The: The History Of The Last Off-Shoot Of An Old Family Tree
Nuorena nukkunut
Matson, Alexander
N.S. Berg: Dunwoody, GA
1974
313
SILLANPÄÄ
Frans E.
Meek Heritage, The
Hurskas kurjuus
Matson, Alex & Pitkin, John R.
P.S. Eriksson: NY
1973
221
SILLANPÄÄ
Frans E.
People In The Summer Night
Ihmiset suviyössä
Blair, Alan
U. of Wisconsin P. : Madison
1966
158
SIMONSUURI
Kirsti
Boy Devil
Paholaispoika
Paddon, Seija
Toronto, Exile Editions.
1992
WALTARI
Mika
Egyptian, The
Sinuhe egyptiläinen
Walford, Naomi

Putnam: New York, NY
1949
503
WALTARI
Mika
Michael The Finn
Mikael karvajalka
48
Walford, Naomi
Dymock's Book Arcade:
Sydney, Australia
1951
363
WALTARI
Mika
Roman The
Ihmiskunnan viholliset
Tate, John
Putnam : NY
1966
637
WALTARI
Mika
Sinuhe The Egyptian
Sinuhe egyptiläinen
45
Walford, Naomi
Dymock's Book Arcade:
Sydney, Australia
1950
503
WALTARI
Mika
Sinuhe The Egyptian
Sinuhe egyptiläinen
Walford, Naomi
Chivers Large Print: Bath
1973
503
WALTARI
Mika
Sultan's Renegade, The
Mijel forfott
1950
Walford, Naomi
Dymock's Book Arcade:
Sydney, Australia
1951
471
Putnam
1951
471
WALTARI
Mika
Tree Of Dreams, The And Other Stories
Leino, L et al
Pocket Books : NY
1966
pb
248
Hodder: London
1965
251
WALTARI
Mika Toimi
Adventurer, The
Walford, Naomi
Putnam: New York, NY
1950
377
WALTARI
Mika Toimi
Dark Angel, The
Johannes angelos
Walford, Naomi
Dymock's Book Arcade:
Sydney, Australia
1953
320
WALTARI
Mika Toimi
Dark Angel, The
Johannes angelos
1952
Walford, Naomi
Putnam: New York, NY
1953
374
Putnam: London
1953
320
WALTARI
Mika Toimi
Dark Angel, The
Johannes angelos
1952
Walford, Naomi
WSOY, Porvoo: Finland
1989
401
New English Library:
London
1964
pb
302
WALTARI
Mika Toimi
Egyptian, The, A Novel
Sinuhe egyptiläinen
Walford, Naomi
G.P. Putnam's Sons
1956
503
WALTARI
Mika Toimi
Egyptian, The, A Novel
Sinuhe egyptiläinen
Walford, Naomi
HKI, Porvoo: Finland
1983
509
WALTARI
Mika Toimi
Etruscan, The
Turms kuolematon
Leino, Lily
Putnam: New York, NY
1958
381
WALTARI
Mika Toimi
Etruscan, The
Turms kuolematon
Ramsden, Evelyn
Hamilton
1958
284
WALTARI
Mika Toimi
Moonscape, And Other Stories
Kuun maisema
1953
Walford, Naomi
Putnam: New York, NY
1956

310
WALTARI
Mika Toimi
Nail Merchant At Midnight, A
Neljä päivänlaskua
Beesley, Alan
Putnam: New York, NY
1954
176
WALTARI
Mika Toimi
Stranger Came To The Farm, A
Vieras mies tuli taloon
1937
Walford, Naomi
Putnam: New York, NY
1952
254
WALTARI
Mika Toimi
Stranger Came To The Farm, A
Vieras mies tuli taloon
1937
Walford, Naomi
Dymock's Book Arcade: Sydney, Australia
1953
243
Brown & Watson
1960
156
WALTARI
Mika Toimi
Wanderer, The
Mikael hakim
Walford, Naomi
Putnam: New York, NY
1951
438
WALTARI
Mika Toimi
Etruscan, The
Pocket Books of Canada
1958
310
WALTARI
Mika Toimi
Secret Of The Kingdom, The
Valtakunnan salaisuus
Walford, N
Hamilton
1963
317
YLIRUUSI
Tauno
Hand In Hand
Käsi kädessä
Impola, Richard
Middlebury Vt., P.S. Eriksson Publisher
1992
164

ICELAND

ANTHOLOGY
Firchow, Evelyn Scherabon (Ed)
Icelandic Short Stories
Firchow, Evelyn Scherabon
Twayne Publishers: New York, NY
1975
214
ANTHOLOGY
Simpson, Jacqueline (Ed)
Northmen Talk, The; A Choice Of Tales From Iceland
U. of Wisconsin P. : Madison
1965
290
ANTHOLOGY
Wolf, Kirsten; Arny Hjaltadóttir (Eds)
Western Icelandic Short Stories
University of Manitoba, Winnipeg
1991
139
ASTTHORSSON
Gisli
Ink And Oilskin
Braudid og astin
Beste, Lawrence F
Winnipeg, Gunnars & Campbell
1985
122
BERGSSON
Gudberger
Swan, The
Scudder, B
Mare's Nest: London
1997
pb
8.95
BJARNSSON
Jóhann Magnús
Icelandic Sherlock Holmes, An
Steffensen, Jan B
Aalborg, Pinkerton (Denmark)
1994
EGGERTS
Thorsten
Paper King's Subjects, The
Excalibur: London
1991
pb
285
7.95
ELDJARN
Thorarinn
Blue Tower, The
1999
pb
Mare's Nest: London
9.95
GRIMSDOTTIR
Vigdis
Z - a Love Story
1998
Anne Jeeves
Mare's Nest: London
pb
9.95
GUDMUNDSSON
Einar Már

Angels Of The Universe
1993
Scudder, B
Mare's Nest: London
1995
pb
168
7.95
GUDMUNDSSON
Einar Már
Epilogue of the Raindrops
1994
Scudder, B
Mare's Nest: London
7.95
GUNNARSSON
Olafur
Trolls' Cathedral
Trollakirkja
1996
Mare's Nest: London
pb
8.95
LAXNESS
Halldór Kiljan
Atom Station, The
Atómstöðin
Magnusson, Magnus
Sag Harbor, N.Y., Second Chance P.
1982
202
Methuen: London
1961
201
LAXNESS
Halldór Kiljan
Fish Can Sing, The
Öll réttindi áskilin
Magnusson, Magnus
Methuen: London
1966
286
LAXNESS
Halldór Kiljan
Happy Warriors, The
Gerpla
1956
John, Katherine
Methuen: London
1958
287
LAXNESS
Halldór Kiljan
Independent People, An Epic
Sjálfstaett fólk
Thompson, J.A.
Greenwood Press: Westport, CT
1976
470
LAXNESS
Halldór Kiljan
Paradise Regained
Paradisaheimt
Magnusson, Magnus
Methuen: London
1962
253
LAXNESS
Halldór
Salka Valka
Lyon, F.H.
Verry : Conn.
1965
429
MAGNÚSSON
Sigurdur A.
Under A Dead Star
Undir kalstjörnu
Hallmundsson, May & Halberg
Winnipeg, Gunnars & Campbell
1985
147
OLAFSSON
Olafur Johann
Absolution
Fyrirgefning syndanna
Pantheon: NY
1991
259
Orion
1994
259
12.99
PILCHER
C.V
Icelandic Christian Classics
Oxford: New York, NY
1951
71
SIUGURDSSON
Olafur Jóhann
Pastor Bodvar's Letter
Penumbra
1985
SIUGURDSSON
Olafur Jóhann
Stars Of Constantinople, The
Boucher, Alan
State University Press
Baton Rouge, ouisiana
1992
224
SIGURDARDÓTTIR
Frída Á
Night Watch
1990
Edwardsen, K
Mare's Nest
1995
pb
168
7.95
THÓRDARSON
Agnar
Called Home
Kellog, Robert
Norvik: Norwich
206
10.95
THÓRDARSON
Agnar
A Medal Of Distinction : A Novel Of Iceland
Cook, Robert
New York, Hippocrene Books
1984
167
THÓRDARSSON

Agnar
Medal Of Distinction, A
Bjartad i bordid
Cook, Robert
New York, Hippocrene Books
1984
167
THÓRDARSON
Agnar
Sword, The
Ef sverd Þitt er stutt
Scach, Paul
Twayne Publishers: New York, NY
1972
277
VALSSON
Pal
Brushstrokes of Blue
David McDuff
Mare's Nest: London
pb
1994
6.95
VILHJÁLMSSON
Thor
Quick Quick Said The Bird
Fljótt fljótt, sagói fuglinn
O'Kane, John
Kapuskasing Ont., Penumbra Press
1987
206
VILHJÁLMSSON
Thor
Justice Undone
1995
Scudder, B
Mare's Nest: London
8.95

LATVIA

ANTHOLOGY
Berzing, Bud
Sex Songs of the Ancient Letts
University Books: NY
1969
306
ANTHOLOGY
Blue Sky will continue, The. Multilingual ed.
Liesma: Riga
1989
311
ANTHOLOGY
Zauberga, Leva et al
Bear's Ears: An Anthology of Latvian Literature
Helsinki University Press: Helsinki
1997
171
BELS
Alberts
Voice Of The Herald, The. The Investigator, Stories.
Sauceja balss. Izmekletajs.
Foreman, David
Moskva, Progress.
1980
368
CAKLAIS
Maris
Premonition. (Parallet Text)
Priekssajuta
Riga, Liesma
1987
145
DZILNA
Peteris
Bankruptcy, The
Bankrots
Riga, Avots.
1989
181
EGLITIS
Andrejs
Gallows Over Europe
London, John Calder
1984
105
EZERA
Regina
Swing, The
Kuehn, Tracy et al
Moskva, Raduga.
1984
318
LAMS
Visvaldis
Life Reviewed, A
Sinclair-Loutit, David
Moskva, Progress.
1979
253
LESINS
Knuts
Wine Of Eternity, The; Short Stories
Speirs, Ruth & Kundzins, Haralds
U. of Minnesota : Minneapolis
1959
179
SAULCERITE
Viese
Rainis. Quotations.
Rainis. Atdomas.
Zalite, Tamara
Riga, Liesma.
1980
125
SEINUS
Ignas
Ordeal Of Assad Pasha, The
Sealey, Raphael
Manyland Books : Woodhaven NY
1963
61
SKUJINS
Zigmunds
Man In His Prime, A
Moskva, Progress.
1981
288
VACIETIS
Ojars
Piano Concerto

Moskva, Raduga.
1983
272
ZARINS
Marger
Mock Faustus; Or, The Corrected Complemented Cooking-Book Ccc
Moskva, Raduga.
1987
302
ZIEDONIS
Imants
Flowers Of Ice
Callaghan, Barry
Riverdale-on-Hudson N.Y., Sheep Meadow Press
1987
127
ZIEDONIS
Imants
Selected Poems And Prose.
Dzejas un prozas izlase
Speirs, Ruth
Riga, Avots.
1980
125
ZIEDONIS
Imants
Thoughtfully I Read The Smoke
Dumus es lasu uzmanigi.
Rottenberg, Dorian
Moskva, Progess.
1980
278

LITHUANIA

ANTHOLOGY
Kelertas, Violeta (Ed)
Come Into My Time : Lithuania In Prose Fiction 1970-90
Urbana, University of Illinois Press.
1992
251
ANTHOLOGY
Skrupskelis, Alina
Lithuanian Writers In The West: An Anthology
Skrupskelis, Alina
Chicago, Lithuanian Library Press and Loyola University Press.
1979
387
BALTRINAS
Valius
Not Changed But Very Different
Ta pati ir visai kita
Armalyte, Olimpija et al.
Vil'njus, Mintis.
1981
163
BARANAUSKA
Antanas
Forest Of Anyksciai, The
Rastenis, Nadas
Lithuanian Days : Los Angeles
1956
41
BIELIAUSKAS
Alfonsas
Hills Of Vilnius, The
Ryley, Maureen
Moskva, Progress.
1990
373
BORUTA
Kazys
Wooden Miracles, Or, The Life And Works Of Vincas Dovine, Maker Of Gods
Translator's ed. Chicago, Morkunas Printing
1988
237
BUBNYS
Vytautas
Under Summer Skies
Po vasaros dangum
Foreman, David
Moskva, Progress.
1979
255
DONELAITIS
Kristionas
Seasons, The
Tempest, Peter
Vil'njus, Vaga
1985
159
GLIAUDA [J. GLIAUDYS]
Jurgis
House Upon The Sand
Namai ant smelio
Sealey, Raphael & Stark, Milton
Manyland Books : NY
1963
168
KAIRYS
Anatolijus
Under The Sword Of Damocles
Po damoklo kardu
Grazulis, Nijole
Chicago, Ill., Lithuanian Literary Associates
1980
251
KALEDA
Algis
Echoes Of The Years
Metu aidai
Dapkute, R.
Vil'njus, Mokslas.
1988
142
KAVALIUNAS
Vacys
Esther
Kavaliunas, Jolita
Vilnius, Vaga
1993
164

KREVE - MICKEVICIUS
Vincas
Herdsman And The Linden Tree, The
Baranauskas, A. ; Prankus P. & Sealey R.
Manyland Books : NY
1964
128

KREVE - MICKEVICIUS
Vincas
Temptation, The
Pagunda
Sealey, Raphael
Manyland Books : NY
1965
102

MARCINKEVICIUS
Justinas
Love Is Like This.
Tokia yra melle.
Pazusis, Lionginas
Vil'njus, Vaga
1983
143

MERAS
Icchokas
Stalemate
Lygiosios trunka akikirka.
Zdanys, Jonas
Secaucus, N.J., Lyle Stuart.
1980
173

NARVILAS
Vytautas
Distant Yet Very Close
Tekoriene, Dalija
Vil'njus, Mintis
1989
203

NERIS
Salomeja
Blue Sister, River Vilija. (Parallel Text)
Sesuo zydrioji - vilija
Rottenberg, Dorian et a
Moskva, Raduga.
1987
261

PAZUSIS
Lionginas
Beads Of Amber
Gintaro verinys
Pazusis, Lionginas
Vil'njus, Vaga
1979
215

TAMULAITIS
Vytautas
Nimblefoot The Ant; Her Adventures
Skruzdelytes greitutes nuotykiai
Baranauskas, Albinas & Mills, Clark
Manyland Books : NY
1965
183

VAICIULAITIS
Antanas
Noon At The Country Inn, Short Stories
Baranauskas, Albinas et al.
Manyland Books : NY
1966
142

VAITKUS
Mykolas
Deluge, The
Tvanas
Baranauskas, Albinas
Manyland Books : NY
1965
172

ZOBARSKAS
Stepas
In Quest Of Nine Brothers
Sealey, Mrs Raphael
Stockwell: Ilfracombe
1960
79

ZOBARSKAS
Stepas
Selected Lithuanian Short Stories
Voyages: NY
1962
263

NORWAY

AGER
Waldemar
Sons Of The Old Country
Gamlelandets sonner
Ager, Trygve M.
Lincoln, University of Nebraska P
1983
254

ANTHOLOGY
Slaves Of Love And Other Norwegian Short Stories.
McFarlane, James; Garton, Janet
Oxford, Oxford University Press.
1982
265

ANTHOLOGY
Garton, Janet (Ed.)
Contemporary Norwegian Women's Writing
Norvik: Norwich
1995
253
10.95

ANTHOLOGY
Hanson, Katherine (Ed)
An Everyday Story: Norwegian Women's Fiction
Seattle, Seal Press
1984
249

ANTHOLOGY
Larsen, Hanna Astrup (Ed)
Norway's Best Stories; An Introduction To

Modern Norwegian Fiction
Orbeck, Anders
Books for Libraries P.: Freeport, NY
1971
369
ANTHOLOGY
Larsen, Hanna Astrup (Ed.)
Told In Norway; An Introduction To Modern Norwegian Fiction
Orbeck, Anders
Books for Libraries P.: Freeport, NY
1972
369
ASKILDSEN
Kjell
Sudden Liberating Thought, A. Selected Stories.
Lyngstad, Sverre
Norvik: Norwich
1994
pb
237
9.95
BJØRG
Vik
Aquarium Of Women, An
Kvinneakvariet
Garton, Janet
Norvik: Norwich
1987
pb
108
BJØRNBOE
Jens
Moments Of Freedom: The Heiligenberg Manuscript
Erihetens øyeblikk
Murer, Esther Greenleaf
Norton: New York, NY
1975
217
BJØRNEBOE
Jens
Least Of These, The
Jonas
Jebsen, Bernt & Stafford, Douglas K.
Bobbs - Merrill : Indianapolis
1961
312
BJØRNEBOE
Jens
Sharks, The. The History Of A Crew And A Shipwreck
Haiene
Mürer, Esther Greenleaf
Norvik: Norwich
1992
241
9.95
BJØRNSON
Bjørnstjerne
Synnövé Solbakken
Sutter, Julie
Books for Libraries Press: Freeport, NY
1972
189
BJØRNSON
BjøRnstjerne
Three Comedies
Sharp, R.F.
Greenwood P.: Westport, CT
1974
198
BOJER
Johan
Emigrants, The
Vor egen stamme
Jayne, A.G.
Greenwood P.: Westport, CT
1974
351
BOJER
Johan
Emigrants, The
St. Paul, Minnesota Historical Society Press
1991
351
BOJER
Johan
Last Of The Vikings, The
Den siste viking
Muir, Jessie
New American Library of Canada : Toronto
1965
256
BOJER
Johan
Last Of The Vikings, The
Den siste viking
Muir, Jessie
New American Library : NY
1964
256
BORGEN
Johan
Lillelord: A Novel
Lillelord
Moen, Elizabeth Brown; Peterson, Ronald E.
New Directions: NYC
1982
312
London, Calder
1982
312
BORGEN
Johan
Scapegoat, The
Jeg
Rokkan, Elizabeth
Norvik: Norwich
1993
pb
187
9.95
BRANTENBERG
Gerd
Daughters Of Egalia, The

Egalias døtre
Louis Mackay in co-operation with Gerd Brantenberg
Seal P; Seattle, WA
1985
269
Journeyman: UK
1985
269
4.95
BRANTENBERG
Gerd
What Comes Naturally
Opp alle jordens homofile
Louis Mackay in co-operation with Gerd Brantenberg
Womens Press: London
1986
112
7.95
BREKKE
Toril
Jacaranda Flower, The
Anne Born
Methuen: London
1987
120
9.95
CARLING
Finn
Commission
Oppdrag
Muinzer, Louis A
P.Owen: London
1993
119
CARLING
Finn
Diary For A Dead Husband
Dagbok til en død
Muinzer, Louis A
P.Owen: London
1998
hb
136
15.50
CARLING
Finn
Under The Evening Sky
Under aftenhimmelen
Muinzer, Louis A
P.Owen: London
1990
hb
120
13.50
CHRISTENSEN
Synnöve
Lindeman Daughters
Dotrene lindeman
1956
Savill, Mervyn
Doubleday : Garden City, NY
1960
408
Barrie Books
1958
426
CHRISTIANSEN
Sigurd Wesley
Chaff Before The Wind
Agner i stormen
Anderson, Isaac
Greenwood P.: Westport, CT
1974
319
CHRISTIANSEN
Sigurd Wesley
Two Living And One Dead
Bjorkman, Edwin
Greenwood P.: Westport, CT
1975
288
COLLETT
Camilla
District Governor's Daughters, The
Amtmandens døttre
Kirsten Seaver
Norvik: Norwich
1991
pb
312
DASS
Peter
Trumpet Of Nordland, The. And Other Masterpieces Of Norwegian
Jorgenson, Theodore
St. Olaf College Press: Northfield, MN
1956
208
DORED
Elisabeth
I Loved Tiberius
Jeg elsket tiberius
Walford, Naomi
Pantheon : NY
1963
302
DUUN
Olav Julius
Floodtide Of Fate
Menneske og maktene
Popperwell, R J
Sidgwick & Jackson
1960
256
DØCKER
Rolf
Marius
Oliver Stallybrass
Brockhampton P: Leicester
1969
145
EGNER
Thorbjorn
Singing Town, The
Ramsden, Evelyn & Berg, Leila
Macmillan : NY
1961
96
Methuen: London
1959
105

ELIASSEN
Sigurd
Dragon Wang's River
Gamle drage wangs elv
John, Katherine
Day: NY
1959
256
FALDBAKKEN
Knut
Adam's Diary
Adams dagboek
Lyngstad, Sverre
Lincoln, University of Nebraska P
1988
246
P.Owen: London
1991
hb
246
12.95
FALDBAKKEN
Knut
Honeymoon, The
Bryllupsreisen. Ek
Myhre, Liv
New York St. Martin's Press
1987
231
FALDBAKKEN
Knut
Insect Summer
Adams dagboek
Hal Sutcliffe and Torbjørn Støverud
P.Owen: London
1991
hb
215
14.50
FALDBAKKEN
Knut
Sleeping Prince, The
Maude danser
Janet Garton
P.Owen: London
1988
hb
208
11.50
FALDBAKKEN
Knut
Sweetwater
Uår sweetwater
Joan Tate
P.Owen: London
1994
hb
184
15.95
FALDBAKKEN
Knut
Twilight Country
Aftenlandet
Joan Tate
Kingston Ont., Quarry Press.
1993
P.Owen: London
1993
hb
216
14.99
FLOGSTAD
Kjartan
Dollar Road
Christensen, Nadia
Baton Rouge, Louisiana State University Press
1989
203
FRIIS-BAASTAD
Babbis
Kristy' S Courage
Kjersti
McKinnon, Lise S.
Harcourt, Brace & World : NY
1965
159
GAARDER
Jostein
Sophie's World
Sofies verden
Paulette Møller
New York, Farrar Straus and Giroux
1994
403
GAARDER
Jostein
Sophie's World
Sofies verden
Paulette Møller
Dolphin: UK
1995
pb
436
6.99
GAARDER
Jostein
Sophie's World
Sofies verden
Paulette Møller
Phoenix: UK
1995
hb
349
16.99
GAARDER
Jostein
Through A Glass, Darkly
Elizabeth Rokkan
Phoenix
1998
hb
154
9.99
GAARDER
Jostein
Through A Glass, Darkly
Elizabeth Rokkan
Phoenix
1999
pb
208
5.99
GAARDER
Jostein
Vita Brevis : A Letter To St Augustine
Vita brevis
Anne Born
Phoenix
1999
164

9.99
GARBORG
Arne
Weary Men
North Western University
P: Evanston, Ill
1999
pb
224
North Western University
Press: UK dist.
Turnaround
1999
pb
224
11.99
GRIFFITHS
Ella
Murder On Page Three
Mord på side 3
J. Basil Cowlishaw
Quartet: London
1984
183
6.95
GRIFFITHS
Ella
Water Widow, The
J. Basil Cowlishaw
Quartet: London
1986
220
8.95
GULBRANSSEN
Trygve
Bjorndal Cycle, The. (Beyond Sing The Woods, The Wind From The Mountains)
Putnam: New York, NY
1949
HAMRE
Leif
Edge Of Disaster
Blå 2 - hopp ut
Ramsden, Evelyn
Harcourt, Brace : NY
1962
125
HAMRE
Leif
Leap Into Danger
Otter tre to kaller
Ramsden, Evelyn
Harcourt, Brace : NY
1961
156
HAMRE
Leif
Leap Into Danger
Ramsden, Evelyne
Harcourt : NY
1966
156
HAMRE
Leif
Operation Arctic
Ryen, Dag
Atheneum: New York, NY
1973
154
HAMSUN
Knut
August
Gay-Tifft, Eugene
New York, H. Fertig.
1990
441
HAMSUN
Knut
Dreamers
Svaermere
Tom Geddes
Souvenir
1995
pb
126
7.99
HAMSUN
Knut
Growth Of The Soil
Worster, W
John Lan: London
1949
hb
416
Knopf: NY
1968
hb
435
HAMSUN
Knut
Growth Of The Soil
Markens grode
Worster, W
Pan
1980
hb
317
HAMSUN
Knut
Growth Of The Soil
Markens grode
Worster, W
Souvenir
1979
hb
435
HAMSUN
Knut
Hunger
Duckworth
1949
hb
320
HAMSUN
Knut
Hunger
Sverre Lyngstad
Rebel Inc: Edinburgh
1996
pb
193
6.99
HAMSUN
Knut
Hunger
Sult
Robert Bly
Pan
1976
pb
189
HAMSUN
Knut
Mysteries
Mysterier
Bothmer, Gerry

Avon: New York, NY
1975
255
Souvenir
1998
pb
352
8.99
HAMSUN
Knut
Mysteries
Mysterier
Bothmer, Gerry
Souvenir
1973
pb
352
HAMSUN
Knut
Mysteries
Mysterier
Bothmer, Gerry
Pan
1976
pb
254
HAMSUN
Knut
Night Roamers And Other Stories
Livsfragmenter.
Nunnally, Tiina
Seattle, Fjord Press.
1992
156
HAMSUN
Knut
On Overgrown Paths
Paa gjengrodde stier
Anderson, Carl L
MacGibbon & Kee
1968
hb
176
HAMSUN
Knut
Pan
Pan: av løitnant thomas glahns papirer
McFarlane, James W.
P. Noonday: New York, NY
1958
192
Artemis P
1957
192
HAMSUN
Knut
Pan: From Lieutenant Thomas Glahn's Papers
Pan: av løitnant thomas glahns papirer
McFarlane, James W.
Avon: New York, NY
1975
160
HAMSUN
Knut
Robert Ferguson
Farrar, Strauss: NY
1969
Souvenir
1974
hb
126
HAMSUN
Knut
Tales Of Love And Loss
Robert Ferguson
Souvenir
1997
pb
224
8.99
HAMSUN
Knut
Victoria
Stallybrass, Oliver
Los Angeles, Sun & Moon Press
1994
HAMSUN
Knut
Wanderer, The Etc.
Under høststjernen. En vandrer spiller med sordin
Stallybrass, Oliver &
Gunnvor
Farrar, Straus & Giroux
1975
281
Souvenir
1976
hb
281
HAMSUN
Knut
Wayfarers
Landstrykers.
McFarlane, James
London, Pan
1982
pb
382
HAMSUN
Knut
Wayfarers
Landstrykers.
McFarlane, James
Farrar
1980
459
Souvenir
1980
hb
460
HAMSUN
Knut
Women At The Pump, The
Konerne ved vandposten.
Stallybrass, Oliver &
Gunnvor
London, Pan
1979
pb
350
HANSEN
Eric Fosnes
Psalm At Journey's End
Salme ved reisens slutt
Joan Tate
Secker: London
1997
pb
325
9.99

HANSEN
Eric Fosnes
Psalm At Journey's End
Salme ved reisens slutt
Joan Tate
Vintage
1998
pb
370
6.99
HANSSON
Per
One In Ten Had To Die
Hver tiende mann måtte dø
Allen & Unwin: London
1970
147
HANSSON
Per
One In Ten Had To Die
Hver tiende mann måtte dø
Fontana
1976
pb
159
HASLUND
Ebba
Nothing Happened
Det hendte ingenting.
Wilson, Barbara
Seattle WA, Seal Press.
1987
134
HAVREVOLD
Finn
Summer Adventure
Sommereventyret
Crampton, P
Abelard-Schuman
1961
127
HE
Dong
Ask The Sun
Spor solen
Katherine Hanson
Women in Translation
1997
120
12.95
HOEL
Sigurd
Meeting At The Milestone
Mote ved milepelen
1947
Ramsden, Evelyn
British Book Centre: New York, NY
1952
284
HOEL
Sigurd
Road To The World's End
1933
Lyngstad, S
Sun & Moon
1995
351
HOEL
Sigurd
Troll Circle, The
Trollringen
1933
Lyngstad, S
Lincoln, University of Nebraska
1991
313
HOEM
Edvard
Ferry Crossing, The
Kjerleikens ferjereiser
Shackelford, Frankie Denton
New York, Garland.
1989
184
HOLM
Hannebo
Beauty Queen
Skjønnhetsdronning
Crampton, P
Abelard
1961
159
HOLMVIK , OYVIND & FAYE - LUND, HANS
Dive To Danger
Dybde - 120 fot
Ramsden, Evelyn
Harcourt, Brace : NY
1964
125
HOLT
Kåre
Race, The: A Novel Of Polar Exploration
Kappløpet
Tate, Joan
Delacorte Press: New York, NY
1976
255
HVIDSTEN
A
Old Caillie
Michael, M A
Hodge: Edinburgh
1949
172
JENSEN
Axel
Epp
Stallybrass, O
Chatto: London
1967
116
JOHNSON
Pål Espolinrad
For Love Of Norway
Royskund, Conrad
1989
147
KIELLAND
Axel
Live Dangerously
Hannay, Carolyn
Collins
1949
256
LARSSON
Bjorn
Celtic Ring, The
George Simpson

22.95
LARSSON
Bjorn
Long John Silver
Harvill: London
1999
pb
352
10.99
LIE
Sissel
Lion's Heart
Loevens hjerte
1988
Born, Anne
Orkney P: Kirkwall
Orkney
1990
126
LIKSOM
Rosa
One Night Stands
Serpents Tail
1993
pb
120
7.99
LOVEID
Cecilie
Sea Swell
Sug
Christensen, Nadia
London, Quartet
1986
pb
115
LØNN
Øystein
Tom Reber's Last Retreat
Boyars
1992
hb
176
12.95
MASTERSON
Louis
Apache Breakout
Corgi: London
1975
pb
125
MASTERSON
Louis
Bell Of Death
Corgi: London
1975
pb
112
MASTERSON
Louis
Between Life And Death
Phil Newth
Corgi: London
1972
pb
127
MASTERSON
Louis
Bloody Earth
Corgi: London
1975
pb
110
MASTERSON
Louis
Bravado
Corgi: London
1973
pb
112
MASTERSON
Louis
Butcher From Guerrero
Corgi: London
1973
pb
124
MASTERSON
Louis
Claw Of The Dragon
I dragons klor
Corgi: London
1971
pb
94
MASTERSON
Louis
Coyoteros
Corgi: London
1975
pb
111
MASTERSON
Louis
Day Od Death, The
De dodes dag
Corgi: London
1975
pb
126
MASTERSON
Louis
Devil's Marshal, The
Djevellens marshall
Phil Newth
Corgi: London
1971
pb
124
MASTERSON
Louis
Duel In Tombstone
Corgi: London
1974
pb
128
MASTERSON
Louis
El Gringo's Revenge
Corgi: London
1978
pb
126
MASTERSON
Louis
Gallows Express
Galge-ekspressen
Corgi: London
1973
pb
126
MASTERSON
Louis
Gunman's Inheritance
Revolvermann's arv
Phil Newth

Corgi: London
1971
pb
143
MASTERSON
Louis
Harder Than Steel
Corgi: London
1979
pb
141
MASTERSON
Louis
Hell Below Zero
Helvete under null
Corgi: London
1974
pb
125
MASTERSON
Louis
Killer Kane
Corgi: London
1979
pb
158
MASTERSON
Louis
Killing For The Law
Drep for loven
Corgi: London
1973
pb
110
MASTERSON
Louis
Law Of The Jungle
Jungelens lov
Phil Newth
Corgi: London
1972
pb
127
MASTERSON
Louis
Marshall And Murderer
Morder og marshall
Corgi: London
1971
pb
112
MASTERSON
Louis
Monster From Yuna, The
Udyret fra yuna
Corgi: London
1971
pb
95
MASTERSON
Louis
New Orleans Gamble
Hoyt spill i new orleans
Corgi: London
1975
pb
110
MASTERSON
Louis
No Tears For Morgan Kane
Ingen tarer for morgan kane
Phil Newth
Corgi: London
1972
pb
127
MASTERSON
Louis
Pistolero
Udyret fra yuna
Transworld
1971
pb
125
MASTERSON
Louis
Ranger's Honour, A
En rangers aere
Transworld
1971
pb
128
MASTERSON
Louis
Ransom
De piskede
Corgi: London
1973
pb
124
MASTERSON
Louis
Return To Action
Phil Newth
Corgi: London
1972
pb
128
MASTERSON
Louis
Revenge
Hevn
Phil Newth
Corgi: London
1971
pb
126
MASTERSON
Louis
Rio Grande
Phil Newth
Corgi: London
1972
pb
128
MASTERSON
Louis
Southern Showdown
Corgi: London
1976
pb
127
MASTERSON
Louis
Storm Over Sonora
Phil Newth
Corgi: London
1971
pb
126
MASTERSON
Louis
To The Death, Senor Kane
Corgi: London
1974
pb

126
MASTERSON
Louis
Without Mercy
Phil Newth
Corgi: London
1972
pb
128
MICHELET
Jon
Orion's Belt
Ellen Nations
Ulverscroft Large Print: Leicester
1987
hb
507
7.25
MICHELET
Jon
Orion's Belt
Ellen Nations
Souvenir
1986
hb
MYKLE
Agnar
Hotel Room, The
Tyven, tyven skal du hete
Michael, Maurice
Dutton : NY
1963
279
Barrie & Rockliff
1963
279
MYKLE
Agnar
Hotel Room, The
Tyven, tyven skal du hete
Michael, Maurice
Panther
1964
pb
319
MYKLE
Agnar
Lasso Round The Moon
Lasso rundt fru luna
1954
Michael, Maurice
Dutton : NY
1962
459
Barrie & Rockliff
1960
459
MYKLE
Agnar
Man And His Sink And Other Stories, A
Michael, Maurice
Panther
1968
pb
190
MYKLE
Agnar
Rubicon
Michael, Maurice
Barrie & Rockliff
1966
282
MYKLE
Agnar
Rubicon
Rubicon
Michael, Maurice
Panther
1968
pb
247
NEDREAAS
Torborg
Music From A Blue Well
Musikk fra en blå bronn.
Lee, Bibi
Lincoln, University of Nebraska P
1988
238
NEDREAAS
Torborg
Nothing Grows By Moonlight
Av måneskinn gror det ingenting
Lee, Bibi
Lincoln, University of Nebraska P
1987
198
NEWTH
Mette
Abduction, The
Bortførelsen
Tina Nunnally and Steve Murray
New York, Farrar Straus & Giroux
1989
247
Sprint
1989
212
3.95
NORDRÅ
Olav
Red Harvest
Rod host
Friis, Erik J.
Twayne Publishers : Boston
1978
190
OBSTFELDER
SigbjøRn
Priest's Diary, A
En prests dagbog.
James McFarlane
Norvik: Norwich
1987
pb
75
2.5
PAULSSON
Bjørn Konow
Blind Landing
Toverud, Constance Ford
Harcourt Brace Jovanovic: NY
1972
123
RØLVAAG
Ole E.
Boat Of Longing, The

Længselens baat
Solum, Nora O.
Greenwood P.: Westport, CT
1974
304
RØLVAAG
Ole
Giants In The Earth
I de dage
Colcord, Lincoln & Rolvaag, Ole
Harper & Row : NY
1965
453
RØLVAAG
Ole E.
Peder Victorious
Peder seier
Solun, Nora O. & Rolvaag, Ole
Harper & Row
1966
330
RØLVAAG
Ole E.
Peder Victorious
Peder seier
Solun, Nora O. & Rolvaag, Ole
Lincoln, Univ. of Nebraska Press.
1982
325
RØLVAAG
Ole E.
Peder Victorious
Solum, Nora O. & Rølvaag, Ole E.
Greenwood P.: Westport, CT
1973
350
RØLVAAG
Ole E.
Pure Gold
To tullinger, et billede fra idag
Erdahl, Sivert & Rølvaag, Ole E.
Greenwood P.: Westport, CT
1973
346
RØLVAAG
Ole E.
Their Fathers' God
Den signede dag
Ager, Trygve M.
Greenwood P.: Westport, CT
1973
338
ROLVAAG
Ole
Their Father's God
Den signede dag.
Ager, Trygve M.
Lincoln, University of Nebraska P
1983
338
ROLVAAG
Ole E.
When The Wind Is In The South And Other Stories
Zempel, Solveig
Sioux Falls S.D., Center for Western Studies
1984
88
RYGG
Pernille
Butterfly Effect, The
Sommerfugleffekten
Joan Tate
Harvill: London
1997
hb
220
15.99
RYGG
Pernille
Butterfly Effect, The
Sommerfugleffekten
Joan Tate
Harvill: London
1998
pb
220
5.99
RYNNING-TONNESEN
Olaf
Secret Transmitter, The
Hemmelig sender
Friis, Erik J.
Bobbs-Merrill : Indianapolis
1965
194
SANDEL
Cora
Alberta Alone
Bare alberte
Rokkan, Elizabeth
Orion : NY
1966
P.Owen: London
1964
284
SANDEL
Cora
Alberta Alone
Bare alberte
Rokkan, Elizabeth
Panther
1967
pb
250
SANDEL
Cora
Alberta Alone
Bare alberte
Rokkan, Elizabeth
Womens P
1980
pb
250
SANDEL
Cora
Alberta And Freedom
Alberte og friheten
Rokkan, Elizabeth
P.Owen: London
1963
241
SANDEL

Cora
Alberta And Freedom
Alberta og frihed
Rokkan, Elizabeth
Panther
1967
pb
235
SANDEL
Cora
Alberta And Freedom
Alberta og frihed
Rokkan, Elizabeth
Womens P
1980
pb
235
SANDEL
Cora
Alberta And Jacob
Alberta og jakob
Rokkan, Elizabeth
Athens Ohio, Ohio University Press
1984
247
Panther
1967
pb
233
SANDEL
Cora
Alberta And Jacob
Alberta og jakob
Rokkan, Elizabeth
Womens P
1980
pb
233
SANDEL
Cora
Coa Sandel: Selected Short Stories
Wilson, Barbara
Seal p; Seattle, WA
1985
204
SANDEL
Cora
Krane's Café
Kranes kondotori
Rokkan, Elizabeth
Athens Ohio, Ohio University P: Athens, Ohio
1985
173
P.Owen: London
1968
173
SANDEL
Cora
Krane's Café
Kranes kondotori
Rokkan, Elizabeth
Womens P
1984
173
SANDEL
Cora
Leech, The
Kjøp ikke dondi
Rokkan, Elizabeth
P.Owen: London
1960
202
SANDEL
Cora
Leech, The
Kjøp ikke dondi
Rokkan, Elizabeth
Athens Ohio, Ohio University Press
1986
202
Womens P
1986
pb
202
7.95
SANDEL
Cora
Silken Thread, The
Rokkan, Elizabeth
Womens P
1988
pb
175
3.95
SANDEL
Cora
Silken Thread, The
Rokkan, Elizabeth
Ohio UP: Athens Ohio
1986
175
P.Owen: London
1986
hb
175
9.95
SANDEMOSE
Aksel
Ross Dane
Winnipeg, Gunnars & Campbell Pub..
1989
170
SANDEMOSE
Aksel
Werewolf, The
Verulven
Lannestock, Gustav
U. of Wisconsin P. : Madison
1966
374
SENJE
Sigurd
Escape!
Stepans skrin
Ramsden, Evelyn
Harcourt, Brace & World : NY
1964
156
SISSEL
Lie
Lion's Heart
Løvens hjerte
1988
Anne Born
Orkney P: Kirkwall, Orkney (Scotland)
1990
126
5.95
SKOUEN
Arne

Stokers' Mess
Birkeland, Joran
Knopf: New York, NY
1948
237
SKRAM
Amalie
Betrayed
Forrådt
1892
Aileen Hennes
Pandora
1996
hb
131
9.95
SKRAM
Amalie
Constance Ring
1885
Hanson, Katherine; Messick, Judith
Seattle WA, Women in Translation.
1988
307
SKRAM
Amalie
Under Observation
Professor hieronimus
Hanson, Katherine; Messick, Judith
Seattle WA, Women in Translation.
1992
369
SPANG
Michael Grundt
Spy Who Longed For Home, The
Cowlishaw, J. Basil
New York, St. Martin's Press.
1989
232
STAALESEN
Gunnar
Yours Until Death
Din til døden
Amassien, Margaret
Constable: London
1993
238
13.99
STAALESEN
Gunnar
Yours Until Death
I morket er alle ulver grå
McDuff, David
London, Quartet.
1986
214
13.99
STIGEN
Terje
Interrupted Passage, An
Vindstille underveis
Langema, Amanda
Twayne Publishers: New York, NY
1974
261
SVINSAAS
Ingvald
Tom In The Mountains
Tom i villmarka
Turner, Marianne
Lothrop, Lee & Shepard :NY
1964
108
STEEN
Thorvald
Don Carlos
1998
Don Carlos
1993
James Anderson
Sun & Moon Press: LA
UNDSET
Sigrid
Four Stories. (Selma Broter. Thjodolf. Miss Smith-Tellefsen. Simonsen.)
Walford, Naomi
Knopf : NY
1961
245
UNDSET
Sigrid
Four Stories
Walford, Naomi
Greenwood Press : Westport, Conn.
1978
245
UNDSET
Sigrid
In The Wilderness
Chater, Arthur G.
Pocket Books : NY
1964
216
UNDSET
Sigrid
Jenny
Emmé, W.
H. Fertig: New York, NY
1975
305
UNDSET
Sigrid
Kristin Labransdatter.
Charles Archer
Abacus
1995
pb
1069
8.99
UNDSET
Sigrid
Kristin Labransdatter.
Charles Archer
Pan
1980
pb
1069
UNDSET
Sigrid
Master Of Hestviken, The
Olav audunssøn i hestviken; olav audunssøn og hans børn
Knopf: New York, NY
1952

994
UNDSET
Sigrid
Snake Pit, The
Chater, Arthur G.
Pocket Books : NY
1964
247
VESAAS
Tarjei
Birds, The
Fuglane
Torbjørn, S et alk
P.Owen: London
1968
hb
224
VESAAS
Tarjei
Bleaching Yard, The
Bleikeplassen.
Torbjørn, S et alk
P.Owen: London
1981
hb
156
VESAAS
Tarjei
Boat In The Evening, The
Båten om kvelden
Rokkan, Elisabeth
W. Morrow: New York, NY
1972
184
VESAAS
Tarjei
Bridges, The
Bruene
Elisabeth Rokkan
P.Owen: London
1969
hb
183
VESAAS
Tarjei
Bridges, The
Bruene
Elisabeth Rokkan
Panther
1972
pb
157
VESAAS
Tarjei
Ice Palace, The
Rokkan, Elizabeth
Los Angeles Calif., Sun & Moon P
1991
VESAAS
Tarjei
Land Of Hidden Fires
Løynde eldars land
König, Fritz & Crisp, Jerry
Wayne State U.P.: Detroit, MI
1973
125
VESAAS
Tarjei
Seed, The. Spring Night
Kimen; vårnatt
Chapman, Kenneth G.
American - Scandinavian Foundation : NY
1964
317
VESAAS
Tarjei
Spring Night
Vårnatt
K.G.Chapman
P.Owen: London
1972
167
VESTLY
Anna Catherina
Hello, Aurora
Aurora i blokk
Aimos, Eileen & Fairfax, Jane
T.Y. Crowell
1974
135
VIK
Bjørg
Aquarium Of Women, An
Kvinneakvarie
Garton, Janet
Norvik: Norwich.
1987
108
VIK
Bjørg
Out Of Season, And Other Stories
En håndfull lengsel
McDuff, David; Browne, Patrick
London, Sinclair Browne.
1983
143
WAAGE
Johan
Narvik Campaign, The
Kampene om narvik
Butler, Ewan
Harrap
1964
211
WASSMO
Herbjørg
Dina's Book
Dinas bok
Nadia M. Christensen
New York, Arcade Publishing
1994
455
Black Swan
1996
pb
527
6.99
WASSMO
Herbjørg
House With The Blind Glass Windows, The
Huset med den blinde glassveranda
Lloyd, Roseann; Simpson, Allen

Seattle Wash., Seal Press.
1987
227
WIESE
Jan
Naked Madonna, The
Kvinnen som kledte seg naken for sin elskede
Tom Geddes
Harvill: London
1995
hb
158
9.99

SAMI ('LAPP')

GASKI
Harald
In the Shadow of the Midnight Sun; Contemporary Sami Prose and Poetry
Davvi Girji: Kárášjohka (Norway)
1996
276
VALKEAPÄÄ
Nils-Aslak
The Sun, My Father
Beaivi, Áhcáza
DAT: Guovdageadnu
1997
s.n.

SWEDEN & FINLAND-SWEDISH

AHLIN
Lars
Cinnamoncandy
Kanelbeiten
Kalter Weiss, Hanna
Garland
1990
256
Garland
1990
256
ALBREKTSON
Arvid
Tariro
Tariro
Kruuse, Elsa
Muhlenberg : Philadelphia
1959
226
ALMQUIST
Carl Jonas Love
Queen's Diadem, The
Drottningens juvelsmycke
1834
Sandstrem, Yvonne L
Skoob
1992
247
ALMQUIST
Carl Jonas Love
Sara Videbeck, The Chapel
Det går an
1839
Benson, Adolph Burnett
Twayne Publishers: New York, NY
1972
194
ANCKARSVÄRD
Karin
Mysterious School-Master, The
Tag fast magistern
MacMillan, Annabelle
Harcourt, Brace : NY
1961
190
ANCKARSVÄRD
Karin
Rider By Night
Varför just krabat?
MacMillan, Annabelle
Harcourt, Brace : NY
1962
192
ANTHOLOGY
Clareus, Ingrid (Ed)
Scandinavian Women Writers: An Anthology From The 1880s To The 1980s
New York, Greenwood Press
1989
ANTHOLOGY
Fulton, Robin (Ed)
Preparations For Flight And Other Swedish Short Stories
Dufour: USA
Forest: London
1990
pb
162
8.95
ANTHOLOGY
Lagerlöf, Karl Erik (Ed)
Modern Swedish Prose
Minnesota UP: Minneapolis
1979
hb
277
ANTHOLOGY
Larsen, Hanna Astrup (Ed)
Sweden's Best Stories; An Introduction To Swedish Fiction
Stork, Charles Wharton
Books for Libraries P.: Freeport, NY
1971
365
ANTHOLOGY
Wästberg, Per
An Anthology Of Modern Swedish Literature
Merrick, N.Y., Cross-Cultural Communications.
1979
217
ANTHOLOGY

Schoolfield, George C. (Ed)
Swedo-Finnish Short Stories
Schoolfield, George C.
Twayne Publishers: New York, NY
1975
388
AXELSSON
Sun
Dreamed Life, A
Drömmen om ett liv.
Printz-Påhlson, Ulla
Athens, Ohio, Ohio University Press
1983
201
BENGTSSON
Frans G.
Long Ships, The; A Saga Of The Viking Age
Röde orm
Meyer, Michael
New American Library of Canada : Toronto
1964
414
BENGTSSON
Frans Gunnar
Long Ships, The
Röde orm
Meyer, Michael
New American Library : NY
1959
414
BENGTSSON
Frans Gunnar
Long Ships, The; A Saga Of The Viking Age
Röde orm
1951
Meyer, Michael
Knopf: New York, NY
1956
503
Collins: London
1956
511
BERGMAN
Ingmar
Best Intentions
Godja viljan
Tate, Joan
Arcade: NY
1993
298
Harvill: London
1993
295
BERGMAN
Ingmar
Fanny And Alexander
Fanny och alexander
Blair, Alan
Penguin: Middx.
1989
216
BERGMAN
Ingmar
Film Trilogy, A
En filmtrilogi
Austin, Paul
Calder: London
1967
143
BERGMAN
Ingmar
Four Stories: The Touch; Cries And Whispers; The Hour Of The Wolf;
Blair, Alan
Anchor Press: Garden City, NY
1976
168
BERGMAN
Ingmar
Four Stories
Blair, Alan
Anchor Press / Doubleday : Garden City, NY
1977
168
Boyars: London
1982
168
BERGMAN
Ingmar
From The Life Of Marionettes.
Ur marionetternas liv.
Blair, Alan
New York, Pantheon Books
1980
98
BERGMAN
Ingmar
Magic Lantern, The
Tate, Joan
Penguin: Middx.
1988
310
BERGMAN
Ingmar
Scenes From A Marriage
Scener ur ett äktenskap
Blair, Alan
Pantheon Books: NY
1974
199
BERGMAN
Ingmar
Sunday's Children
Söndagsbarn
Tate, Joan
Arcade Pub: NYC
1994
153
Harvill: London
1994
pb
107
13.99
BERGMAN
Margareta
Karin : A Novel.
Karin vid havet
Austin, Paul Britten
New York, St. Martin's Press.
1985
253

BLOM
K. Arne
Moment Of Truth, The
Sanningens ögonblick
Friis, Erik J.
Harper & Row : NY
1977
147
BORNEMARK
Kjell-Olof
Dividing Line, The
Skiljelinjenan
Thompson, Laurie
New York, Dembner Books.
1988
231
BORNEMARK
Kjell-Olof
Henchman, The
Handgången man
Thompson, Laurie
New York, Dembner Books.
1990
215
BORNEMARK
Kjell-Olof
Messenger Must Die, The
Legat till en trolös
McGraw-Hill: NY
1986
236
Hale: London
1989
hb
236
12.95
BOYE
Karin
Kallocain
Kallocain
Lannestock, Gustav
U. of Wisconsin P. : Madison
1966
193
BOYE
Karin
Kallocain
Kallocain
Lannestock, Gustav
New York, Fromm International Pub. Corp.
1985
193
BRICK
Anna Rikwin
Elle Kari
Jannes, Elly
Macmillan: New York, NY
1952
BURÉN
Märtha
Need To Love, A
Att gå vidare
Tate, Joan
Dodd, Mead. : NY
1964
230
Michael Joseph: London
1964
230
BURMAN
Edor
Three Wolverines Of Rushing Valley
Tre järvar
McMIllan, Annabelle
Dutton: NY
1966
160
BREMER
Fredrika
Colonel's Family
Sarah Death
Dufour
24.95
Norvik: Norwich
240
10.95
CARPELAN
Bo
Axel
Paladin
1991
pb
374
5.99
CARPELAN
Bo
Axel
Axel
McDuff, David
Carcanet; Manchester
1989
hb
374
14.95
CARPELAN
Bo
Urwind
Urwind
Carcanet; Manchester
1996
pb
189
9.95
CARPELAN
Bo
Voices At The Late Hour
Rösterna i den sena timmen
Martin, Irma Margareta
Georgia UP: Athens, Ga.
1988
hb
183
Georgia UP: London
1988
hb
183
17.50
COMBUECHEN
Sigrid
Byron
Byron
Heinemann
1991
hb
518
14.99
CLAESSON
Stig
Ancient Monuments.
Vem älskar yngve frej?
Scobbie, Irene
Stornaway, Thule.

1980
142
DAGERMAN
Stig
Burnt Child, A
Bränt barn
1948
Alan Blair
Quartet: London
1991
pb
272
6.95
DAGERMAN
Stig
Burnt Child, A
Bränt barn
1948
Blair, Alan
Morrow: New York, NY
1950
hb
264
Chatto: London
1950
hb
264
DAGERMAN
Stig
Burnt Child, A
Bränt barn
1948
Alan Blair
Quartet: London
1991
pb
272
6.95
DAGERMAN
Stig
Games Of The Night And Other Writings, The
Naomi Walford
Quartet: London
1986
pb
224
4.95
DAGERMAN
Stig
Games Of The Night And Other Writings, The
Meyer, Michael
Bodley Head
1960
hb
DAGERMAN
Stig
German Autumn
Tysk höst
Robin Fulton
Quartet: London
1988
pb
120
5.95
DAGERMAN
Stig
German Autumn
Robin Fulton
Quartet: London
pb
4.95
DAGERMAN
Stig
Island Of The Doomed
De dömdas ö
Laurie Thompson
Quartet: London
1991
hb
338
17.95
DAGERMAN
Stig
Snake, The
Quartet: London
1995
pb
243
9
DAHLIN
Doris
Sit-In Game, The
Ockupationsleken
Tate, Joan
Viking Press: New York, NY
1973
DELBLANC
Sven
Castrati, The; A Romantic Tale
Kastrater
Williams C. W.
Karoma : An Arbor, MI
1979
151
DELBLANC
Sven
Speranza
Speranza
Austin, Paul Britten
Viking P.: NYC
1983
153
London, Secker & Warburg
1984
153
EDQVIST
Dagmar
Black Sister
Den svarta systern
Tate, Joan
Doubleday for the Crime Club: Garden City
1963
234
Michael Joseph: London
1963
271
EDQVIST
Dagmar
Catalan Incident
Angela Teresa's gäster
1953
Gunvaldsen, I E
Angus & Robertson: London
1958
hb
258
EKLAND
Britt
Sweet Life
Ljuva livet

Headline: UK
1993
hb
373
15.99
EKLAND
Britt
Sweet Life
Ljuva livet
Headline
1994
pb
501
5.99
EKMAN
Kerstin
Blackwater
Händelser vid vatten
Joan Tate
Chatto: London
1995
pb
444
9.99
EKMAN
Kerstin
Forest Of Hours, The
Rövarna i skuleskogen
Joan Tate
Chatto: London
1998
hb
488
15.99
EKMAN
Kerstin
Forest Of Hours, The
Rövarna i skuleskogen
Joan Tate
Chatto: London
1998
hb
488
15.99
EKMAN
Kerstin
Under The Snow
De tre små mästarna
Vintage: London
1997
pb
164
5.99
EKMAN
Kerstin
Witches' Rings
Häxringarna
Shenck, Linda
Norvik: Norwich
1997
pb
358
7.95
EKSTRÖM
Jan
Ancestral Precipice
Ättestupan
Tate, Joan
London, Macmillan.
1983
219
EKSTRÖM
Jan
Deadly Reunion
Ättestupan.
New York, Scribner
1983
243
EKSTRÖM
Jan
Death's Midwives: Stories
Claeson, Eva
Princeton, Ontario Review Press
1985
149
ENGSTROM
Albert Laurentius Johanes
Twelve Tales
Harrap
1949
160
ENQUIST
Per O.
Legionnaires, The; A Documentary Novel
Legionärerna
Blair, Alan
Delacorte P./S. Lawrence: New York, NY
1973
508
ENQUIST
Per Olov
Captain Nemo's Library
Kapten nemos bibliotek
Paterson, Anna
Quartet: London
1992
hb
14.95
ENQUIST
Per Olov
Downfall: A Love Story
Nedstörtad ängel
Quartet: London
1986
109
7.95
ENQUIST
Per Olov
Fallen Angel
Paterson, Anna
Quartet: London
ENQUIST
Per Olov
Magnetist's Fifth Winter, The
Magnetisörens femte vinter
Austin, Paul
Quartet: London
1989
240
10.95
ENQUIST
Per Olov
March Of The Musicians, The
Musikanternas uttåg
Tate, Joan
Collins
1985
hb
255
ENQUIST
Per Olov

March Of The Musicians, The
Musikanternas uttag
Tate, Joan
Quartet: London
1985
pb
255
7.95
ERICSON
Stig
Dan Henry In The Wild West
Dan henry i vilda västern
Teal, Thomas
Delacorte Press / S. Lawrence : NY
1976
148
EKELUND
Vilhelm
Second Light, The
Bruce, Lennart
San Francisco, North Point Press.
1986
186
FAGERHOLM
Monika
Wonderful Women By The Water
Underbara kvinnor vid vatten
Tate, Joan
Harvill: London
1998
pb
282
6.99
FALK
Ann M.
Place Of Her Own, A
Ingen vanlig stina
MacMillan, Annabelle
Harcourt, Brace & World : NY
1964
127
FALK
Ann Mari
Who Is Erika?
Vem är ulla?
MacMillan, Annabelle
Harcourt, Brace & World : NY
1963
124
FOKKER
Nicolas
Tamer, The
Där växer inga rosor i s ågspånet
Harper & Row : NY
1979
260
Harper & Row : London
1979
260
FOSS
Hans Andersen
Cotter's Son, The
Husmandsgutten
Winkjer, Joel G.
Park Region Pub. Co.: Alexandria, Minn.
1963
127
FRANZEN
Nils-O
Agaton-Sax And The Colossus Of Rhodes
Tareget
1975
hb
128
FRANZEN
Nils-O
Agaton-Sax And The Max Brothers
Agaton sax och broderna max
Deutsch
1970
hb
126
FRANZEN
Nils-O
Agaton-Sax And The Scotland Yard Mystery
Agaton sax och de okontante miljardärerna
Deutsch
1969
hb
128
FRANZEN
Nils-O
Agaton-Sax And The Scotland Yard Mystery
Agaton sax och de okontante miljardärerna
Target
1973
pb
128
FRANZEN
Nils-O
Agaton-Sax And The Bank Robbers
Agaton sax och broderna max
Target
1973
pb
128
FRANZEN
Nils-O
Agaton-Sax And The Criminal Doubles
Agaton sax och bykopings gastabud
Deutsch
1971
hb
128
FRANZEN
Nils-O
Agaton-Sax And The Criminal Doubles
Agaton sax och bykopings gastabud
Target
1973
pb
128
FRANZEN
Nils-O
Agaton-Sax And The

Diamond Thieves
Agaton sax och de slipade diamanttjuvama
Target
1973
pb
110
FRANZEN
Nils-O
Agaton-Sax And The Haunted House
Agaton sax och det vita mössmysteriet
Tareget
1975
hb
128
FREDERIKSSON
Marianne
Hanna's Daughters
Orion
1998
hb
352
16.99
FRIDEGÅRD
Jan
I, Lars Hård
Jag lars hård
Robert E. Bjork
Nebraska UP: Lincoln, Neb
1983
105
Nebraska UP: London
FRIDEGÅRD
Jan
Jacob's Ladder & Mercy
Tack för himlastegen & barmhartighet
Robert E. Bjork
Nebraska UP: Lincoln, Neb
1991
186
FRIDEGÅRD
Jan
Land Of Wooden Gods
Robert E. Bjork
Nebraska UP: Lincoln, Neb
1989
211
Nebraska UP: London
FRIDEGÅRD
Jan
People Of The Dawn
Gryningsfolket
Robert E. Bjork
Nebraska UP: Lincoln, Neb
1990
203
Nebraska UP: London
FRIDEGÅRD
Jan
Sacrificial Smoke
Offerrökt
Robert E. Bjork
Nebraska UP: Lincoln, Neb
1991
190
Nebraska UP: London
GIERTZ
Bo Harald
Hammer Of God, The
Stengrunden
Nelson, Clifford A.
Augustana : Rock Island, Ill.
1962
335
GIERTZ
Bo Harald
With My Own Eyes; A Life Of Jesus
Michael, Maurice
Macmillan : NY
1962
236
GOLOWANJUK
Jascha
My Golden Road From Samarkand
Min gyllene vag fran samarkand
Quartet: London
1993
202
14.95
GUILLOU
Jan
Enemy's Enemy
Fiendens fiende
1989
Keeland, Thomas
Knopf: NY
1992
401
Bloomsbury: Lonon
1994
pb
402
10.99
GUSTAFSSON
Lars
Bernard Foy's Third Castling
Bernard foys tredje rockad hunden
Sandstroem, Yvonne L.
New Directions: NY
1988
260
GUSTAFSSON
Lars
Death Of A Beekeeper, The
Biodlares dod
Janet K. Swaffar and
Guntram H. Weber
New Directions: NY
1981
Harvill: London
1990
pb
167
6.99
GUSTAFSSON
Lars
Funeral Music For Freemasons
Sorgemusik för frimurareg, en
Sandstroem, Yvonne L.
New York, New Directions

Pub. YC
1987
151
GUSTAFSSON
Lars
Sigismund : From The Memories Of A Baroque Polish Prince
Sigismund
Weinstock, John
New York, New Directions
Pub. YC
1985
191
GUSTAFSSON
Lars
Stories Of Happy People
Sandstroem, Yvonne L.; Weinstock, John
New York, New Directions
Pub. YC
1986
134
GUSTAFSSON
Lars
Tale Of A Dog, The
Historien med hunden
Janet K. Swaffar and Guntram H. Weber
New Directions: NY
1981
Harvill: London
1990
pb
167
6.99
GUSTAFSSON
Lars
Tennis Players, The
Tennisperlarna
Sandstroem, Yvonne I.
New York, New Directions
Pub. YC
1983
92
GUSTAFSSON
Lars
Tiler's Afternoon, A
Kakelsattares eftermiddag, en
Geddes, Tom
New Pub Corp: NYC
1993
117
Harvill: London
1993
pb
117
7.99
GYLLENSTEN
Lars
Testament Of Cain, The
Kains memoarer
Bradfield, K
Calder
1967
123
GÖRLING
Lars
491; A Novel
491
Hollo, Anselm
Grove : NY
1966
282
HAGERFORS
Lennart
Whales In Lake Tanganyika, The
Valarna i tanganyika asj÷n
Penguin: Middx.
1991
pb
172
4.99
HAGERFORS
Lennart
Whales In Lake Tanganyika, The
Valarna i tanganyika asj÷n
Hollo, Anselm
Grove P: NYC
1989
172
Andre Deutsch
1989
hb
HALLQVIST
Britt G
Bettina's Secret
Bettinas hemlighet
Parker, Anne
Dent
1968
152
HAMMARSKJÖLD
Dag
Markings
Sjöberg, Leif & Auden W.H.
Knopf : NY
1966
216
HAMORI
László
Adventure In Bangkok
Äventyr i bangkok
McMillan, Annabelle
Harcourt, Brace & World
1966
188
HAMORI
László
Dangerous Journey
McMillan, Annabelle
Harcourt : NY
1966
190
HARTMAN
Olov
Sudden Sun, The
Innanför
Kruuse, Elsa
Fortress P. : Philadelphia
1964
138
HEDBERG
Carl O
Animals In Cages
Djur i bur
Schubert, E
Weidenfeld
1962
126
HELANDER
Gunnar

Big City Zulu
Osberg, Margery
Augustana Press: Rock Island. Ill
1959
235
HELANDER
Gunnar
Black Rhapsody
Svart symfoni
Osberg, Margery
Harper: New York, NY
1958
214
HELLBERG
Hans-Eric
Grandpa's Maria
Morfars maria
Crampton, Patricia
Morrow: New York, NY
1974
189
HOLMSEN
Sverre
Singing Coral
Sjungende korall
1946
Bulman, Joan
Barrie
1951
292
HUBERT
Tord
Trap, The
Fällan
Selberg, Ingrid
D. McKay Co. : NY
1977
160
Gollancz
1976
160
HÖGSTRAND
Olle E.
Debt, The
Skulden
Tate, Joan
Pantheon Books: New York, NY
1975
217
HÖGSTRAND
Olle E.
Gambler, The
Spelarna
Blair, Alan
Pantheon Books: NY
1974
216
HÖGSTRAND
Olle E.
On The Prime Minister's Account
Maskerat brott
Levy, Elina
Pantheon Books: New York, NY
1972
217
Gollancz: London
1972
217
HÖGSTRAND
Olle E.
On The Prime Minister's Account
Maskerat brott
Levy, Elina
Quartet: London
1974
pb
217
IDSTROM
Annika
My Brother Sebastian
Forest: London
1991
8.95
INGER
Nan
Katrin
Tate, J
H.Hamilton
1967
160
JANSSON
Tove
Summer Book, The
Sommarboken
Teal, Thomas
Pantheon Books: New York, NY
1975
166
JERSILD
Per Christian
After The Flood : A Novel.
Efter floden
Blecher, Löne Thygesen; Blecher, George
New York, Morrow.: New York, NY
1986
251
JERSILD
Per Christian
Animal Doctor, The
Djurdoktorn
Paul, David Mel & Paul, Margareta
Pantheon Books: New York, NY
1975
267
JERSILD
Per Christian
Children's Island
Tate, Joan
Nebraska UP
1988
hb
23.35
JERSILD
Per Christian
Children's Island.
Tate, Joan
Nebraska UP
1988
pb
JERSILD
Per Christian
Living Soul
En levanden själ
Lesser, Rika
Norvik: Norwich
1988
pb
205

7.95
JERSILD
Per Christian
House Of Babel
Babels hus
Tate, Joan
Lincoln, University of Nebraska
1987
321
JOHNSON
Eyvind
Dreams Of Roses And Fire.
Friis, Erik J.
New York, Hippocrene Books
1984
384
JOHNSON
Eyvind
Return To Ithaca, The Odyssey Retold As A Modern Novel
Strändernas svall
1946
Michael, M.A.
Thames and Hudson: New York, NY
1952
474
Thames & Hudson
1952
474
JÖNSSON
Reidar
My Father, His Son
En hund begraven.
Ruuth, Marianne
New York, Arcade Pub.
1991
226
Faber
1989
220
9.99
JÖNSSON
Reidar
My Life As A Dog
Mitt liv som hund
Farrar
1989
219
Faber: London
1989
220
9.99
KALLIFATIDES
Theodor
Peasants & Masters (First Volume Of Trilogy : A Greek Chronicle)
Bönder och herrar.
Teal, Thomas
Seattle, Fjord Press.
1990
203
KIHLMAN
Christer
All My Sons
Alla mina söner
P.Owen: London
1984
hb
10.95
KIHLMAN
Christer
Blue Mother, The
Tate, Joan
Nebraska UP
1990
308
Nebraska UP
1990
KIHLMAN
Christer
Dear Prince
P.Owen: London
KIHLMAN
Christer
Downfall Of Gerdt Blath
Gerdt blath undergang
Tate, Joan
P.Owen: London
1989
hb
221
12.95
KIHLMAN
Christer
Sweet Prince
Dyre prins.
Tate, Joan
P.Owen: London
1983
hb
232
KURTÉN
Björn
Dance Of The Tiger: A Novel Of The Ice Age
Den svarta tigern.
Pantheon: NYC
1980
255
London, Abacus.
1982
256
LAGERKVIST
Pär
Barabbas
Barabbas
Blair, Alan
Random House: New York, NY
1951
180
LAGERKVIST
Pär
Barabbas
Barabbas
Blair, Alan
Random House: New York, NY
1957
180
London, New English Library
1983
128
LAGERKVIST
Pär
Death Of Ahasuerus, The
Ahasuerus död.
Walford, Naomi
New York, Vintage

Books.New York, NY
1982
118
LAGERKVIST
Pär Fabian
Dwarf, The
Dick, Alexander
Hill & Wang : NY
1960
228
Chatto: London
1953
LAGERKVIST
Pär Fabian
Dwarf, The
Dvärgen
Dick, Alexander
Quartet: London
1986
175
LAGERKVIST
Pär Fabian
Eternal Smile, The And Other Stories
Random House: New York, NY
1956
389
Chatto: London
1971
206
LAGERKVIST
Pär Fabian
Evening Land
Aftonland
Auden, W.H. & Sjöberg, Leif
Wayne State U.P.: Detroit, MI
1975
193
LAGERKVIST
Pär Fabian
Guest Of Reality
Gäst hos verkligheten
Robin Fulton
Quartet: London
1989
pb
147
5.95
LAGERKVIST
Pär Fabian
Herod And Mariamne.
Mariamne.
Walford, Naomi
New York, Vintage Books.New York, NY
1982
115
LAGERKVIST
Pär Fabian
Holy Land, The
Det heliga landet.
Walford, Naomi
New York, Vintage Books.New York, NY
1982
85
LAGERKVIST
Pär
Holy Land, The
Det helige landet
Walford, Naomi
Random House : NY
1966
85
Chatto: London
1967
LAGERKVIST
Pär
Marriage Feast, The, Etc.
Blair, A. & Lindin, C.E.
Hill & Wang: NY
1973
222
LAGERKVIST
Pär
Pär Lagerkvist: Five Early Works.
Swanson, Roy Arthur
Edwin Mellon P: Lewiston, NY
Edwin Mellon P: Lampeter
1989
LAGERKVIST
Pär
Pilgrim At Sea
Pilgrim på havet.
Walford, Naomi
New York, Vintage Books.New York, NY
1982
116
LAGERKVIST
Pär
Sibyl, The
Sibyllan
1956
Walford, Naomi
Random House : NY
1960
154
Quartet: London
1985
pb
175
4.95
LAGERLÖF
Selma
Changeling, The
Bortbytingen
Susanna Stevens
New York, Knopf
1992
LAGERLÖF
Selma Ottiliana Lovisa
Diary Of Selma Lagerlöf, The
Dagbok, mårbacka iii
Howard, Velma Swanston
Kraus Reprint: Millwood, NY
1975
241
LAGERLÖF
Selma
Gösta Berlings Saga
Gösta berlings saga
Bly, Robert
Karlstad, Press: Sweden
1982
310
LAGERLOF
Selma
Löwensköld Ring, The

Löwensköldska ringen
Schenk, Linda
Norvik: Norwich
1991
pb
117
7.95
LAGERLÖF
Selma Ottiliana Lovisa
Mårbacka
Swanston Howard, Velma
Kraus Reprint Co. :
Millwood, NY
1975
288
LAGERLÖF
Selma Ottiliana Lovisa
Marbacka
Howard, Velma Swanston
Gale Research Co.:
Detroit, MI
1974
288
LAGERLÖF
Selma
Memories Of My Childhood: Further Years At Mårbacka
Ett barns memoarer
Howard, Velma Swanston
Kraus Reprint Co.:
Millwood, NY
1975
290
LAGERLÖF
Selma O.L.
Treasure, The
Herr arne's penningar
Daughters Inc: Plainfield, VT
1973
159
LANG
Maria
No More Murders
Inte flera mord
Tate, J
Hodder
1967
190

LAURING
Palle
Roman, The
Vitellius
1954
Spink, Reginald
Museum P: London
1961
223
LENGSTRAND
Rolf
Horse Astray In Stockholm, A
Häst på villovägar
Lerner Publns Co. :
Minneapolis
1965
LIDMAN
Sara
Naboth's Stone
Nabots sten
1981
Tate, Joan
Norvik: Norwich
1989
pb
262
9.50
LIDMAN
Sara
Rain Bird, The
Regnspiran
1962
Schubert, Elspeth H
Hutchinson: London
1963
pb
326
9.5
LIE
Jonas
Seer & Other Stories, The
Morton, Brian & Trevor, R.
Forest: London
1990
pb
148
9.95

LINDER
Erik Hjalmar
Hjalmar Bergman
Djurklou, Catherine
Twayne: Boston MA
1975
197
LINDERHOLM
Helmer
Land OfThe Beautiful River
Den sköna flodens land
Folke, Ellis I. &
Conradson Edgar A.
St Martin' s : NY
1963
389
LINDGREN
Astrid
Cherry Tree At Bullersby
Tate, Joan
Mammoth?
1991
pb
92
2.5
LINDGREN
Astrid Ericsson
Brothers Lionheart, The
Bröderna lejonhjärta
Tate, Joan
Viking Press: New York, NY
1975
183
LINDGREN
Torgny
Bathsheba
Geddes, Tom
Harper: NYC
1989
249
Harvill: London
1990
pb
5.95
LINDGREN
Torgny

Bathsheba
Batseba
Geddes, Tom
Faber: London
1987
pb
250
LINDGREN
Torgny
In Praise Of Truth
Till sanningens lov
Harvill: London
1994
pb
211
14.99
LINDGREN
Torgny
Light
Ljuset
Geddes, Tom
Harvill: London
1994
pb
336
8.99
LINDGREN
Torgny
Light
Ljuset
Geddes, Tom
Harvill: London
1992
hb
336
14.99
LINDGREN
Torgny
Merab's Beauty And Other Stories
Sandbach, Mary; Geddes, Tom
Harper: NY
1989
243
Harvill: London
1990
pb
156
5.95
LINDGREN
Torgny
Way Of The Serpent
Ormens võg põ hõlleberget
Geddes, Tom
Harvill: London
1990
hb
104
11.5
LINDGREN
Torgny
Way Of The Serpent
Ormens võg põ hõlleberget
Geddes, Tom
Harvill: London
1997
pb
104
5.99
LO-JOHANSSON
Ivar
Bodies Of Love
Lyckan
Allan Tapsell
Souvenir
1971
316
LO-JOHANSSON
Ivar
Bodies Of Love
Lyckan
Allan Tapsell
Sphere
1974
pb
300
LO-JOHANSSON
Ivar
Breaking Free
Wright, Rochelle
Lincoln, University of Nebraska P
1990
478
LO-JOHANSSON
Ivar
Only A Mother
Bara en mor
Bjork, Robert E
Lincoln, University of Nebraska P
1991
505
LUNDKVIST
Artur
Journeys In Dream And Imagination
Färdas i drömmen och
Weissmann, Ann B.; Planck, Annika
New York, Four Walls Eight Windows
1991
129
LÄNSBERG
Olle
Dear John
Käre john
Gunilla Kronvall
Universal-Tandem Pub
1970
MANKELL
Henning
Faceless Killers
Steven T. Murray
hb
23.00
MARTINSON
Harry
Road, The
Vägen till klockrike
Michael, M.A.
Reynal: New York, NY
1958
276
Cape
1957
276
MARTINSON
Moa
My Mother Gets Married
Mor gifter sig
Lacy, Margaret
Feminist Press: NY
1988
287
MARTINSON
Moa

Women And Apple Trees
Kvinnor och äppelträd
Lacy, Margaret
Reynal: New York, NY
1958
276
Womens P: London
1987
hb
213
8.95
MARTINSON
Moa
Women And Apple Trees
Kvinnor och äppelträd
Lacy, Margaret
Feminist Press: NY
1985
MOBERG
Vilhelm
Emigrants, The
Utvandrarne
1953
Lannestock, Gustaf
Simon & Schuster: New York, NY
1951
381
Reinhardt: London
1958
366
MOBERG
Vilhelm
Emigrants, The
Utvandrarne
1953
Lannestock, Gustaf
Reinhardt
1971
366
MOBERG
Vilhelm
Last Letter Home, The
Nybyggarna: sista brevet till sverige
Lannestock, Gustaf
Minnesota Historical Society
1995
pb
230
15.95
Reinhardt
1961
383
MOBERG
Vilhelm
Settlers, The
Roger McKnight
Minnesota Historical Society
1995
pb
399
15.95
MOBERG
Vilhelm
Time On Earth, A
Din stund på jorden
Walford, Naomi
Simon & Schuster :NY
1965
252
MOBERG
Vilhelm
Unto A Good Land, A Novel
Invandrarna
1953
Lannestock, Gustaf
Simon and Schuster: New York, NY
1956
371
Reinhardt
1957
372
MOBERG
Vilhelm
Unto A Good Land, A Novel
Invandrarna
1953
Lannestock, Gustaf
Reinhardt
1972
372
MOBERG
Vilhelm
When I Was A Child
Soldat med brutet gevär
1947
Lannestock, Gustaf
Knopf: New York, NY
1958
280
Heinemann
1957
245
MYRDAL
Jan
Another World
Alan Bernstein
Ravenswood Books
1994
22.95
MYRDAL
Jan
Childhood
Barndom.
Swanson, Christine
Chicago, Lake View Press.
1991
182
22.95
MÖRNE
Arvid Hakon
Slaves To The Sea
Havets bröd
Michael, Maurice A
Elek
1958
182
NISSER
Peter William
Red Marten, The
Den röda mården
Walford, Naomi
Knopf : NY
1959
325
OHLSSON
Berndt
Noah
Noa
Tate, Joan
Hutchinson: London

1964
223
OLSSON
Hagar
Woodcarver And Death, The
Träsnidaren och döden
Schoolfield, George C.
U. of Wisconsin P.
1965
136
PARLAND
Oscar
Enchanted Way
Den förtrollade vägen
Tate, Joan
P.Owen: London
1991
hb
202
13.95
PARLAND
Oscar
Year Of The Bull
Tjurens
P.Owen: London
1991
hb
198
14.5
PETERZÉN
Elisabet
Last Draw
Desertrain, Laura
Seattle Wash., Seal Press.
1988
228
PETERZÉN
Elisabet
Till Life Us Do Part
Äktenskaps brott
Madsen, Marianne Kold
Wingate: New York, NY
1970
160
PETERZÉN
Elisabet
Till Life Us Do Part
Sista sticketrott
Desertrain, Laura
Seattle Wash., Seal Press.
1988
228
PLEIJEL
Agneta
Dog Star, The
Hundstjõrnan
Tate, Joan
P.Owen: London
1991
hb
120
13.95
SANDGREN
Gustav E
As The Naked Wind From The Sea
...Som havets nakna vind
Marianne Kola Neilson
Tandem
1970
175
SCHERER
Maria
Emperor Waltz, The
Silvertrumpeten maskerad balen
Quartet: London
1989
pb
359
5.95
SCHOULTZ
Solveig Von
Heartwork
Marlaine Delargy & Joan Tate
Forest: London
pb
144
7.95
SJORGEN
Peder
Bread Of Love
Kärlekens bröd
Voeles, Richard B.
U. of Wisconsin P. : Madison
1965
113
SJÖWALL
Maj
Laughing Policeman
Skrattande polisen, den
Blair, Alan
Vintage
1992
Gollancz: London
1991 (1971)
pb
3.99
SJÖWALL
Maj
Laughing Policeman
Skrattande polisen, den
Chivers Large Print
1993
380
9.45
SJÖWALL
Maj
Man On The Balcony, The
Mannen põ balkongen
Gollancz: London
1990
180
SJÖWALL & WAHLÖÖ,
Maj, Per
Abominable Man, The
Den vedervärdige mannen från säffle
Teal, Thomas
Pantheon Books: New York, NY
1972
215
Gollancz: London
1973
205
SJÖWALL & WAHLÖÖ,
Maj, Per
Abominable Man, The
Den vedervärdige mannen från säffle
Teal, Thomas

Vintage Books: New York, NY
1980
182
SJÖWALL & WAHLÖÖ
Maj & Per
Cop Killer: The Story Of A Crime
Polismördaren
Teal, Thomas
Vintage Books : NY
1978
324
SJÖWALL & WAHLÖÖ,
Maj & Per
Cop Killer: The Story Of A Crime
Polismördaren
Teal, Thomas
Pantheon Books: New York, NY
1975
296
Penguin: Middx.
1978
pb
256
SJÖWALL & WAHLÖÖ,
Maj, Per
Fire Engine That Disappeared, The
Brandbilen som forsvann
Tate, Joan
Bantam: New York, NY
1972
218
Gollancz: London
1972
213
SJÖWALL & WAHLÖÖ,
Maj & Per
Locked Room, The: The Story Of A Crime
Det slutna rummet
Austin, Paul Britten
Pantheon Books: New York, NY
1973
311
Gollancz: London
1974
hb
311
SJÖWALL & WAHLÖÖ,
Maj & Per
Locked Room, The: The Story Of A Crime
Det slutna rummet.
Austin, Paul Britten
Vintage Books: New York, NY
1980
279
SJÖWALL & WAHLÖÖ,
Maj & Per
Locked Room, The: The Story Of A Crime
Det slutna rummet
Austin, Paul Britten
Penguin: Middx.
1977
pb
265
SJÖWALL & WAHLÖÖ,
Maj & Per
Man Who Went Up In Smoke, The
Mannen som gick upp i rök
Tate, Joan
Vintage Books: New York, NY
1976
153
SJÖWALL & WAHLÖÖ,
Maj & Per
Man Who Went Up In Smoke, The
Mannen som gick upp i rök
Tate, Joan
Gollancz: London
1970
183
SJÖWALL & WAHLÖÖ,
Maj & Per
Man On The Balcony, The: The Story Of A Crime
Mannen på balkongen
Blair, Alan
Vintage Books: New York, NY
1976
179
SJÖWALL & WAHLÖÖ,
Maj & Per
Man On The Balcony, The: The Story Of A Crime
Mannen på balkongen
Blair, Alan
Vintage Books: New York, NY
1993
180
SJÖWALL & WAHLÖÖ,
Maj, Per
Murder At The Savoy
Polis, polis, potatismos
Anny & Ken Knoespel
Gollancz: London
1972
216
SJÖWALL & WAHLÖÖ,
Maj & Per
Roseanna
Roseanna
Roth, Lois
Vintage Books: New York, NY
1976
201
Gollancz: London
1968
hb
212
SJÖWALL & WAHLÖÖ,
Maj & Per

Roseanna
Roseanna
Roth, Lois
Vintage Books: New York, NY
1993
Goll
SJÖWALL & WAHLÖÖ,
Maj & Per
Terrorists, The
Terroristerna
Tate, Joan
Pantheon Books: New York, NY
1976
281
Penguin: Middx.
1984
277
SJÖWALL & WAHLÖÖ,
Maj & Per
Terrorists, The
Terroristerna
Tate, Joan
Gollancz: London
1977
280
SKJÖNSBERG
Gunnar
Joueney To The End Of The Earth
Resan till världens ände
Ware, Kay & Sutherland, Lucille
Webster : St. Louis
1963
SOYA
Carl E.
Grandmother' S House
Hansen, Agnes C.
Taplinger : NY
1966
293
STOLPE
Sven
Night Music
Spel i kulisser
Devlin, John
Sheed & Ward
1962
286
STRINDBERG
August
Cloister, The
Klostret
Mary Sandbach
Secker: London
1969
160
STRINDBERG
August
Dance Of Death, The
Dödsdansen
Paulson, Arvid
Norton: New York, NY
1976
125
STRINDBERG
August
Inferno: From An Occult Diary
Inferno
Mary Sandbach
Penguin: Middx.
1979
pb
432
STRINDBERG
August
Madman's Defence, A
En däres forsvarstal
Cape
1969
303
STRINDBERG
August
On The Seabord; A Novel Of The Baltic Islands
I havsbandet
Westergren, Elizabeth Clarke
H. Fertig: New York, NY
1974
300
SWAHN
Sven Christer
Island Through The Gate, The
Havsporten
Crampton, Patricia
Macmillan: New York, NY
1974
183
SILBERSKY, LEIF;
SVE DELID, OLOV
Last Witness, The
Hale
1979
175
SUNDMAN
Per O
Expedition, The
Expeditionen
Sandbach, Mary
Secker: London
1967
236
SUNDMAN
Per O
Expedition, The
Expeditionen
Sandbach, Mary
Panther: London
1970
pb
190
SUNDMAN
Per O
Flight Of The Eagle, The
Ingenjor andrees luftfard
Sandbach, Mary
Secker: London
1970
hb
383
SÖDERBERG
Hjalmar
Doctor Glas, A Novel
Doktor glas
Austin, Paul B.
Little, Brown : Boston
1964
150
Chatto: London

1963
150
SÖDERBERG
Hjalmar
Short Stories
Carl Lofmark
Little, Brown : Boston
1964
150
Norvik: Norwich
1987
pb
149
SÖDERHJELM
Kai
Free Ticket To Adventure
Fribiljett till äventyret
MacMillan, Annabelle
Lothrop, Lee & Shepard : NY
1964
192
SÖDERBERGH
Bengt
Mysterious Barricades, The
De gåtfulla barrikaderna
Eivor Martinus
P.Owen: London
1986
hb
267
12.95
SÖDERHJELM
Martin
Christine. 'Five Shards For The Lady'.
Christine. 'fem skärvor åt damen'.
Bradfield, K
Chatto: London
1964
223
TEGNÉR
Esias
Frithiof's Saga
Fritiofs saga
Longfellow, Henry
Wadsworth et al.
G. Macy: New York, NY
1953
TIKKANEN
Märta
Love Story Of The Century, The
Århundradets kärlekssaga.
Katchadourian, Stina
San Bernardino Calif.,
Borgo Press.
1984
132
TIKKANEN
Märta
Manrape
Män kan inte våldtasga.
Wein, Alison
Chicago, Academy
Chicago
1979
143
Corgi: London
1979
144
TIKKANEN
Märta
Manrape
Män kan inte våldtasga.
Wein, Alison
V irago
1978
pb
144
TIKKANEN
Henrik
30 Years' War, The
30-Åriga kriget
Blecher,
George;Thygesen-Blecher, Lone
Lincoln, University of Nebraska
1987
157
TIKKANEN
Henrik
Snobs' Island.
Sandbach, Mary
London, Chatto &
Windus.
1980
122
TIKKANEN
Henrik
Winter's Day, A
Sandbach, Mary
New York, Pantheon Books.
1980
128
TUNSTROM
Goran
Christmas Oratorio, The
Paul Hoover
Godine: Boston
1995
23.95
WAHLSTEDT
Viola
Come Back Jock
Kom tilbaka, jock!
Calley, L
Collins
1961
160
WAHLSTEDT
Viola
Travel Alone, Eva
Res ensam, eva!
Leupold, Nancy S.
Holt, Rinehart & Winston
1966
158
WAHLÖÖ
Per
Assignment, The
Uppdraget
Tate, John
Knopf : NY
1966
243
Sphere: London
1979
220
WAHLÖÖ
Per
Generals, The
Tate, Joan

Pantheon Books: New York, NY
1974
277
WAHLÖÖ
Per
Murder On The Thirty-First Floor.
Mord på 31: a våningen.
Tate, Joan
New York, Pantheon Books.
1982
207
WAHLÖÖ
Per
Steel Spring, The
Stalsspranget
Tate, Joan
Michael Joseph: London
1970
187
WASTBERG
Per
Air Cage, The
Luftburen
Thomas Teal
Souvenir
1973
377
WIJKMARK
Carl-Henning
Hunters Of Karinhall, The
Jägarna på karinhall
Bisset, George
Avon Books: New York, NY
1976
320
WINBERG
Anna-Greta
When Someone Comes Along
När narg ot bara händer.
Crampton, Patricia
London, Macmillan.
1979
112
WINBERG
Anna-Greta
When Someone Splits.
När nagon bara sticker
London, Macmillan.
1979
128
WÄRNLÖF
Anna Lisa
Fredrika' S Children
Fredrikes barn
MacMillan, Annabelle
Harcourt, Brace & World : NY
1964
156
WÄRNLÖF
Anna Lisa
Boy Upstairs, The
Pojken en trappa upp
MacMillan, Annabelle
Harcourt, Brace & World
1963
128
WÄSTBERG
Per
Air Cage, The
Luftburen
Teal, Thomas
Delacorte P.: New York, NY
1972
377

check out the series!

The Babel Guides are a series of illustrated guides in a lively, accessible style to *world fiction available in English*. Each Guide has around 100 reviews of novels or short story collections and each review is an enjoyable 'trailer' for the book, with a long quote as a taster. As well as reviews there is a unique *database* with information on fiction from the country published since 1945.

'Absolutely wonderful, accessible and fun'
British Centre for Literary Translation
'A brilliant idea'
BBC Radio 3
'A novel way to travel'
The Observer
'intelligent, comprehensible and entertaining'
Library Review

Babel Guide to Italian Fiction in Translation
ISBN 1899460004 £7.95/$14.95
Babel Guide to the Fiction of Portugal, Brazil & Africa in Translation
ISBN 1899460055 £7.95/$14.95
Babel Guide to French Fiction in Translation
ISBN 1899460101 £9.95/$18.95
Babel Guide to German Fiction in Translation
ISBN 1899460209 £9.95/$16.95
Babel Guide to Jewish Fiction in Translation
ISBN 189946025X £9.95/$18.95
[Spanish, Modern Greek, Dutch, Arab and other Babel Guides to be announced.]

Keep up to date on the series and related information on our website: www.raybabel.dircon.co.uk. Please contact series editor Ray Keenoy if you would like to contribute to future Babel Guides or have comments or corrections.

Available in bookshops or from the publisher, post and packing free in the European Union, elsewhere please add 10%, US$ or UK£ cheques/eurocheques accepted.

Boulevard Books 8 Aldbourne Road London W12 OLN UK
Tel/Fax 0181 743 5278 email: raybabel@dircon.co.uk
UK & Europe Trade orders & Credit Card orders from
Kuperard/Bravo London 0171 424 0554 fax 0171 424 0556
US & Canada: Paul & Co. Publishers Consortium Inc.
c/o COSI 2 Christie Heights St.Leonia NJ 07605
tel 201 840 4748 fax 201 840 7148